# T.M. SuperCalc!

## The Book

# T.M. SuperCalc!
# The Book

---

## Donald H. Beil
### National Technical Institute for the Deaf
### Rochester Institute of Technology

Reston Publishing Company, Inc.

A Prentice-Hall Company
Reston, Virginia

**Library of Congress Cataloging in Publication Data**

Beil, Donald H.
  SuperCalc! the book.

  Bibliography: p.
  Includes index.
  1. SuperCalc (Computer program) I. Title.
  QA76.6.B432      1983        001.64′25      82-20507
  ISBN 0-8359-7306-9
  ISBN 0-8359-7305-0 (pbk.)

Care has been taken to ensure that accurate information has been provided in this book; however, neither the author nor the publisher
assumes any responsibility for its use. The version of SuperCalc and
the hardware used in preparing this book are described in Chapter 1,
Introduction.

©1983 by
Reston Publishing Company, Inc.
A Prentice-Hall Company
Reston, Virginia

10    9    8    7    6    5    4    3    2

Printed in the United States of America
SuperCalc® is a trademark of Sorcim Corporation.
The Answer Key is a trademark of Sorcim Corporation.
CP/M is a registered trademark of Digital Research, Inc.

Artist: Marian Haley Beil

# Dedication

My thanks to those who help me write:

Bob Blackburn and John Fanselow who, after pizza at a reunion of Somali Volunteers, convinced me to complete my first book.

John Coyne and Rick Curwin with whom I've shared many talks about writing and publishing.

Larry Benincasa and Ellen Cherry, my friends at Reston who make publishing a pleasure.

Charles Casale whose one extraordinary letter will keep me writing for a long time.

# Contents

# Preface

In writing about SuperCalc, I hope to serve a variety of SuperCalc users.

**New SuperCalc users** will find a series of presentations that help the user become familiar with SuperCalc capabilities and manner of functioning. The book is organized to present a straightforward approach to using SuperCalc productively on a computer and to understanding the relationships between hardware, SuperCalc, spreadsheets, data, and the people who use this system. The large number of practice problems is included to help the new user become a skilled user. Many figures illustrate and explain how SuperCalc can be used.

**Potential SuperCalc purchasers** will find a presentation of both the capabilities and the limitations of using SuperCalc. This book can place this product in perspective and help in deciding if SuperCalc can be productive for solving problems for a potential user. There are several versions of SuperCalc; all function similarly, but have some differences. The versions described in this book are cited in Chapter 1, Introduction.

**Data Processing managers** who are responsible for evaluating and approving software purchases within their corporation or institution can use this book to evaluate with the user the appropriateness of this product to meet the needs of those requesting it.

**Experienced SuperCalc users** will find presentations on creating templates, on preparing documentation, on user training, and on recognizing, preventing, and correcting errors. The book is also an indexed reference guide, which presents the features of SuperCalc. It provides a general orientation to producing SuperCalc sheets that are useful parts of the system that we use or may be used by our clients, secretary, or supervisor. A short training session is outlined; it can be used to train those who will work with the templates that we prepare.

**Educators and trainers** can use the book as a framework for coursework and training on the use of SuperCalc. The book provides an understanding of the power of SuperCalc and of the cautions necessary with this system. Practice problems are included; these can be assigned to students or trainees to help them in developing their skills.

**Managers, clients, and others** who use results obtained from SuperCalc models or who work with models prepared by others can use the book to develop an understanding of how those models are built and how reliable they are when used.

I want to recognize and thank Larry Benincasa of Reston Publishing Company for his continued enthusiasm and support.

I discussed the book regularly with Dominic Fantauzzo of the National Technical Institute for the Deaf at the Rochester Institute of Technology (NTID/RIT) and benefited from his enthusiasm, suggestions, and interest. He, John Sweeney, and Paul Taylor each asked to read the manuscript and each offered valuable comments. Others at NTID/RIT who have helped or provided support include Rick Curwin, Robert Taylor, Lorna O'Brien, Warner Strong, William Castle, Nancy Fabrize, Barry Keesan, Mike Kleper, Sondra Milko, Bruce Peterson, Sheila Reasoner, Rosanne Rivers, Doug Sargent, and Alan Willett.

David Cole got me started on this project.

From Sorcim, I've had help from B.G. Robertson, Brad S. Chin, Jennifer Jernigan, Venetia Johnson, and Kathleen Ward.

I recognize Dan Bricklin and Bob Frankston for their pioneering work with VisiCalc.

Others who have been supportive or helpful, often in ways unknown to them, include Roz Beil; Sikandar Shaikh and Nick Francesco of The Computer Center in Rochester, New York; C.R. Myers, Frank Hacknauer, Marc Nodell, Philip F. Paul, Linda DiBiasio, and Stephen G. Lindemann.

David Kroenke's framework for considering a computer system influenced my thinking and the organization of my writing in several chapters.

Many word-processing technicians have participated in preparing the manuscript. Although by choice they are usually not recognized by name, I want to do so. They are Laura Beiderbecke, Sharyn Bendzus, Dorothy Cerniglia, Petr J. Chudoba, Debra Dietch, Kathy Exner, Barbara Hall,

Marcia Hood, Mary Jo Ingraham, Jane Johnson, Irene Kulesa, Tammy Marin, Theresa Northrup, Katrina Poquette, Betty Shaffer, Anita Sherman, and Gary Stape.

Ellen Cherry's work as production editor on this book for Reston Publishing Company was thorough and was done with great care. It was a pleasure to work with her again.

Others at Reston who have been helpful include Nikki Harden, Debbie Balboni, Carol King, Joellen Kinzer, and Erin Loftus.

My wife Marian and our sons Noah and Gabriel support me continually.

Donald H. Beil

# CHAPTER 1

# Introduction

Using SuperCalc™ successfully involves an understanding of this product as part of a full system that includes not only SuperCalc itself but a number of other considerations as well. This environment or system includes

- The SuperCalc program we use.
- The computer on which we use the program.
- Uses to which we put SuperCalc, that is, the worksheets which we prepare and use.
- Data we enter when we use electronic sheets.
- People who use this system.

In this chapter, we'll briefly discuss the importance of each of these.

## THE SUPERCALC SOFTWARE PROGRAM

SuperCalc is a computer program that is sold for many microcomputers that are CP/M® based. It is written and marketed by Sorcim Corporation. The program is sold as a package consisting of the SuperCalc program on a diskette, an accompanying manual, and a reference card, all packaged in a binder.

Its capabilities are discussed generally in Chapter 2, The Capabilities of

---

SuperCalc is a trademark of Sorcim Corporation. CP/M is a trademark of Digital Research. IBM is a registered trademark of the International Business Machine Corp.

a SuperCalc System, and specifically throughout other chapters. Likewise, its limitations are discussed in Chapter 12, The Limitations of a SuperCalc System, and throughout the book. Other chapters describe how we use this system. A thorough understanding of what SuperCalc can and cannot do and how it is used is vital for us if we want to determine if and how it can be used to solve problems that we face.

All examples in the book have been prepared on an IBM® Personal Computer using Version 1.10 of SuperCalc. Users of other available versions will find that the versions are conceptually similar, but that there are some variations in capabilities and functioning.

## THE COMPUTER ON WHICH WE USE SUPERCALC

SuperCalc is available for a number of computers. For each, it's a different program, one that will function on a particular model of a particular brand of computer. Although there are variations from version to version, the differences are slight in comparison to the commonalities between them.

The computer, or hardware, on which we use, or run, SuperCalc will make a difference in how we can use it. For example, the size of the memory will directly affect our use of SuperCalc, since it can limit the problem solution we prepare. Other considerations include the screen capabilities of the system—that is, how many characters (letters, numbers, decimal points, etc.) can be on one line and how many lines can appear on the screen, the availability of arrow keys, etc. Other topics are also discussed in Chapter 12, The Limitations of a SuperCalc System.

Each of us must decide on the importance of these capabilities and limitations to our applications for SuperCalc. We must also consider the uses for our computer other than SuperCalc and how well the system meets those needs as well as our SuperCalc needs.

## THE USES FOR SUPERCALC

This area, using SuperCalc productively to solve our problems, is a major emphasis of this book.

We will see that as we use SuperCalc to solve problems, we create what are called worksheets. To prepare them we'll need to know how to build these sheets. We'll discuss this in the following chapters: 3, Getting Started; 4, Commands; 5, Text, Numbers and Formulas; 6, Built-in Functions; and 7, Other Topics.

In Chapter 9, Creating Templates, we'll discuss how to prepare models or patterns called templates. These are worksheets on which we've prepared models with some, but not all, of the values needed to calculate relationships. We'll complete these by entering the required values and rapidly obtaining our desired results.

We'll present ways of dealing with errors in our work in Chapter 8, Recognizing, Preventing, and Correcting Errors. Chapter 10, Documentation, provides some simple formats that we can use to record information of value to users (including ourself) of our work.

## THE DATA WE ENTER

With SuperCalc, as with any computer system, the results are heavily dependent upon the data provided, the numeric values and label information (for example, budget dollar amounts, employee names, etc.) that we enter. If we have a worksheet accurately prepared, and then we enter data incorrectly, our results will most likely also be incorrect. We'll see that a SuperCalc system has limited capabilities for verifying the accuracy of data, a limitation that requires cautious use on our part. In Chapter 9, Creating Templates, we'll discuss this topic thoroughly.

## SYSTEM USERS

If we want to use SuperCalc productively, we must be fully informed regarding its use. In addition, we'll find that others may use the Super-Calc models, or templates, that we prepare. If others use our work, we must ensure that they are properly trained and have sufficient knowledge of their crucial responsibilities in the functioning of the full system. Chapter 11, What Our Client, Secretary, or Supervisor Needs to Know, contains an outline of a training session that we could conduct to ensure appropriate results.

Chapter 13, Practice Problems, is designed to provide a variety of problems to assist SuperCalc users in developing skills to use this system. The problems also suggest a wide range of potential uses of SuperCalc.

The Preface contains a short review of how other current or potential SuperCalc users may find this book useful.

# CHAPTER 2

# The Capabilities of a SuperCalc System

## INTRODUCTION

SuperCalc is a powerful versatile software tool available for a number of popular computer systems. Its power lies in its ability to provide the capabilities found in our use of a pencil, a sheet of paper, and a calculator. But because it provides this power on a computer, the power of the computer is combined with this software to give results accurately and readily and with great flexibility. It is useful in a wide variety of applications.

Budgeting and forecasting are two prime examples. In this chapter, we'll combine these two topics into one area, ''budget forecasting,'' and discuss the capabilities of SuperCalc. In Chapter 12, The Limitations of a SuperCalc System, we'll examine the limitations of a SuperCalc-based system.

## A SAMPLE PROBLEM: BUDGET FORECASTING

We'll begin our budget forecasting cycle with information about our current budget. Figure 2-1 shows our starting point. Notice that we've started with a simplified version of an expense budget; we'll build toward a more realistic example. The example of Figure 2-1 contains only a few lines with one column total. But even at this level, the complexities of budget forecasting can be demonstrated. PERSONNEL costs are dependent on the number of people employed (EMPLOYEES). BENEFITS are forecast as a percentage of PERSONNEL costs. TRAVEL expenses also depend on the number of people (EMPLOYEES).

As we sit down to do this forecast by hand, we have the budget worksheet of Figure 2-1 and some assumptions about the future. We expect to grow at 5 people per year, meaning that we'll go from 50 people in the current fiscal year (FY 0), to 55 next year (FY+1), to 60 in two years (FY+2), and finally to 65 people in three years (FY+3). Total PERSONNEL costs for the current year (FY 0) are calculated by multiplying the number of EMPLOYEES by the average salary of $20,000. Salaries are expected to rise 10% per year, with salaries for new employees calculated at the average salary for the year.

The computations of future PERSONNEL costs alone are not simple, as amounts are extended and increases for current employees are combined with costs for future new employees. However, once the PERSONNEL costs are determined, the BENEFITS computation is straightforward. In our example, BENEFITS are 25% of PERSONNEL costs. For the other lines, we'll need to make some assumptions about the future, for example, TELEPHONE, HOSPITALITY, and EQUIPMENT each increase at 10% per year, RENT is constant at $60,000 per year, and TRAVEL costs, currently budgeted at $800 per person, will increase 20% per year per person. We'll need to be careful with this line (TRAVEL) as it's also a function of the number of people working.

Figure 2-2 contains our budget, prepared by hand with a calculator for FY+1 through FY+3, following the rules established for ourselves in the preceding paragraphs.

Figure 2-2 is prepared by working carefully through the rows and columns and by recalling our assumptions as each item is calculated. Now suppose that we decide not to hire 5 new people per year but 6. Our hand calculations require a fresh worksheet, transfer of some numbers that we can carry from Figure 2-2 as is (although simply copying numbers introduces the potential for errors), and the recalculation of the PERSONNEL costs, BENEFITS, TRAVEL, and TOTAL lines; that is, everything affected by the number of EMPLOYEES.

Although we may get faster at the calculations, our tools are simply inadequate for the process. Our abridged budget of Figure 2-2 contains 27 values that we have entered or calculated (nine each for three years, including the totals). Most entries are a function of some other entry as established by our own budgeting rules. If we want to change those values, we need to recalculate each entry dependent on its assumption.

*Inadequate tools* is an understatement. The tools available are so weak that we can be prevented from doing a thorough analysis. The effort can easily go into preparing a numerically accurate budget rather than a planned one.

```
                                   Budget Forecast
                    ************** Year ******************
                         FY 0         FY+1         FY+2         FY+3
                        *******      *******      *******      *******

Employees                  50


Personnel             1000000
Benefits               250000
Telephone               10000
Rent                    60000
Travel                  40000
Hospitality              1000
Equipment               18000
                      ----------

        TOTAL $       1379000
```

**Figure 2-1.** A budget forecasting worksheet for four fiscal years showing data for the current year (FY 0).

```
                                   Budget Forecast
                    ************** Year *******************
                         FY 0         FY+1         FY+2         FY+3
                        *******      *******      *******      *******

Employees                  50           55           60           65


Personnel             1000000      1210000      1452000      1730300
Benefits               250000       302500       363000       432575
Telephone               10000        11000        12100        13310
Rent                    60000        60000        60000        60000
Travel                  40000        52800        69120        89856
Hospitality              1000         1100         1210         1331
Equipment               18000        19800        21780        23958
                      ----------      -----        -----        -----

        TOTAL $       1379000      1657200      1979210      2351330
```

**Figure 2-2.** Our budget worksheet with values calculated by hand for the next three fiscal years.

## THE POWER OF SUPERCALC

SuperCalc is an excellent tool for solving this problem and many others. Working at the computer, we can create a worksheet, also called an electronic sheet or spreadsheet, consisting of our budget line-item names, column headings, our FY 0 actual values, and then "formulas" for calculating all other entries based on our assumptions.

The simple budget used in earlier figures appears on the screen of a computer, as shown in Figure 2-3. Notice that the worksheet on the screen follows the format in our earlier work. We have used SuperCalc to prepare the sheet in a format to match our desires; we are able to create these worksheets to meet our needs. (We'll discuss the information displayed on the lower lines of the screen in Chapter 3, Getting Started.)

Now let's see how we can use this SuperCalc sheet as a replacement for the inadequate tools discussed earlier.

Suppose we want to hire 6 people instead of 5 in each of the three future years. We can ask this type of "what if..." question easily with SuperCalc. We can change the entries for EMPLOYEES to 56, 62, and 68 and in a second or so have the complete budget revised to include the new values on the screen, as shown in Figure 2-4. The values for the years FY+1, FY+2 and FY+3 have been updated to reflect the new forecasts for the additional employees.

Similarly, we could ask: "What if" we change our BENEFITS percentage? "What if" we change the cost of TRAVEL per employee? Other similar "what if" questions could be asked, and with SuperCalc we immediately have the impact of such a change displayed for us.

This is the power of SuperCalc.

The preparation of this particular budget spreadsheet requires approximately the same amount of time as preparing the values of Figure 2-2 by hand (this will not be true for all problems). In this time, we can create all relationships that we've discussed. Doing this job with SuperCalc gives us an astounding advantage in our forecasting calculations. Once the relationships are established, we can change any one value or relationship (called a formula) and immediately see the impact of that new assumption.

## A REALISTIC EXAMPLE

Let's move from here to a real budget rather than the preceding abridged, invented version. Figure 2-5 shows a full expense budget in its final form as we want it to be prepared. Values must be calculated for each FY other than FY 0. The unabridged budget actually contains 34

```
                           Budget Forecast
                 ******************* Year *******************
                     FY 0          FY+1          FY+2          FY+3
                    *******       *******       *******       *******


     Employees          50            55            60            65


     Personnel      1000000       1210000       1452000       1730300
     Benefits        250000        302500        363000        432575
     Telephone        10000         11000         12100         13310
     Rent             60000         60000         60000         60000
     Travel           40000         52800         69120         89856
     Hospitality       1000          1100          1210          1331
     Equipment        18000         19800         21780         23958
                    --------      --------      --------      --------

        TOTAL $     1379000       1657200       1979210       2351330

 v A20
Width: 11   Memory: 84 Last Col/Row:F19      ? for HELP
   1>
     Function keys:  F1 = HELP ;   F2 =    ERASE LINE/RETURN TO WORKSHEET
```

**Figure 2-3.** Our budget forecast on the screen of a computer using SuperCalc.

```
                           Budget Forecast
                 ******************* Year *******************
                     FY 0          FY+1          FY+2          FY+3
                    *******       *******       *******       *******


     Employees          50            56            62            68


     Personnel      1000000       1232000       1500400       1810160
     Benefits        250000        308000        375100        452540
     Telephone        10000         11000         12100         13310
     Rent             60000         60000         60000         60000
     Travel           40000         53760         71424         94003
     Hospitality       1000          1100          1210          1331
     Equipment        18000         19800         21780         23958
                    --------      --------      --------      --------

        TOTAL $     1379000       1685660       2042014       2455302

 v A20
Width: 11   Memory: 84 Last Col/Row:F19      ? for HELP
   1>
     Function keys:  F1 = HELP ;   F2 =    ERASE LINE/RETURN TO WORKSHEET
```

**Figure 2-4.** Our SuperCalc screen after revising the number of new EMPLOY-EES, assuming that we hire six new people per year instead of five.

Ten Year Fiscal Forecast Based On a
10 % Increase per Year

| Code | Description | Fiscal Year 0 | Fiscal Year+1 | Fiscal Year+2 | Fiscal Year+3 | Fiscal Year+4 | Fiscal Year+5 | Fiscal Year+6 | Fiscal Year+7 | Fiscal Year+8 | Fiscal Year+9 |
|---|---|---|---|---|---|---|---|---|---|---|---|
| | | (000) | (000) | (000) | (000) | (000) | (000) | (000) | (000) | (000) | (000) |
| #110 | Prof. Salr. | 1553 | 1708 | 1878 | 2065 | 2271 | 2498 | 2747 | 3021 | 3323 | 3655 |
| #120 | P/T Prof. | 28 | 30 | 33 | 36 | 39 | 42 | 46 | 50 | 55 | 60 |
| #141 | Consultant | 99 | 108 | 118 | 129 | 141 | 155 | 170 | 187 | 205 | 225 |
| | Sub. | 1680 | 1846 | 2029 | 2230 | 2451 | 2695 | 2963 | 3258 | 3583 | 3940 |
| 142 | P/T I | 116 | 127 | 139 | 152 | 167 | 183 | 201 | 221 | 243 | 267 |
| 143 | P/T II | 54 | 59 | 64 | 70 | 77 | 84 | 92 | 101 | 111 | 122 |
| | Sub. | 170 | 186 | 203 | 222 | 244 | 267 | 293 | 322 | 354 | 389 |
| 144 | P/T III | 107 | 117 | 128 | 140 | 154 | 169 | 185 | 203 | 223 | 245 |
| 145 | P/T IV | 18 | 19 | 20 | 22 | 24 | 26 | 28 | 30 | 33 | 36 |
| | Sub. | 125 | 136 | 148 | 162 | 178 | 195 | 213 | 233 | 256 | 281 |
| 150 | Hourly I | 62 | 68 | 74 | 81 | 89 | 97 | 106 | 116 | 127 | 139 |
| 152 | Hourly II | 15 | 16 | 17 | 18 | 19 | 20 | 22 | 24 | 26 | 28 |
| 155 | Hourly III | 0 | 0 | 0 | 0 | 0 | 0 | 0 | 0 | 0 | 0 |
| | Sub. | 77 | 84 | 91 | 99 | 108 | 117 | 128 | 140 | 153 | 167 |
| #200 | Benefits | | | | | | | | | | |
| 210 | Soc Sec | 209 | 229 | 251 | 276 | 303 | 333 | 366 | 402 | 442 | 486 |
| 220 | Retirmt | 112 | 123 | 135 | 148 | 162 | 178 | 195 | 214 | 235 | 258 |
| 232 | L/T Dis | 12 | 13 | 14 | 15 | 16 | 17 | 18 | 19 | 20 | 22 |
| 240 | Hlth In | 51 | 56 | 61 | 67 | 73 | 80 | 88 | 96 | 105 | 115 |
| 260 | Maj Med | 15 | 16 | 17 | 18 | 19 | 20 | 22 | 24 | 26 | 28 |
| 270 | Wkm Com | 27 | 29 | 31 | 34 | 37 | 40 | 44 | 48 | 52 | 57 |
| | Sub. | 426 | 466 | 509 | 558 | 610 | 668 | 733 | 803 | 880 | 966 |
| 310 | Supplies I | 44 | 48 | 52 | 57 | 62 | 68 | 74 | 81 | 89 | 97 |
| 320 | Supplies II | 62 | 68 | 74 | 81 | 89 | 97 | 106 | 116 | 127 | 139 |
| | Sub. | 106 | 116 | 126 | 138 | 151 | 165 | 180 | 197 | 216 | 236 |
| 408 | Consultants | 72 | 79 | 86 | 94 | 103 | 113 | 124 | 136 | 149 | 163 |
| 590 | Cons. Trvl. | 12 | 13 | 14 | 15 | 16 | 17 | 18 | 19 | 20 | 22 |
| | Sub. | 84 | 92 | 100 | 109 | 119 | 130 | 142 | 155 | 169 | 185 |
| 430 | Telephone | 25 | 27 | 29 | 31 | 34 | 37 | 40 | 44 | 48 | 52 |
| | Sub. | 25 | 27 | 29 | 31 | 34 | 37 | 40 | 44 | 48 | 52 |
| 470 | Travel I | 48 | 52 | 57 | 62 | 68 | 74 | 81 | 89 | 97 | 106 |
| 515 | Travel II | 27 | 29 | 31 | 34 | 37 | 40 | 44 | 48 | 52 | 57 |
| | Sub. | 75 | 81 | 88 | 96 | 105 | 114 | 125 | 137 | 149 | 163 |
| 520 | Hospitality | 10 | 11 | 12 | 13 | 14 | 15 | 16 | 17 | 18 | 19 |
| 544 | Recruiting | 36 | 39 | 42 | 46 | 50 | 55 | 60 | 66 | 72 | 79 |
| 580 | Advsrs I | 0 | 0 | 0 | 0 | 0 | 0 | 0 | 0 | 0 | 0 |
| 585 | Advsrs II | 0 | 0 | 0 | 0 | 0 | 0 | 0 | 0 | 0 | 0 |
| | Sub. | 46 | 50 | 54 | 59 | 64 | 70 | 76 | 83 | 90 | 98 |
| 620 | Equip. Rent | 57 | 62 | 68 | 74 | 81 | 89 | 97 | 106 | 116 | 127 |
| | Sub. | 57 | 62 | 68 | 74 | 81 | 89 | 97 | 106 | 116 | 127 |
| 630 | Repair | 38 | 41 | 45 | 49 | 53 | 58 | 63 | 69 | 75 | 82 |
| 631 | Maintenance | 42 | 46 | 50 | 55 | 60 | 66 | 72 | 79 | 86 | 94 |
| | Sub. | 80 | 87 | 95 | 104 | 113 | 124 | 135 | 148 | 161 | 176 |
| #755 | Contingency | 10 | 11 | 12 | 13 | 14 | 15 | 16 | 17 | 18 | 19 |
| 756 | Contng756 | 10 | 11 | 12 | 13 | 14 | 15 | 16 | 17 | 18 | 19 |
| | Sub. | 20 | 22 | 24 | 26 | 28 | 30 | 32 | 34 | 36 | 38 |
| ##912 | Equipment | 120 | 132 | 145 | 159 | 174 | 191 | 210 | 231 | 254 | 279 |
| ##914 | Equip>200 | 104 | 114 | 125 | 137 | 150 | 165 | 181 | 199 | 218 | 239 |
| | Sub. | 224 | 246 | 270 | 296 | 324 | 356 | 391 | 430 | 472 | 518 |
| TOTAL $ | | 3195 | 3501 | 3834 | 4204 | 4610 | 5057 | 5548 | 6090 | 6683 | 7336 |

**Figure 2-5.** Our full budget with forecast information supplied for FY+1 through FY+9.

line items plus 14 subtotal lines, plus a total line—that is, 49 lines, not the 8 shown in the earlier example in this chapter. The "real" job requires a significant amount of time for the calculations when performed by hand. Also consider the impact if we wished to forecast for 20 years, not 10 as shown here.

Notice that the budget has line items, subtotals, and final totals; that it has underlines; and that there are assumed but invisible relationships between entries. For example, the BENEFITS may be computed as a percentage of the salary line items. SuperCalc has all these capabilities. However, we are working at a computer system with a screen that has limitations on the number of lines and characters (numbers, letters, punctuation, blanks, etc.) that can be displayed simultaneously. Different versions of SuperCalc for various computer systems display a different number of characters on the screen. Our entire real budget will not fit on the screen of any of these systems. This is a consideration when SuperCalc is used to solve problems.

However, SuperCalc has a series of commands to control which portion of the sheet appears on the screen. It is possible to "move" the sheet "under" the screen and therefore see parts of it as we desire. Some of these screen capabilities are discussed and demonstrated later in this chapter; all will be fully explained in the book.

## SCREEN FORMATTING

SuperCalc offers an on-line window onto the worksheet. The sheet seems to move or "scroll" under the window. This action is like reading microfiche in a microfiche reader. The microfiche contains much more than we can see at one time. With SuperCalc, we can reposition the window so that it shows portions of the sheet, as in Figure 2-6. This shows the "screen" overlaid on the larger budget sheet. The window moves over the sheet like a magnifying glass.

SuperCalc, in its screen formatting capabilities, is much more powerful than a microfiche reader or a magnifying glass. For example, it can change the width of the columns shown. In this way, if we narrow the columns, we can "see" more of the sheet, as in Figure 2-7, where 9 columns appear on the screen instead of 7 in the previous figure.

These two figures show only numerical values; our column headings (top) and budget identification (left) have scrolled from view. Another capability of SuperCalc is a Title Lock command that allows us to fix, or freeze, titles corresponding to what is on the remainder of the screen. Titles can be fixed vertically (columnwise), horizontally (rowwise), or in both directions. Figure 2-8 is similar to Figure 2-7 except that both the

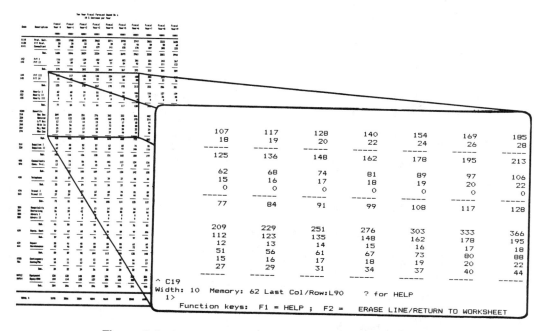

**Figure 2-6.** A screen overlaid on the budget sheet illustrating how SuperCalc provides a window onto the sheet.

column labels and row labels are shown on the screen in correspondence to the numeric values shown.

In addition to these capabilities, the screen can be split horizontally or vertically into two windows each of which displays part of the sheet. Each portion can then be scrolled separately, and each can have separate titles and column widths. This is a powerful capability, as shown in Figure 2-9, in Figure 2-10, and again in Figure 2-11.

Figure 2-9 shows a horizontal split in the screen. We can observe the effect on the fiscal year (FY) totals at the bottom of each column while changing other parts of the screen, for example, the percentage increase per year in our budget. Figure 2-9 shows several of the fiscal year totals for a 10% increase per year in each line item starting in FY+1, and Figure 2-10 shows the same window for a 14% increase starting in that year. At our computer we can quickly see the impact on the total annual budget caused by this projected increase in our budget. The second window occurs within seconds after we change the percentage.

In the next illustration, we've selected a vertical split in the screen. In Figure 2-11, we see the effects on some of the line items of our FY+9 budget caused by the change to a 14% per year increase in our budget.

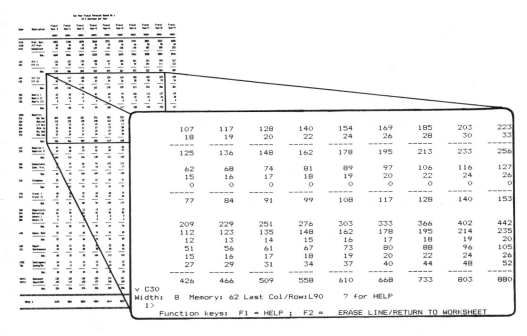

```
         107     117     128     140     154     169     185     203     223
          18      19      20      22      24      26      28      30      33
        -----   -----   -----   -----   -----   -----   -----   -----   -----
         125     136     148     162     178     195     213     233     256

          62      68      74      81      89      97     106     116     127
          15      16      17      18      19      20      22      24      26
           0       0       0       0       0       0       0       0       0
        -----   -----   -----   -----   -----   -----   -----   -----   -----
          77      84      91      99     108     117     128     140     153

         209     229     251     276     303     333     366     402     442
         112     123     135     148     162     178     195     214     235
          12      13      14      15      16      17      18      19      20
          51      56      61      67      73      80      88      96     105
          15      16      17      18      19      20      22      24      26
          27      29      31      34      37      40      44      48      52
        -----   -----   -----   -----   -----   -----   -----   -----   -----
         426     466     509     558     610     668     733     803     880

v C30
Width:   8  Memory: 62 Last Col/Row:L90    ? for HELP
   1>
     Function keys:   F1 = HELP ;   F2 =    ERASE LINE/RETURN TO WORKSHEET
```

**Figure 2-7.** A window onto our budget with the budget displayed with narrower columns than in Figure 2-6.

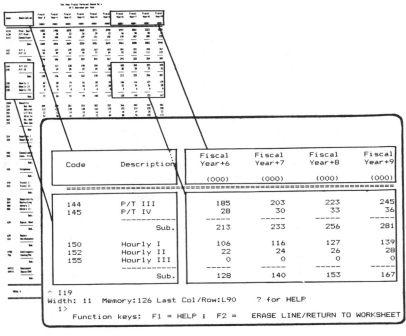

```
                           | Fiscal  | Fiscal  | Fiscal  | Fiscal
   Code       Description  | Year+6  | Year+7  | Year+8  | Year+9
                           | (000)   | (000)   | (000)   | (000)
   ==================================================================
   144        P/T III      |   185   |   203   |   223   |   245
   145        P/T IV       |    28   |    30   |    33   |    36
                           | ------  | ------  | ------  | ------
                  Sub.     |   213   |   233   |   256   |   281

   150        Hourly I     |   106   |   116   |   127   |   139
   152        Hourly II    |    22   |    24   |    26   |    28
   155        Hourly III   |     0   |     0   |     0   |     0
                           | ------  | ------  | ------  | ------
                  Sub.     |   128   |   140   |   153   |   167

^ I19
Width: 11  Memory:126 Last Col/Row:L90    ? for HELP
   1>
     Function keys:  F1 = HELP ;  F2 =    ERASE LINE/RETURN TO WORKSHEET
```

**Figure 2-8.** A window onto the budget sheet illustrating fixed titles.

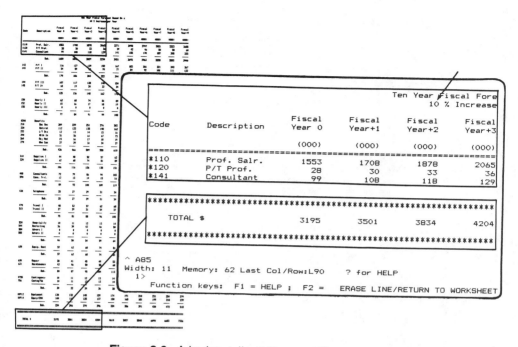

**Figure 2-9.** A horizontally split screen illustrating our totals (bottom) and another portion from the sheet (top).

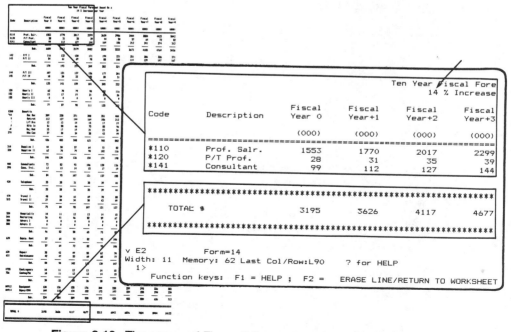

**Figure 2-10.** The screen of Figure 2-9 moments after revising our line-item percentage increase from 10% to 14% per year.

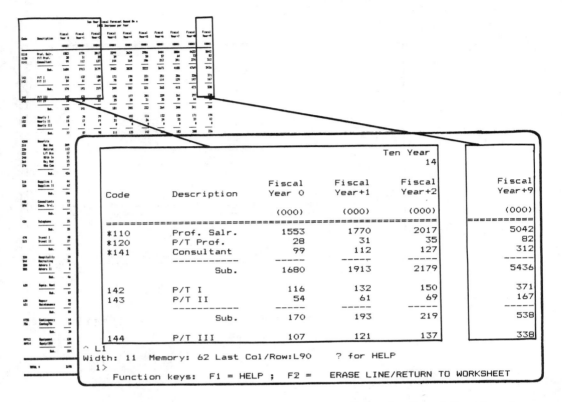

**Figure 2-11.** A vertical split in the screen illustrating the relationship between early fiscal years and FY+9.

## USING THE WORKSHEET

Preparing the relationship between entries of the sheet involves creating formulas which actually become entries of the sheet. For example, look at the part of the sheet shown in Figure 2-12. We'll provide a brief description of the sheet here and a full description in Chapter 3, Getting Started.

First notice the columns and rows of information, like a large accounting sheet. Each column on the screen is labeled at the top. The columns now on the screen are B, C, D, ... G. Each row also is labeled, but with numbers, not letters. We can see rows 26, 27, ... 44, 45 on the screen in Figure 2-12. SuperCalc allows us the choice of including or ignoring this border. In all earlier figures, we ignored it. Each place where a column and row meets is called a cell, or entry. Each cell is named with the column label, then row label, for example, A1, G35, or C29.

At any entry on the sheet, we can write text, or labels, such as the word

BENEFITS

at cell B37. Or, we can write a numeric value such as the value

209

at location C38. Or we can write a relationship, called a formula, on the sheet at an entry, as we'll see. We write all this information by typing the characters on the keyboard of the computer.

In Figure 2-12, the value at location C29 is the total of the values stored in entries C26 and C27. This formula itself is entered into position C29 of the sheet. The formula does not print on the screen as the entry; instead, its value (currently 125) is displayed. Then when values for C26 or C27 are entered or changed, C29 is changed. The formula at C29 remains the same, but its current value may change, depending on the contents of C26 and C27.

At location C29, we actually enter the formula relating C26 and C27. We type

C26+C27

at the keyboard. This provides our formula for this entry.

| | B | | C | | D | | E | | F | | G | |
|----|--------|---|------|---|------|---|------|---|------|---|------|---|
| 26 | P/T III | | 107 | | 121 | | 137 | | 156 | | 177 | |
| 27 | P/T IV | | 18 | | 20 | | 22 | | 25 | | 28 | |
| 28 | ----------- | | ----- | | ----- | | ----- | | ----- | | ----- | |
| 29 | Sub. | | 125 | | 141 | | 159 | | 181 | | 205 | |
| 30 | | | | | | | | | | | | |
| 31 | Hourly I | | 62 | | 70 | | 79 | | 90 | | 102 | |
| 32 | Hourly II | | 15 | | 17 | | 19 | | 21 | | 23 | |
| 33 | Hourly III | | 0 | | 0 | | 0 | | 0 | | 0 | |
| 34 | ----------- | | ----- | | ----- | | ----- | | ----- | | ----- | |
| 35 | Sub. | | 77 | | 87 | | 98 | | 111 | | 125 | |
| 36 | | | | | | | | | | | | |
| 37 | Benefits | | | | | | | | | | | |
| 38 | Soc Sec | | 209 | | 238 | | 271 | | 308 | | 351 | |
| 39 | Retirmt | | 112 | | 127 | | 144 | | 164 | | 186 | |
| 40 | L/T Dis | | 12 | | 13 | | 14 | | 15 | | 17 | |
| 41 | Hlth In | | 51 | | 58 | | 66 | | 75 | | 85 | |
| 42 | Maj Med | | 15 | | 17 | | 19 | | 21 | | 23 | |
| 43 | Wkm Com | | 27 | | 30 | | 34 | | 38 | | 43 | |
| 44 | ----------- | | ----- | | ----- | | ----- | | ----- | | ----- | |
| 45 | Sub. | | 426 | | 483 | | 548 | | 621 | | 705 | |

```
^ C29           Form=C26+C27
Width: 11   Memory: 62 Last Col/Row:L96     ? for HELP
  1>
     Function keys:  F1 = HELP ;   F2 =   ERASE LINE/RETURN TO WORKSHEET
```

**Figure 2-12.** Part of the budget electronic sheet used to illustrate the establishment of formulas created to provide relationships between entries.

Let's look at another feature of SuperCalc. Look at column E. In our budget, the formulas that we want here are similar to all those in column D.

SuperCalc provides the capability, in a single step, of replicating these formulas down a column or across a row. We enter the formulas in one area of the sheet, for example, in column D. We then have the ability to reproduce these formulas automatically in columns E through H with one command. In doing so, the formulas can be replicated relative to their locations; that is, all summation formulas will add numbers from the correct columns (not from column D). This powerful command enables us to build and revise these relationships rapidly and easily.

## FUNCTIONS

SuperCalc includes approximately twenty-five built-in functions, which can greatly simplify formula preparation. For example, at location C45 of the sheet in Figure 2-12, we can enter the formula

$$C38+C39+C40+C41+C42+C43$$

which is similar to the formula used at C29. However, we can also use the SUM built-in function (which is explained fully later in the book). This is a timesaver because with it we only have to enter

$$SUM(C38:C43)$$

There are many built-in functions, including summation, averaging, counting, finding the maximum or minimum, and the net present value. There are also scientific functions such as logarithms (LN, LOG10, and EXP), sine, cosine, tangent, square root, arcsine, arccosine, arctangent, a value for pi, etc.

## CREATING MODELS (OR TEMPLATES)

There are other features of SuperCalc, of which the capability to create templates is an extremely important one. Look at Figure 2-13. It's our budget again, but many of the entries show ..... instead of a value. For example, entry E7 contains a series of periods, and not a numeric percentage. Similarly, entries C14, C15, C16, and others show the periods and not numeric values. Many others show the value 0 (zero).

This is an example of a template. The dots are printed at locations at which values are to be entered. In creating this, we are providing a blank form for a user to complete. The user then fills in the blanks and, in doing so, obtains results for chosen values. The template can be established so that when the user enters values at one location, SuperCalc will automatically advance to the next location where data should be entered, skipping intermediate cells.

The steps needed to enter numbers in these positions can be taught to another person by the creator of the template. Thus, the function of entering the data can be performed by someone without the skill necessary to create the templates. This can be an extremely important timesaver and means that the template designer's skill can be used in preparing additional templates while a client, secretary, or supervisor uses the model.

The templates are reusable, meaning that once written, they can be used repeatedly or can be distributed to many units of an organization. For the experienced user who also performs the data entry function, the existence of the template is also important for many reasons, including use with different projections and the general flexibility that they provide.

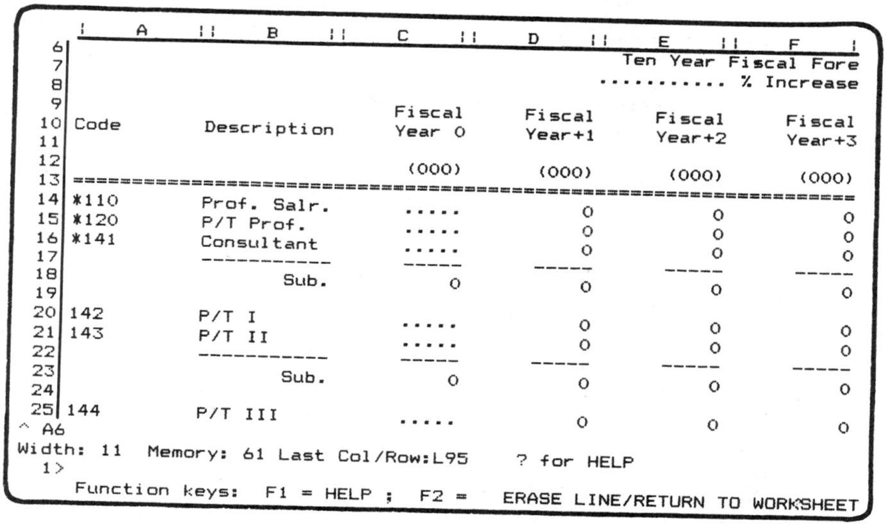

| | A | B | C | D | E | F |
|---|---|---|---|---|---|---|
| 6 | | | | | | |
| 7 | | | | | Ten Year | Fiscal Fore |
| 8 | | | | | ........... | % Increase |
| 9 | | | | | | |
| 10 | Code | Description | Fiscal Year 0 | Fiscal Year+1 | Fiscal Year+2 | Fiscal Year+3 |
| 11 | | | | | | |
| 12 | | | (000) | (000) | (000) | (000) |
| 13 | ============ | ============ | ============ | ============ | ============ | ============ |
| 14 | *110 | Prof. Salr. | ..... | 0 | 0 | 0 |
| 15 | *120 | P/T Prof. | ..... | 0 | 0 | 0 |
| 16 | *141 | Consultant | ..... | 0 | 0 | 0 |
| 17 | | ----------- | ----- | ----- | ----- | ----- |
| 18 | | Sub. | 0 | 0 | 0 | 0 |
| 19 | | | | | | |
| 20 | 142 | P/T I | ..... | 0 | 0 | 0 |
| 21 | 143 | P/T II | ..... | 0 | 0 | 0 |
| 22 | | ----------- | ----- | ----- | ----- | ----- |
| 23 | | Sub. | 0 | 0 | 0 | 0 |
| 24 | | | | | | |
| 25 | 144 | P/T III | ..... | 0 | 0 | 0 |

^ A6
Width: 11 Memory: 61 Last Col/Row:L95 ? for HELP
1>
Function keys: F1 = HELP ; F2 = ERASE LINE/RETURN TO WORKSHEET

**Figure 2-13.** Our budget shown in model, or template, form.

## ADDITIONAL CAPABILITIES

Other capabilities of SuperCalc include the ability to insert, delete, or move rows and columns.

Individual entries, or the entire sheet, can be formatted in a variety of ways, for example, values rounded to integers, or numbers shown with two decimal places (dollars and cents), etc.

Selected cells can be protected which prevents them from being inadvertently destroyed. We'll see that this is an important capability.

All or part of the sheet may be printed.

We can prepare simple bar graphs as shown in Figure 2-14, where the budget amounts from our forecast are shown graphically.

SuperCalc also has capabilities for storage and retrieval of sheets on diskettes. This means that an application that has been placed on a spreadsheet can be reexamined as needed when conditions change or that reports can be generated periodically or on an as-needed basis. Since these data diskettes can be copied, multiple copies of the sheets and templates can be distributed to various SuperCalc users or can be stored as backup copies. At several places in the book, we'll discuss the importance of this backup capability.

SuperCalc contains a powerful 'help' capability which allows us to obtain on-screen assistance while we are working with this product. To access help, we press the ''?'' key, or the designated function key if available.

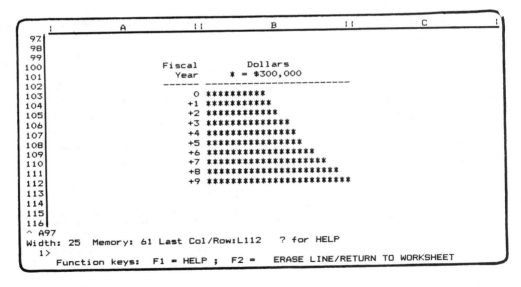

**Figure 2-14.** An illustration of the limited graphing capabilities of SuperCalc.

## SUMMARY

This chapter has provided an introduction to the capabilities of Super-Calc:

- A worksheet on which we write text (column or row titles, underlines, etc.), numbers, or formulas.
- The capability to recalculate values rapidly when new values are entered.
- A variety of screen formatting facilities to allow for the sheet to scroll under the screen, for titles to be fixed in place over columns or next to rows, for the screen to be split horizontally or vertically, for column widths to be changed, etc.
- The ability to use built-in functions to simplify formula preparation.
- The capability to create templates that can be used like blank forms on which we write our data.
- Commands to insert, delete, move, and copy rows and columns.
- Formatting commands to control the display format of individual entries of the sheet or of all entries on the sheet.
- Commands to print all or parts of the sheet.
- The ability to store electronic sheets, in various stages or with a variety of calculations, on diskettes for repeated use as required.
- The option to receive help on the screen when needed.

The remainder of this book provides the knowledge to use these capabilities and the others of SuperCalc, as well as to understand their limitations.

# CHAPTER 3

# Getting Started

---

## INTRODUCTION

This chapter helps us to begin using SuperCalc to solve problems. The chapter assumes that the reader is able to load SuperCalc successfully into the memory of the system in use. This implies the ability to turn on the system, load a diskette properly into the disk drive, format diskettes, prepare backup copies of diskettes and take the steps necessary to install, load and run SuperCalc.

Those unable to complete these steps should refer to either the manuals accompanying the computer hardware or the SuperCalc manual. These steps become routine for a regular user, while an occasional user may at times require assistance from another user, a vendor, or a manual to help recall the necessary steps.

All readers who have a computer available are encouraged to follow the examples in this chapter, as well as throughout the book, on that system and to develop skills with SuperCalc by completing the exercises in Chapter 13, Practice Problems.

We'll begin our work assuming we have formatted several diskettes for later use.

## THE SUPERCALC WORKSHEET AND THE COMPUTER WINDOW

We're beginning with SuperCalc loaded properly into our computer and producing the screen like the one in Figure 3-1 at the top. When we press "return" we'll see a screen like that of Figure 3-1 at the bottom. For now we'll ignore the lines at the bottom of the lower half of the figure.

Throughout the book we'll use

## RETURN

to indicate that we should press the return key (however it may be labeled) on our keyboard. This key is labeled in different ways on different keyboards.

SuperCalc provides us with a large worksheet which has columns and rows named as follows: the columns are named with letters, and the rows with numbers. Notice columns A, B, C, ... H, and rows 1, 2, 3, ... 19, 20 on the screen. These names, called labels, allow us to identify locations where columns and rows intersect.

Look closely at the intersection of column A and row 1, which is named, or labeled, A1 in SuperCalc. A1 is called the coordinate of that cell on the sheet. Notice a shaded rectangle at this position. This rectangle, pointing to A1, is called the worksheet cursor and acts like a highlight of one entry. Different versions of SuperCalc use different methods of indicating the location of the cursor on the sheet. The cell where the cursor rests is called the active or current cell. On the keyboard, locate the arrow keys; while watching the screen, we'll push the key on which the arrow points to the right. When we do so, the rectangular cursor moves. The cursor is now positioned at the intersection of column B and row 1, called entry B1, or simply B1.

If our keyboard does not have four arrow keys, then we obtain the same action by pressing and holding down the control key (CTRL or CNTRL or CONTROL) while we then press either E, D, X, or S. These keys provide the following cursor moves:

CTRL-E   up
CTRL-D   right
CTRL-X   down
CTRL-S   left

Since these keys are normally located as:

```
        E
   S        D
        X
```

their relative location on the keyboard makes their function easy to remember. In this book we'll simply refer to the up, right, down, or left arrow key, meaning produce this action with the keys available on your keyboard.

Now depress the left arrow key, which returns the cursor to A1. Push the left arrow key again. Nothing has happened; we have stopped at the left-hand edge of the sheet.

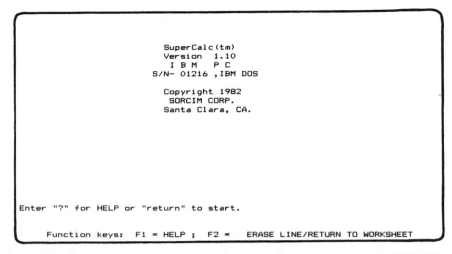

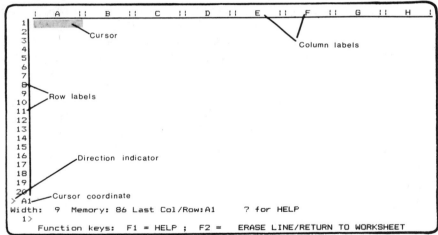

**Figure 3-1.** The screen after SuperCalc has been successfully loaded into the memory of the computer, top, and after pressing the RETURN key, bottom. (Refer to Chapter 1, Introduction, for details of the specific hardware and SuperCalc versions used in this book.)

Let's move right again, to B1, then C1, then D1 ... bringing us to I1. All of the column labels have changed and now instead of A, B, C, ... H we have labels B, C, D, ... I. Press the right arrow again several times and notice that we are moving across the columns with new columns coming into view while others move off to the left. This action, called scrolling, can be reversed by pressing the left arrow key repeatedly, which returns us to the left.

As we move, notice that the cursor coordinate contains the name (or coordinate), of the entry at which the cursor points. This changes each time the cursor moves. (Refer to Figure 3-1.)

Move the cursor repeatedly to the right to location Z1, and then once to the right, revealing location AA1. Continued movement reveals AB1, AC1, ... AZ1, BA1, BB1, ... and finally we bump into the right-hand edge of the sheet at location BK1.

In total we have 63 columns on this worksheet, columns A through Z, AA through AZ, and BA through BK.

Let's return to A1 from our current location at BK1. We can do so by pressing the left arrow key repeatedly, by using this key in conjunction with the repeat key (which we'll abbreviate to REPT) of the keyboard, or by using the auto-repeat capability if available (press a key and hold it down to repeat its function). Using one of these methods, the cursor moves quickly across the sheet, returning us to location A1. In one version, the HOME key automatically jumps the cursor to location A1.

Let's discover the bottom of the sheet by moving down from A1 with the "down" arrow key. The bottom occurs at row 254. Now from location A254 move horizontally across the sheet with the right arrow key. We find that entry BK254 is the bottom right corner of the sheet.

Suppose that we want to move into the middle of the sheet, for example, to G45. Do so using the methods that we've presented.

For practice we'll return to entry BK254 but do so without the arrow keys or the REPT key. SuperCalc provides a simple action allowing us to move the cursor directly from one entry to another. It's called the GO TO. In order to use it, we first press the = key, after which the screen looks like Figure 3-2. Notice the line near the bottom now says

ENTER CELL TO JUMP TO.

This is the prompt line used by SuperCalc to communicate to us its expectations of our next action. Here we are being told that we have entered a GO TO and that SuperCalc is waiting for us to enter the coordinate of the location that we want.

Notice the entry line, also near the bottom of the screen. In this situation, what we now type will appear on this line. We want to move to entry BK254. To do so, first type the letter B. The B appears on the entry line; the cursor on this line moves one position to the right, awaiting our next keystroke. This cursor may take a different form in various versions of SuperCalc, for example an underline, a blinking underline, etc. Enter a K and notice that the line now has BK. Also notice that the number at the left of the entry line changes as we build the line. It indicates the current position of the cursor on the entry line and can be helpful to us by providing the length of the line we are entering. Enter the value 254 by typing the 2, then the 5, then the 4. At this point we have entered the desired coordinate. (If an error is made, read the next few paragraphs.) To indicate to SuperCalc that we're finished entering the coordinate, we press the RETURN. When we do so, the window changes completely and the cursor is now at location BK254 on the screen.

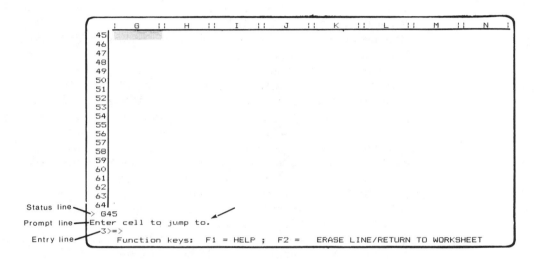

**Figure 3-2.** Our SuperCalc screen after we have begun the GO TO instruction but before entering the coordinate of the location we want.

When we are typing non-text items, SuperCalc allows us to type either upper or lower case letters interchangeably. This means that either

BK or bk

would be acceptable here.

Let's return to G45 and deliberately type an error so that we learn one way of correcting typing errors with SuperCalc. Again we'll type the = key and enter our coordinate. Suppose that instead of entering G45, we type G456 and press RETURN. A move of the cursor does not occur. Our coordinate G456 is not on the sheet and nothing happens. In this instance SuperCalc did not accept the error.

However, SuperCalc communicated to us by printing

RANGE ERROR

in the lower right area of the screen. SuperCalc provides a wide variety of error messages to indicate improper actions.

At this point we still have

G456

on the entry line. Now we can use the arrow keys to move the cursor on this line to perform ''in-line editing'' of what we are typing. The arrow keys perform the functions below. Each also works with the repeat capability.

| Arrow key | Function |
| --- | --- |
| left | Moves the entry line cursor one position to the left each time it is pressed. We can then type over whatever appears on the line. |
| right | Moves the entry line cursor one position to the right, again with the typeover capability. |
| up | Places the cursor in an insert mode on the line, allowing us to insert spaces, and then characters. Some SuperCalc versions support an INSERT key (if it is available on the keyboard) for the same function. If available it permits character insertion without the need to first insert spaces. |
| down | Places the cursor in a delete mode on the line, allowing us to delete characters. Some versions support the same action with the DELETE key (if present on the keyboard). |

Using this information, we can now press the left arrow key (to position the entry line cursor on the 6) then press the down arrow key (to delete this character). A RETURN will jump us to G45.

Move the active cell back to BK254.

Let's try again (to jump to G45), entering the = followed by number 45 (without the G). To cancel the whole line we can use the left arrow repeatedly and we will back out of the line.

The same effect can be obtained by pressing the control key (CTRL) and, while holding it down, pressing the Z key. This fully cancels what we have entered, assuming that we have not yet entered the RETURN key. Finally, on keyboards with function keys, one of those keys may also serve to erase a line. This is indicated in Figure 3-2 where the bottom line of the screen says the function key F2 erases a line. Not all versions of SuperCalc use function keys, or display this line.

Let's start again from location G45 and put the whole sheet into perspective by looking at Figure 3-3. Here we've superimposed the current screen over a representation of the entire worksheet.

The screen is really a window onto the electronic sheet. As we described in Chapter 2, The Capabilities of a SuperCalc System, this window is like a magnifying glass moving over the sheet at our direction or like a piece of microfiche in a reader. The sheet moves under the window, enabling us to view only a part of it at a time. However, as we'll see, our sheet is much more powerful than the microfiche, whose images cannot be changed.

Move the cursor back to entry A1 and let's start learning how to change the sheet by writing information of our own on it.

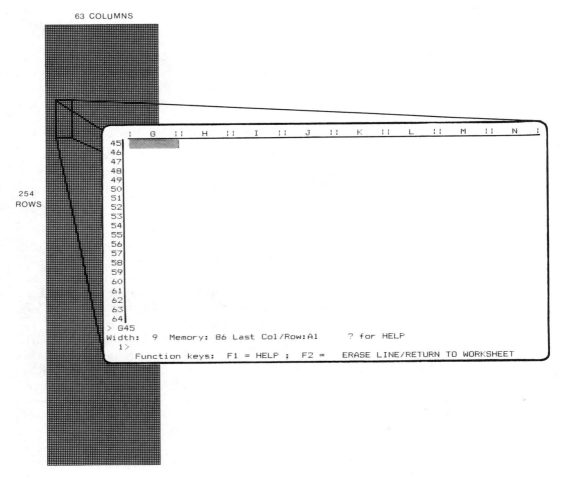

**Figure 3-3.** An example of a SuperCalc screen superimposed over a representation of the entire sheet.

## WRITING ON THE ELECTRONIC SHEET

We will begin with four values that we want to total. Suppose that they are the number of units of a new product, which our company introduced in the FIRST quarter and then sold during the SECOND and THIRD quarter of the year. Now, the end of the third quarter, we are forecasting that we will sell 25 during the FOURTH quarter. We want to use Super-Calc to produce a report like the following.

|          | UNITS |
|----------|-------|
| QUARTER  | SOLD  |
| FIRST    | 8     |
| SECOND   | 12    |
| THIRD    | 15    |
| FOURTH   | 25    |
|          | ------- |
| TOTAL    | 60    |

In this section we'll introduce the steps necessary to prepare this report with SuperCalc. In the next section we'll expand this example to project our future sales and to demonstrate additional SuperCalc capabilities.

Let's start by noticing that this report really contains three different types of information:

• Column and row identification (QUARTER, FIRST, TOTAL, UNITS SOLD, ---------, etc.), called text.

• Numbers (8, 12, etc.), called values.

• Finally, the TOTAL (60), a value but also the sum of the four quarterly values. This relationship, the sum, is called a formula.

We are able to begin writing anywhere on the sheet. Let's write our text down the first column starting at cell A2. Move the cursor to location A2, and we are ready to start entering our text—the word QUARTER.

With SuperCalc all text must start with a quotation mark (''). This indicates that what follows is text. We will type it, and then type the first letter, Q. Both characters,

''Q

appears on the entry line.

We will finish typing the word, and correct any errors that we make with the arrow keys as we did earlier in this chapter.

When we're satisfied with what we have entered, we press the RE-

TURN key. Move the cursor to A2 again. A2 now shows the word QUARTER in the cursor, and the status line shows

$$\vee \text{A2} \qquad \text{TEXT}=\text{''QUARTER}$$

at the left of the line.

A2 is the coordinate of the cursor, TEXT indicates that a label has been written at this position, and the word ''QUARTER is the text itself.

If we notice an error now, for example, a spelling error, we can enter the full label again and the old spelling will be removed and replaced by the new spelling. We will learn other ways of doing this later.

With SuperCalc, the RETURN key also includes an automatic move of the cursor. The first character on the status line is an arrow ''tip'' indicating the direction of this automatic movement. This can be useful for many applications and can assist us in moving the cursor. We'll also see that we can turn off this automatic advance and have the RETURN key not include this automatic cursor movement.

Let's finish the column by moving the cursor down to A4, with the RETURN or down arrow. As we do so we see that we have left the word QUARTER at A2; that is, we have successfully written text on the sheet. At A4 we'll enter the word ''FIRST. When it's correct, we'll push RE-TURN. Now (at A5) type ''SECOND. Continue down the column, entering the words THIRD and FOURTH, then skipping row 8, and entering the word TOTAL at entry A9.

If we forget to enter the quote (''), we'll see

### FORMULA ERROR

at the right of the status line. Use the arrow keys to change, or edit, this, and insert the quote then a RETURN.

We have now finished column A. Use the arrow keys to move up and down column A, noticing how the status line repeats the contents of each entry where the cursor rests.

Move to B1 and enter the word UNITS (don't forget ''), then to B2 and enter the word SOLD, and then to entry B4, where we are ready to enter our first value (as compared to the labels that we've entered so far). Here we press the 8 key, and an 8 followed by a cursor appears on the edit line. Now, as with a label, the RETURN is used to indicate that we're finished entering our value. Let's use the RETURN key and notice that the status line shows, in part,

$$\text{B4} \qquad \text{FORM}=8$$

and that the value 8 also appears at location B4. FORM indicates a formula, here a simple value. Moving down the column, we'll enter the other values, 12, 15, then 25.

For now we'll skip over the underline, and position the cursor at location B9. If we want, we can simply enter the value 60 at this point; however, we want the SuperCalc system to calculate this sum for us. If our UNIT SALES were not the simple values shown here or if our column listed monthly sales (12 lines) or daily sales (several hundred lines), the importance of allowing the computer to perform this calculation for us is clear. Remember also that our FOURTH quarter sales is a forecast, which we may want to change without the necessity of recomputing the total ourselves (more on this example later).

## USING FORMULAS

At entry B9 we want SuperCalc to compute our sum. Here we'll enter our first formula. We want this entry to be the total of the values stored at entries B4, B5, B6, and B7. We'll examine two ways to do this.

One way to accomplish this is to write the full formula, the sum of the other four entries, at this entry. We'll write

$$B4 + B5 + B6 + B7$$

as the formula. This means that at location B9 we will type the B, then 4, then +, then B, then 5, then +, and so on until we have entered the full formula, as shown in Figure 3-4 on the entry line. This figure shows the screen before pressing the RETURN key.

In typing this formula, a number of possible errors can be made, especially by those who are not regular computer users. In particular, in this formula, we may have problems in entering the plus signs correctly. We may discover that we have not entered what we wanted. If this occurs, use the arrow keys to correct the formula. If the formula has been accepted incorrectly (if it appears on the status line), then simply enter it again at the same location. Doing this will destroy the old incorrect formula and replace it with the new one. In Chapter 4, Commands, we'll learn how to use the Edit command in such situations.

If we enter the formula as we want and if we then type the RETURN key, several things occur:

- The formula appears on the status line near the bottom of the screen.
- More important, our sum, 60, appears at location B9.
- The cursor moves to B10.

The screen, after the RETURN key is pressed, and after we move back to B9, appears as shown in Figure 3-5.

We have successfully entered our formula and have learned how to enter labels, numbers, and formulas.

It is significant to recognize that when a formula is stored, the current

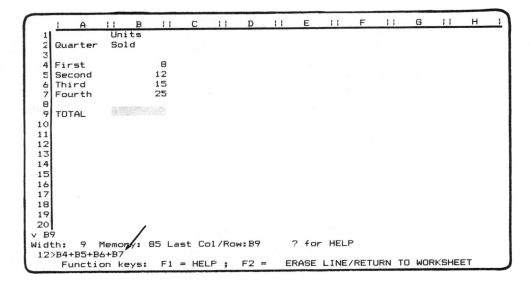

**Figure 3-4.** We have entered the formula for our total at location B9 but have not yet pressed the RETURN key.

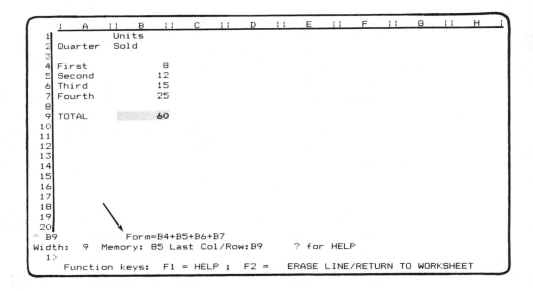

**Figure 3-5.** After pressing the RETURN key of the sheet in Figure 3-4, Super-Calc accepts and lists our formula on the status line and displays the value of this formula, 60, at entry B9 of the sheet.

computed value of the formula is displayed. On the sheet we see the value 60, and not the long formula. This is different from the other entries on this particular sheet, where the item stored was identical to the item displayed. When we study formatting, we'll learn that we can control how items are displayed. We'll also learn that we can display the formulas if we wish.

To illustrate the significance of this, let's suppose that we want to change our forecast for our FOURTH quarter entry: suppose that we want to forecast sales of 35, not 25. We'll move the cursor up to B7 and enter

35 RETURN

The results are shown in Figure 3-6, where our displayed total has changed from 60 to 70.

If we wish, we can continue this forecasting process, determining in turn the results of a series of "what if..." projections for the FOURTH quarter.

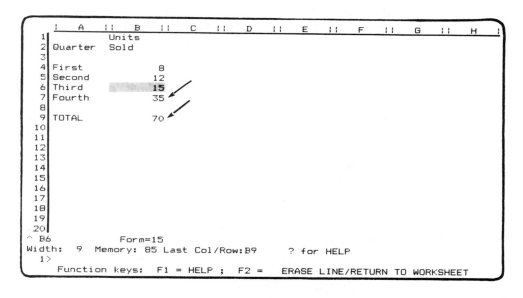

**Figure 3-6.** Our electronic sheet after changing the FOURTH quarter UNITS SOLD to 35 (instead of 25 as shown in Figure 3-5). Notice that the total is instantly recomputed and displayed as 70 (not 60).

## USING ONE OF THE BUILT-IN FUNCTIONS

Let's return the cursor to location B9 and examine a second way of writing our formula for this sum. Recall the possibility that our record-keeping period may be monthly or daily instead of quarterly as shown here. If that is true, it means that our formula for the TOTAL will become extremely long, and therefore both time-consuming and difficult to enter accurately.

SuperCalc provides another way to total a column of numbers, called the SUM function. We'll use it here, simply writing it on top of the old entry and thus replacing the previous formula.

We begin by entering the four characters

SUM(

which indicate that we want to use the SUM function. In Chapter 6, Built-in Functions, we'll learn that there are many others available in SuperCalc, and we'll study how each one is used.

At this point, after the left parenthesis we want to request a sum for the "series" of entries from B4 through B7. To do so, we'll first type

B4

then a colon. We then type

B7)

of which the B7 ends the series and the right parenthesis ends the built-in function. If we press RETURN, and then move the cursor back to B9, we will see the screen of Figure 3-7.

Let's illustrate how this entry can be provided in a somewhat more convenient manner. Now we'll type

SUM(

to begin the sum built-in function again. At this point we're ready to enter the coordinate of the first entry of our series. To do so, we typed the location; however, here we'll demonstrate another way of doing this by pointing the cursor to the desired location.

Press the ESC key. This changes the function of the four arrow keys and also places B9 in the formula we are building after the left parenthesis. Press the up arrow key. As we do so, B8, the current cursor location, appears on the entry line. Push the up arrow again and observe that B8 changes to B7. Push it again and we have B6; again, B5; and finally, B4. If we pass B4, simply press the down arrow key to return to location B4. With B4 correctly on the line, press the colon (:). B4 becomes a part of the entry line; B4 also appears after the colon.

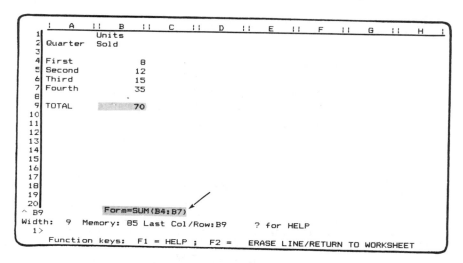

**Figure 3-7.** Entry B9 illustrates the use of the built-in SUM function to calculate the sum of the entries from B4 through B7. (The darker rectangular highlight at the arrow has been added for emphasis and does not appear on the screen.)

Now the arrow keys control the coordinate that appears *after* the colon. Let's complete the series by moving the cursor to B7, using the same technique used for B4. We'll press the down arrow key several times until the cursor is positioned at entry B7. Now we'll type

)

which, like the preceding colon, results in B7 being accepted on the edit line, followed by the right parenthesis, and also causes the cursor to jump back to B9, our original location. The RETURN key completes the action.

The ESC key acts like a switch capable of changing the action of the arrow keys while in the middle of entering information at the active cell. The four arrow keys can therefore serve to edit information or to point to a cell coordinate while entering a line.

The use of the cursor to point to entries that we want included in our formulas is a powerful tool with many applications.

With the SUM function, as with this formula, we can change any or all of the values in locations B4, B5, B6, and B7, and our numeric value displayed at B9 will be instantly updated.

In developing this sheet, we have used only a miminum of the available capabilities of SuperCalc; in fact we have not used any of the commands available. We will introduce a number of these in the next section.

## SOME OF THE SUPERCALC COMMANDS

We'll continue with our quarterly report and present a number of the commands available with SuperCalc. Move the cursor to location B1. Notice that the text UNITS is at the left of this column, and not to the right of this column over the numbers. Let's introduce the commands of SuperCalc by using one of them to move this word to the right of this entry. First press the

/

key, and notice, as shown in Figure 3-8, that the prompt line shows

ENTER B,C,D,E,F,G,I,L,M,O,P,Q,R,S,T,U,W,X,Z,?

We are being prompted to enter one of the many letters following the word ENTER on the line. Each separate letter represents one of the SuperCalc commands. *Some* of these are described below.

| Character | Means |
|-----------|-------|
| B | Blank, or erase, one or more cells. |
| F | Provide a particular display format for selected cells of the sheet. |
| G | Take an action that affects the entire sheet, a global action. |
| I | Insert a row or a column. |
| R | Replicate one part of the sheet in another location on the sheet. |
| S | Save a worksheet. |
| T | Freeze titles in place on the screen. |
| W | Split the screen into two windows in order to display part of the sheet in one area of the screen and another part in a separate area. |
| Z | Zap, or clear, the entire sheet so that we can begin a new example with a clean sheet. |

We'll briefly demonstrate these. All are fully explained in Chapter 4, Commands.

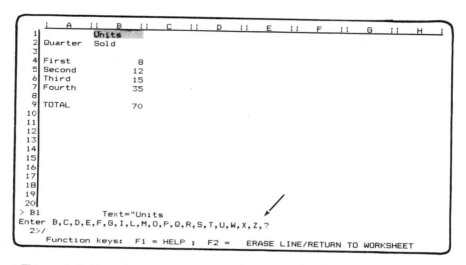

**Figure 3-8.** The screen after pressing the / key to begin a SuperCalc command.

## THE FORMAT COMMAND

Let's start with the Format command. Press the F key, and notice the new prompt line

ENTER LEVEL: G(LOBAL), C(OLUMN), R(OW), OR E(NTRY)

which appears as in Figure 3-9.

Again we are presented with a series of choices (they are not called commands at this point). Notice that we see full English words for the choices. We are prompted to enter only the first letter. As we do so the full word appears on the entry line. This timesaver is called interpretive prompting.

The meanings of the current choices are

| Character | Means |
|---|---|
| G | This format will be global, that is it will affect the entire sheet. |
| C | The format will apply to a column. |
| R | The format will apply to a row. |
| E | The format will apply to one cell or a group of cells. |

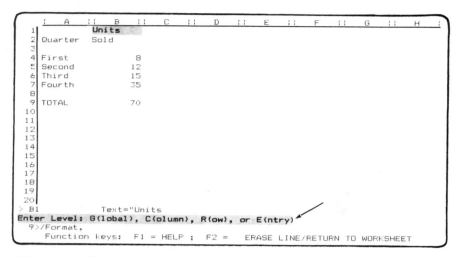

**Figure 3-9.** The same screen after typing F for the Format command. (The darker rectangular highlight at the arrow has been added for emphasis and does not appear on the screen.)

Here we want E since we want to change the format for cell B1 only. We press E and see

ENTER RANGE

on the prompt line. We now can type

B1,

or    ESC RETURN

or    RETURN

each of which will place the coordinate B1 on the entry line, and cause the prompt line to change to

DEFINE FORMATS: (I, G, E, $, R, L, TR, TL, *, D)

*Some* of these additional choices are

| Character | Means |
|---|---|
| I | Display this value as an integer. Notice that an I as a *command*, after a slash, has a different meaning. In one usage I means the Insert command, and in another usage I means integer. This is true of many characters in SuperCalc. |
| TL | Display text to the left of the entry, called left justified. |
| TR | Display text at the right of the column, called right justified. |

Right justification is what we want at this point, as we want to move the word UNITS to the right of the column. We press

TR RETURN

and observe the screen shown in Figure 3-10.

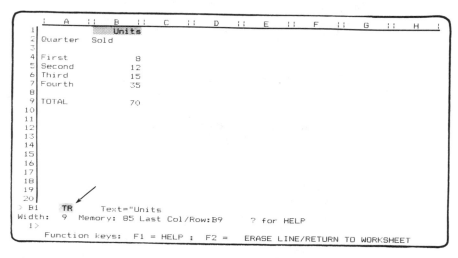

**Figure 3-10.** After typing an R, the word UNITS has been right justified in the field. (The darker rectangular highlight at the arrow has been added for emphasis and does not appear on the screen.)

The status line  now includes the characters

TR

indicating right justification for this text; the entry itself, the word UNITS, has been moved to the right. Move the cursor to position B2, and repeat the process, now by simply typing

/FE RETURN TR RETURN

while mentally thinking

| Character | Means |
|---|---|
| / | Command |
| F | Format |
| E | Format an entry |
| RETURN | Include the active cell. We could also type B1 RETURN. |
| TR RETURN | Right justification |

Let's add one more bit of text. Move to location B8, which is blank. Let's obtain an underline at this entry by typing

''-----

Right justify this text.

## THE BLANK COMMAND

To remove the underline, we can use another command, the Blank command. With B8 as the active cell (the cursor is at B8), type

/B RETURN

and the underline disappears. In this case the cursor was at B8. If it was not at B8, we could type

/B B8 RETURN

and cause B8 to be blanked without moving the cursor to B8. SuperCalc is flexible in the way in which this is permitted.
Now at location B8 type

''===== RETURN /FE RETURN TR RETURN

and notice that a row of double lines composed of equal signs appears right justified at this cell as shown in Figure 3-11. Notice that the double quote is used at the start of our keystrokes for the underline, and not at the end.

## THE INSERT COMMAND

As we look again at the report we've been building, suppose we realize that it would be desirable to have the word PROJECTIONS appear on the first row of the report, above the current column labels. Let's demonstrate how to add it. Move the cursor to position B1 and type

/I

to initiate the Insert command. This places

R(OW) OR C(COLUMN)?

on the prompt line. Press the R to insert a row (the C inserts a column). When we do so, we are prompted to enter the row number. Type

1 RETURN

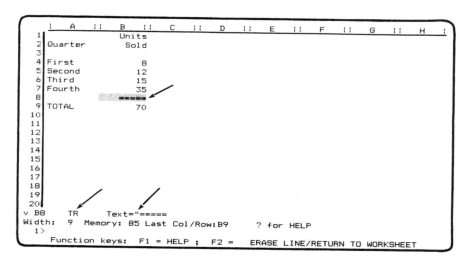

**Figure 3-11.** We'll add the double underline as shown at location B8.

The entire report is shifted down one row. Repeat this action, and it shifts down again. Since we enter the row number, we do not need to move the active cell to row 1 to accomplish this; we can insert a new row as row 1 no matter where the active cell is located.

Before we add our report heading (the word PROJECTIONS), move the cursor to location B11 and observe

SUM(B6:B9)

on the status line. The series, which had previously been

B4:B7

has been updated to accommodate the new locations of our quarterly values for UNITS SOLD. This is an extremely powerful feature, which allows us significant flexibility in building our sheets.

Let's return to row 1 and add the title that we want, the word PROJEC-TIONS. We want to center the word over the report, which means that we'll want it split between column A and column B. At location A1 we'll type

''          PROJECTIONS

and notice the text, which is stored at A1, is spread out over both cell A1 and B1. SuperCalc will continue to spill text into adjacent blank cells until it encounters a cell which has an entry. This simplifies the entry of report headings and other text.

MORE ON THE FORMAT COMMAND

Our sheet has the appearance shown in Figure 3-12. Let's change that appearance again, this time by displaying the sheet with columns that are narrower than the 9-character wide columns displayed here. Why do we change the width? There may be several reasons; for example in our problem we might want to move the two columns closer together to make them easier to read. We'll discuss another reason shortly.

We'll enter

/FG

to initiate the global option of the Format command and indicate that we want to take a format action affecting the entire sheet. The location of the cursor is unimportant. The prompt line is similar to the one we saw earlier for the Format command, except that COLUMN WIDTH is now an option. (It could not be an option in our other example since we were working with a single cell.)

Now we must decide what width we want and enter that width at this point. Let's enter a width of 7 by typing

7 RETURN

All our report still appears, although it has been compressed to the left; significantly, columns I and J (here all blank) appear on the screen.

We see another reason for using narrow columns; where appropriate we can increase the part of the sheet displayed on the screen.

Let's narrow the columns again, to a width of 5, by typing

/FG5 RETURN

Figure 3-13 shows the resulting screen. We observe a number of things. We've again increased the number of columns (here to 15); that is, columns A though O appear. We've lost parts of our labels. For example, at A4, where the cursor is located in the figure, the letters QUART and not QUARTER appear. However, look at the status line that shows

A4        TEXT = ''QUARTER

This is important. We're displaying something different from what is stored on the sheet. We'll discover that many of the SuperCalc commands deal with the way information is displayed and not with the way it is stored. When we change the display format, we do not change what is stored on the sheet. Let's demonstrate this by returning the column width to 9, by typing

/FG9 RETURN

which returns our complete report.

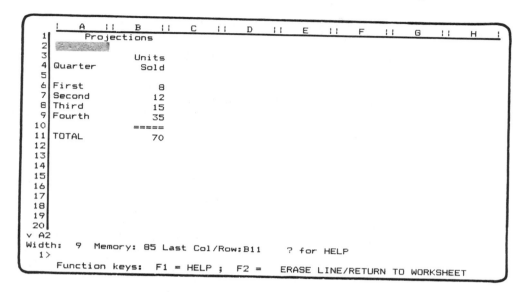

**Figure 3-12.** We've added two rows at the top of our sheet and centered the word PROJECTIONS between columns A and B.

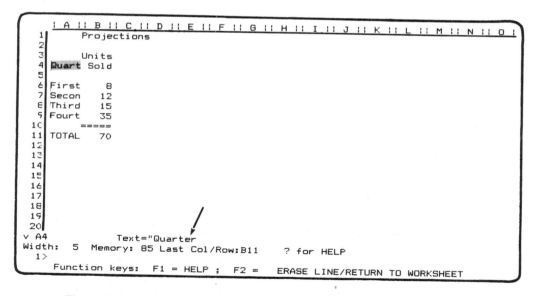

**Figure 3-13.** Our sheet after narrowing the column width to five characters.

## ADDING FORECASTING TO OUR SALES REPORT

The report that we've worked on shows our activity for this year but not for future years. Let's add some forecasts, for example, for each quarter for the next 9 years, making this a 10-year report, including this year. We'll start by revising our column titles slightly. Let's blank locations B3 and B4. We do so by positioning the cursor at each one separately and typing

/B RETURN

or by combining this into one step and typing

/B B3:B4 RETURN

independently of the location of the active cell. As we do so, notice that the format we entered earlier, TR, is deleted. At location B3 enter the word YEAR, a TR format, and at location B4, the value 1. We've produced a simple column label

YEAR

1

over the values in column B. Using the Replicate command, let's take the steps necessary to enter

| YEAR | YEAR | YEAR | | YEAR |
|------|------|------|----|------|
| 2 | 3 | 4 | .... | 10 |

over columns C, D, E, ... K.


## THE REPLICATE COMMAND

Move the cursor to B3, and type

/R

which initiates the Replicate command. We'll use it to reproduce the word YEAR, instead of typing it nine additional times. It will also reproduce the associated format (here TR), which again saves us from repeating this entry nine times. When we look at the screen now, we see a prompt line

FROM? ENTER RANGE

Press the RETURN. If the cursor was not at location B3 when we started, we can type

B3 RETURN

instead. This changes the line. It now shows

TO? (ENTER RANGE), THEN RETURN; OR '','' FOR OPTIONS

At this point we have entered a FROM range, which is the location of the item that we want to replicate. This range is the area from which we want to copy some items. In our example the location is B3, since we want to reproduce the single item in location B3. What's the TO range; that is, where do we want to reproduce this value? We want it from C3 through K3. To indicate this we'll type the now familiar ''series'' entry

C3:K3 RETURN

The word YEAR appears in location C3...H3, visible on the screen, and in locations I3, J3, and K3, which we can verify by moving the cursor to these cells.

Let's move down to the next row, row 4, and discuss how we will replicate our year values, to produce 2, 3, 4, ... 10 in the desired locations. Place the cursor at location C4, and enter the formula

B4+1 RETURN

which places the value 2 at this position on the sheet. This formula says that the value placed at C4 should be one greater than the value at location B4. That is, C4 should be equal to B4+1 as shown on the preceding line.

This seems awkward, when simply entering the number 2 would have done the same thing. We'll see why this formula is useful when we replicate again; however, instead of a label, we'll replicate a formula. With the cursor at location C4, type

/R RETURN

indicating that C4 is our FROM location. If the cursor is not at C4, type

/R C4 RETURN

Our TO area starts at D4, which we can type or which we can enter by cursor move. Let's do the latter, pressing ESC, and then moving the cursor to D4 with the right arrow key. This is the same type of cursor move used earlier in the chapter.

Press the colon. Now let's locate the end of our target by cursor move, pressing the right arrow key until we are at position K4, under the last occurrence of the word YEAR. Now press the RETURN key, and study the screen in Figure 3-14.

What happened? To explain it, move the cursor to D4, then E4, then F4, etc., and watch the formula stored at each location. It changes from B4+1 at location C4, to C4+1 at location D4, to D4+1 at location E4, etc. The coordinate in each formula has automatically changed *relative* to the entry.

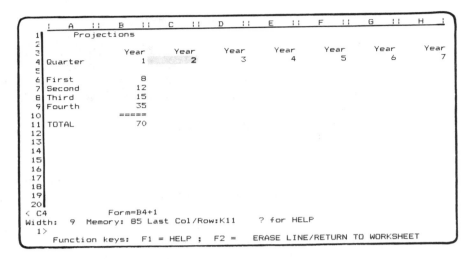

**Figure 3-14.** The screen after we have replicated the year value relatively across row 4.

We'll explain this command in a number of additional examples in Chapter 4, Commands, at which time we will examine the meaning of

### '','' FOR OPTIONS

In our example we are ready to include the quarterly forecasts for each of the next nine years. We need to supply the assumptions for the forecast: SuperCalc cannot do that. Let's make a simple assumption, that UNIT SALES will increase by 10% over the same quarter of the previous year. We have a business in which sales are seasonal, and we want to know what to expect for the quarters of the coming years.

At location C6 of Figure 3-15, we have entered the formula

$$B6*1.1$$

using the * to indicate a multiplication and using 1.1 to indicate a 10% growth; that is, C6 is equal to 110% of B6, or B6 times 1.1. Location C6 shows a value of 8.8, and our formula appears on the status line of the screen.

Let's replicate this formula down the C column into a range of C7 through C9. This is identical in concept to the process that we followed to label the years 1, 2, 3, ... 10.

We'll place the cursor at location C6 and then enter the following keystrokes

/R RETURN C7:C9 RETURN

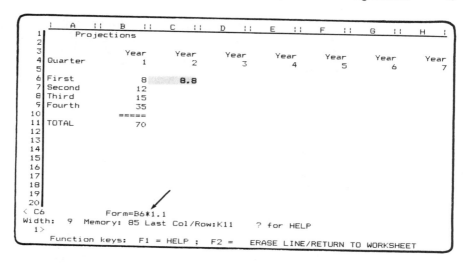

**Figure 3-15.** The beginning step of forecasting sales for each quarter of the next nine years.

Let's explain each item that we've typed.

| Keystrokes | Purpose |
| --- | --- |
| / | Enter the command structure of SuperCalc. |
| R | Select the Replicate command. |
| RETURN | Indicate that we're replicating from the active cell C6. We can also use the ESC and arrow keys as we did in the earlier example in this chapter. Finally, we can also type C6 after the R to indicate the TO range. The three techniques function similarly. |
| C7 | Enter the first coordinate of the FROM range. A cursor move can also be used to specify this entry. |
| : | Indicate a series. |
| C9 | Enter the end of the TO range. Again the cursor can be used. |
| RETURN | Indicate the close of the series. |

Now let's turn on the true power of the Replicate command by replicating the relationships that we've just established in column C across all the remaining eight years of our report. With the cursor again at C6 we type

/R C6:C9 RETURN D6:K6 RETURN

Let's explain again.

| Keystrokes | Purpose |
| --- | --- |
| / | Enter the command structure of SuperCalc. |
| R | Select the Replicate command. |
| C6: | This is different from our earlier examples. Instead of a single entry as the source, we now have a series, beginning with C6. We'll see the end with the next keystrokes. |
| C9 | Enter the coordinate of the end of the series. |
| RETURN | Close this series (the comma key can also be used). We now have as our FROM range a portion of a column rather than a single entry. |
| D6: | Enter the start of the TO range. |
| K6 | Enter the end coordinate of the TO range. Notice that our TO, or target area, is across row 6 while our FROM, or source area, is down column C. When this occurs—that is when the source and target areas are perpendicular—SuperCalc replicates the source onto a two dimensional rectangular area rather than onto a row or column as illustrated earlier. This is a powerful tool. |
| RETURN | End the command. |

Let's move the cursor to the right to see some of the values that we've placed on the sheet. Figure 3-16 shows YEAR 3 through YEAR 10.

We notice that the results are shown with five decimal places for many of the entries here. Let's use the Format command to reduce the number of decimal places, first to two places and then to none. We'll enter

/FG$ RETURN

and notice that these few keystrokes change all values to two decimal places as explained next.

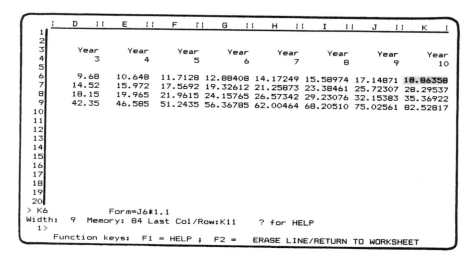

**Figure 3-16.** Our forecast of quarterly sales for YEAR 3 through YEAR 10.

| Keystrokes | Purpose |
|---|---|
| / | Enter the command structure. |
| F | Select the Format command. |
| G | Select the global option, whose action affects the entire sheet. |
| $ | Select the dollars and cents option from the formats available. Here we do not have dollar values but are using this option to obtain two decimal places. |

After entering these keystrokes, we have the screen shown in Figure 3-17.

Notice that unfortunately we have also changed the column labels of row 4 to two places. We now have YEAR 3.00, YEAR 4.00, etc. To correct this, we can enter the Format command, and indicate that an integer, I, format is desired for all of row 4.

Instead of doing this only for the individual year labels, let's change all values to integer. To do so, we enter

/FGI RETURN

where all keystrokes have the preceding explanations except for I, which indicates integer format. When we enter these keystokes, our screen is again promptly revised and appears as in Figure 3-18.

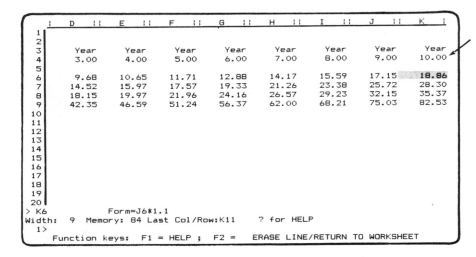

**Figure 3-17.** The forecast with values printed with two decimal places (a dollars and cents format).

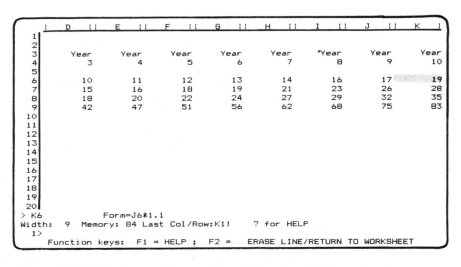

**Figure 3-18.** The forecast shown with an integer format for each entry.

We'll return the cursor to location B10 (=B10 RETURN), and replicate the double underline and the SUM function of column B across the other columns by entering

/R B10:B11, C10:K10 RETURN

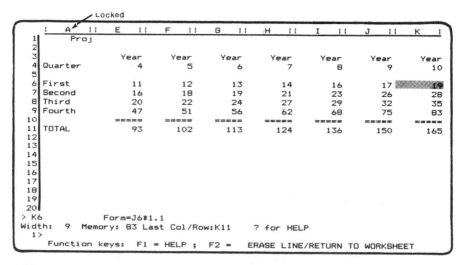

**Figure 3-19.** A demonstration of the use of the Title Lock command to lock titles at the left of the screen.

In this case we did not need the intermediate step of entering formulas in column C. These two lines contain entries that can be replicated as is.

Look carefully at the total for YEAR 2 (see Figure 3-20). It is not correct, as the sum of the four numbers shown is 78, not 77 as shown. (We'll discuss the >> symbols in that figure later in this chapter.) Super-Calc, at our direction, is displaying these values as integers; however, the values stored on the sheet have several decimal places. In the SUM function, and in all formulas, the values used are the values stored on the sheet, not necessarily the values displayed on the screen. In this example, if we want the totals to be correct, we'll need to use the integer function, which is INT and which we'll describe in Chapter 6, Built-in Functions.

## THE TITLE LOCK COMMAND

Move to A1, then scroll (move the active cell) to YEAR 10 and notice that the text at the left moves off the screen, which can make it difficult to identify our values correctly. Return to A6 with the arrow keys and enter

/TV

Then scroll to YEAR 10. As we do so, our labels in column A remain on the screen, providing us with an easy way to identify our data, as shown in Figure 3-19. Our actions worked as follows:

| Keystrokes | Purpose |
|------------|---------|
| /T | Use the Title Lock command. |
| V | Establish a vertical title at, and to the left of, the active cell. |

Let's remove the titles, indicating clear (C) the titles by entering

/TC

which returns us to where we were.


## THE WINDOW COMMAND

If we want to see all our forecast on the screen, we can try to narrow the columns, for example, by entering

/FG3 RETURN

to obtain a global column width of 3. The results of this are shown in Figure 3-20. Notice that the totals for YEAR 5 through YEAR 10 are no longer on the screen; instead we see

>>

at each total location. In this example the sum is too large to fit into a column three characters wide (and leave a blank at the left to separate it from the next column). When this occurs SuperCalc prints a series of greater-than symbols to indicate the problem to us. With this example a global column width of 7 allows us to see the whole sheet; however, let's enter

/FG9 RETURN

to set the column width to 9 and examine another way to solve this problem.

SuperCalc provides a split window capability for the screen, which can be helpful in problems like this. Move row 1 off the top of the screen, and then move the cursor to location A12 with the arrow keys, and type

/WH

which produces the screen of Figure 3-21. The functioning of the keystrokes here is

| Keystrokes | Purpose |
|---|---|
| /W | Enter the Window command. |
| H | Establish a horizontally split window. |

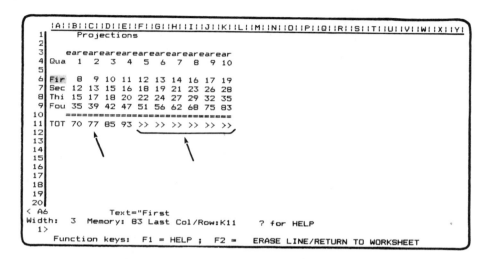

**Figure 3-20.** All columns of our report show on this screen when we reduce the column width to 3, but we no longer have room for the sum at the bottom of every column.

**Figure 3-21.** The screen has been split horizontally into two windows.

```
  ! A   !!   B   !!   C   !!   D   !!   E   !!   F   !!   G   !!   H   !
 2|
 3|        Year        Year        Year        Year        Year        Year        Year
 4|Quarter    1           2           3           4           5           6           7
 5|
 6|First       8           9          10          11          12          13          14
 7|Second     12          13          15          16          18          19          21
 8|Third      15          17          18          20          22          24          27
 9|Fourth     35          39          42          47          51          56          62
10|         =====       =====       =====       =====       =====       =====       =====
11|TOTAL      70          77          85          93         102         113         124
  ! I   !!   J   !!   K   !!   L   !!   M   !!   N   !!   O   !!   P   !
 3|        Year        Year        Year
 4|           8           9          10
 5|
 6|          16          17          19
 7|          23          26          28
 8|          29          32          35
 9|          68          75          83
10|         =====       =====       =====
11|         136         150         165

>  P11
Width:   9   Memory: 83  Last Col/Row:K11      ? for HELP
   1>
     Function keys:  F1 = HELP ;   F2 =    ERASE LINE/RETURN TO WORKSHEET
```

**Figure 3-22.** After scrolling in the lower window, we have our full forecast on the screen at once.

Now press the ; key. Press it again and again. This key jumps the cursor back and forth between the two windows. With the cursor in the bottom screen, use the arrow keys to move YEAR 8 through YEAR 10 into view as in Figure 3-22.

It's important to recognize that we are working with a limitation of a SuperCalc system. The size of the electronic sheet is often larger than the capability of the hardware to display on the screen. In our forecast, if we had a larger report, for example, a 20-year forecast, we simply could not see it all on the screen at one time. Even though SuperCalc provides powerful screen formatting capabilities, we are nevertheless often limited by the hardware.

Use the ; key to jump to the top screen and then position the cursor to location B9. Remember that we started by forecasting for the next quarter, the FOURTH quarter of YEAR 1. We then added the additional years. Let's return to the FOURTH quarter and change that value. Enter the value 40 followed by a RETURN. As we do so, we can watch a rippling as SuperCalc updates each FOURTH quarter value (each is dependent on the previous one). Also notice that the word

CALCULATING..

appears on the prompt line while the recalculation occurs. Change the value and watch this recur.

## THE SAVE COMMAND

We've completed a significant amount of work and want to retain this sheet. To do so, we'll introduce and use the Save command. Chapter 4, Commands, contains additional information about this whole process.

Saving an electronic sheet requires a formatted work diskette (not the SuperCalc diskette). Place the formatted diskette into disk drive B:, and we are now ready to save our sales forecast sheet on the diskette. We type

/S B:FORCAST RETURN A

meaning

| Keystrokes | Purpose |
|---|---|
| /S | Enter the Save command. |
| B: | Select disk drive B: which has the working diskette. |
| FORECAST | This is a name selected for the sheet that we'll store on the diskette. Since we may store many sheets on one diskette, we need to name each one separately. |
| RETURN | Indicate the end of the name of the file. |
| A | Select A(LL) to save *all* of the sheet (we will explain this in the next chapter). |

We have successfully stored our sheet on a diskette ready to be copied into memory when we need it again, perhaps after the FOURTH quarter, when we can enter the actual UNIT SALES.

## THE QUIT COMMAND

To leave SuperCalc we use the Quit command which we initiate by typing /Q. We can then confirm our action (meaning we will destroy the sheet in memory—not on the disk—and return to the operating system) by typing Y (yes), or cancel by typing N (no). We can also remove our diskettes and power off the system.

## SUMMARY

Let's summarize all that we have done.

Beginning with SuperCalc correctly loaded into the memory of our computer, we have gone through a series of steps to create a worksheet that forecasts unit sales over a 10 year period. In doing so, we have introduced many actions, all of which are explained in depth in subsequent chapters.

We have seen that SuperCalc provides a two-dimensional worksheet. We have learned how to scroll the sheet, how to move the cursor, and how to write text, numbers, and formulas on the sheet.

We have used formulas in a number of entries and introduced and demonstrated one of the available built-in functions. Built-in functions can be a powerful tool in simplifying our work and reducing the possiblity of error.

A number of commands were demonstrated, including the Format, Blank, Insert, Replicate, Title Lock, Window, Save, and Quit commands. One of them, the Replicate command, provides a powerful tool that we used in several instances to generate a large number of relationships with a limited amount of typing on our part.

In subsequent chapters all of these, in addition to the remaining commands and built-in functions, will be explained.

# CHAPTER 4

# Commands

## INTRODUCTION

This chapter contains a detailed explanation of each of the commands of SuperCalc. The commands are accessed by entering the slash (/) followed by the letter indicating the desired command. When a slash is entered, the following appears on the prompt line:

ENTER B,C,D,E,F,G,I,L,M,O,P,Q,R,S,T,U,W,X,Z,?

Entering any of these characters initiates the desired command.

Let's use the Answer Key™ to obtain "help" in presenting a brief explanation of the available commands. To do so we press the "?" key, or the designated function key if available. Figure 4-1 shows the screen after we request help.

Notice that the first character is used in choosing the desired command. We press the desired key, and SuperCalc places the full English word on the entry line for us.

When using commands, a number of prompts occur that we'll need to define. The help function can also be used at any level while entering commands to obtain definitions as needed when working at the computer.

We respond to prompts by entering the first character of the word representing the action we desire. After we select the desired action in this way, the full word appears on the entry line followed by a comma. This is called interpretive prompting. We then respond based on the subsequent prompt.

---

The Answer Key™ is a trademark of Sorcim.

```
SuperCalc    AnswerKey (tm)  slash commands :
B(lank)-----> Removes contents of cells.
C(opy)------> Copies contents of cells.
D(elete)----> Deletes entire row or column.
E(dit)------> Allows editing the contents of a cell.
F(ormat)----> Change display format of cells, rows, or entire worksheet.
G(lobal)----> Change global display or calculation options.
I(nsert)----> Create new row or column.
L(oad)------> Read worksheet (or portion) from disk.
M(ove)------> Swap rows or columns.
O(utput)----> Display contents or values of cells on printer, console or disk.
P(rotect)---> Prevent future alteration of cells.
Q(uit)------> Exit SuperCalc.
R(eplicate)-> Reproduce partial rows or columns.
S(ave)------> Write worksheet to disk.
T(itle)-----> Lock first rows or columns against scrolling.
U(nprotect)-> Allow alteration of protected cells.
W(indow)----> Split or unsplit the screen display.
X(eXecute)--> Accept commands and data from a file.
Z(ap)-------> Clear worksheet and all settings.


   Press any key to continue
   Function keys:  F1 = HELP ;  F2 =   ERASE LINE/RETURN TO WORKSHEET
```

**Figure 4-1.** The "help" screen that appears when we type /? (Screen copyright Sorcim Corporation, 1982.)

Below are the terms we'll need to learn, their definitions, and samples of what we enter after we've selected this option.

| Term | Definition | Examples of next entry |
|------|-----------|------------------------|
| C(ell) | The coordinate of one location of the worksheet, composed of a column label followed by a row label. | BB47 AK9 RETURN (see below) |
| R(ow) | A complete row, indicated by entering the desired row label, a number from 1 to 254 | 1 17 200 RETURN (see below) |
| C(olumn) | A complete column, indicated by entering the desired column label, a letter (or two letters) from A to BK. | C AJ BC RETURN (see below) |

| B(lock) | A rectangular section of the worksheet indicated by entering the cells of opposite corners separated by a colon (:). | A1:G7<br>J30:AA4 |
| E(ntry) | A cell or group of cells. | (Cell, row, column, or block.) |
| R(ange) | A single cell, a complete column, a complete row, or a block | (Cell, row, column or block.) |

In addition to these definitions, there are a number of keys that have important functions when entering commands. They are:

| Key | Function |
| --- | --- |
| , | Used to separate items while building command actions on the entry line. |
| RETURN | Provides the same function as the comma, and depending on the context, includes the active cell, current row, or current column on the entry line. |
| control-Z | Cancels the full line. A function key may also do this depending on the version. |
| arrow keys | Provide editing capability as expected on the entry line (left arrow means move left one character; right arrow means move right one character; up arrow means insert one space; down arrow means delete a character) except as noted below. |
| ESC | ESC changes the function of the four arrow keys. After ESC, the arrow keys move the cursor and cause the coordinate of the active cell to appear on the entry line. Press ESC again to return the arrow keys to their other function. |
| ← | If the left arrow causes the cursor on the entry line to move over a comma, the preceding full item will be deleted. for example, with |

$$16>/FORMAT,GLOBAL,\_$$

on the entry line, pressing the left arrow changes that line to

$$9>/FORMAT,$$

The commands of SuperCalc allow us to manipulate a cell or group of cells independently of the active cell; however, since the actions of the keys above do include the capability of defaulting to the active cell, or current row or column, we may often want to reposition the cursor before entering a command.

## WORKING WITH FILES ON DISKETTES

The following comments apply to those commands that access files on diskettes, including the Delete, Load, Output, and Save commands. In working with these commands, a number of general considerations apply:

- Files are stored for a variety of reasons. We may want to revise a worksheet at a later time with different values. We may be trying a new command, or a new formula, and want to preserve the sheet momentarily while we experiment. We may be creating a backup or duplicate copy, which can be used if we inadvertently destroy the original. We may wish to stop work on a sheet that we've only partially finished and will finish later. For these reasons, and others, the ability to save and reuse our work is important.

- SuperCalc works with a single worksheet at a time. That sheet must be in memory. If it's a sheet on a diskette, we must first load it into memory before SuperCalc can be used with it. The sheet in memory may be composed of all or parts of other sheets previously stored on diskettes.

- We can manipulate a sheet in memory as desired without affecting the stored sheet. If we change a sheet in memory, we do not change the corresponding sheet if it was previously stored on a diskette.

- SuperCalc accesses disk storage only under our control. If we revise a sheet, it is not changed on the diskette until we act to store it again.

- Files on diskettes have unique names that are one to eight characters in length. They may or may not be preceded by a disk drive code of a single letter followed by a colon. The characters of the name may be letters or digits.

- When prompted by SuperCalc to enter a filename, we can respond in one of two ways. First we can type the name directly. Second, we can follow the prompts to have SuperCalc list the disk directory for us. This gives us a listing of the names of the files that are already stored on the diskette. When we identify the desired name, we can return to the command as prompted and enter the name.

We are now ready to examine each SuperCalc command.

**/B   THE BLANK COMMAND**

The Blank command, /B, is used to blank, or clear, a single cell or group of cells on the sheet. The action occurs when we type

/B

followed by the range or the RETURN key. To cancel the action (after typing /B), type the control-Z combination of keys. Canceling the Blank command leaves the contents of the entry unchanged.

As an example of the action of this command, study Figure 4-2. We want to blank entries A10 and B10.  To do so type

/B A10:B10 RETURN

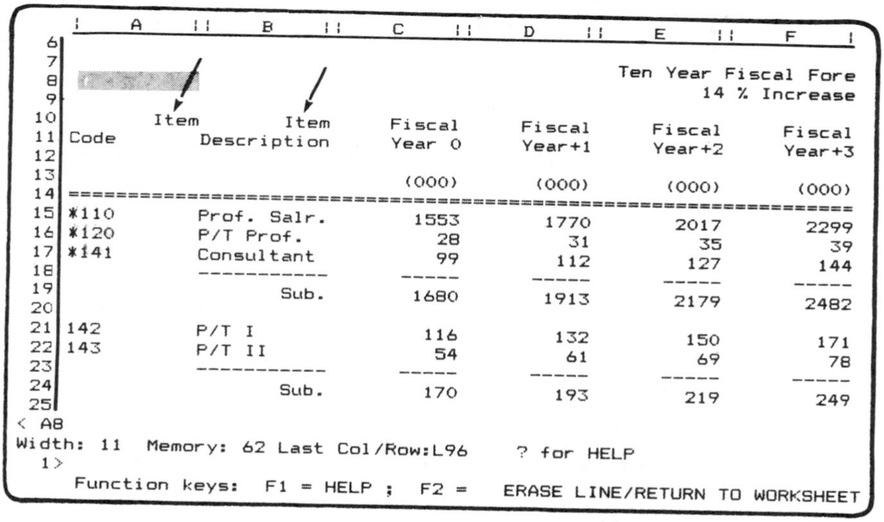

**Figure 4-2.** A sheet on which we want to blank A10 and B10.

Figure 4-3 shows the screen after this action.

We could also use ESC and then the arrow keys to place the two coordinates on the entry line.

The Blank command deletes the contents of the entries and any local formats.

To blank the active cell, we can simply type

/ B RETURN

since the RETURN will place the cell coordinate here.

The command, when executed, does not become the entry of the location and does not itself require storage if the sheet is saved.

Blank entries are evaluated as zero (0) when they are referenced in formulas in other entries.

This command can be used to blank large areas of the sheet.

When we want simply to replace one entry with a new value, text, or formula, it is not necessary to use the Blank command as an intermediate step. Simply moving the cursor to the desired location and then typing the new entry will result in replacing the old contents with the new contents.

```
  !   A   !!   B   !!   C   !!   D   !!   E   !!   F   !
 6|
 7|                                       Ten Year Fiscal Fore
 8|                    /           /                 14 % Increase
 9|
10|                              Fiscal    Fiscal    Fiscal    Fiscal
11|Code          Description     Year 0    Year+1    Year+2    Year+3
12|
13|                              (000)     (000)     (000)     (000)
14|========================================================================
15|*110          Prof. Salr.      1553      1770      2017      2299
16|*120          P/T Prof.          28        31        35        39
17|*141          Consultant         99       112       127       144
18|              -----------     -----     -----     -----     -----
19|              Sub.             1680      1913      2179      2482
20|
21|142           P/T I             116       132       150       171
22|143           P/T II             54        61        69        78
23|              -----------     -----     -----     -----     -----
24|              Sub.              170       193       219       249
25|
^ A8
Width: 11  Memory: 62 Last Col/Row:L96    ? for HELP
  1>
     Function keys:  F1 = HELP ;  F2 =   ERASE LINE/RETURN TO WORKSHEET
```

**Figure 4-3.** The same screen after the blank command is used.

## /C    THE COPY COMMAND

The Copy command is used to copy one area of the sheet to another area. The command is initiated by typing

/ C

at which time we're asked for the range of the area FROM which we wish to copy. We enter it followed by a RETURN or comma, and then are prompted for the TO cell. Notice that the FROM area is a range and the TO area is a single cell. The TO coordinate serves as the upper left corner of the TO area.

In the copy we can request "Options" by pressing the comma (,) and control how formulas are adjusted when they are moved to their new locations. The default (press RETURN and not comma) adjusts each coordinate relative to its new location. The "options" selection is explained under the Replicate command later in this chapter.

Let's look at an example. In Figure 4-4 suppose that we need to add another complete column to this report for FY+4. The Copy command can be used for this. First notice that SuperCalc provides us with the information

LAST COL/ROW:E19

```
         A    ::    B    ::    C    ::    D    ::    E    ::    F    :
 1                          Budget Forecast
 2       ******************** Year *******************************
 3               FY 0        FY+1        FY+2        FY+3
 4               *******     *******     *******     *******
 5
 6
 7 Employees      50          55          60          65
 8
 9
10 Personnel    1000000     1210000     1452000     1730300
11 Benefits      250000      302500      363000      432575
12 Telephone      10000       11000       12100       13310
13 Rent           60000       60000       60000       60000
14 Travel         40000       52800       69120       89856
15 Hospitality     1000        1100        1210        1331
16 Equipment      18000       19800       21780       23958
17              --------    --------    --------    --------
18
19    TOTAL $   1379000     1657200     1979210     2351330
20
v F7
Width: 11  Memory: 84 Last Col/Row:E19     ? for HELP
  1>
     Function keys:  F1 = HELP ;  F2 =   ERASE LINE/RETURN TO WORKSHEET
```

**Figure 4-4.** A simple budget forecast on which we need to add a new column for FY+4. We'll do so with the Copy command.

on the status line at the bottom of this screen. We'll use this information with this command. To copy the full column we'll type

/ C E3:E19 RETURN F3 RETURN

which produces the screen of Figure 4-5.

Let's explain the keystrokes:

| We type | Meaning |
|---------|---------|
| / C | Initiate the Copy command. |
| E3:E19 | Enter the range of the area that we will copy FROM. Here we can see a use for the |
| | LAST COL/ROW:E19 |
| | of the status line. On a large sheet we can quickly locate the bottom of the sheet when we want to complete an action such as the one here. |
| RETURN | End the FROM range. |
| F3 | Enter the single cell indicating the top left of the TO area. |
| RETURN | We do not want ''options'' (since we want coordinates of formulas to be adjusted) so we end the command with a RETURN. |

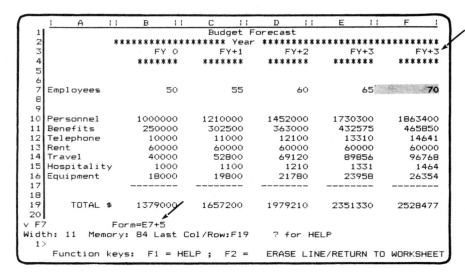

**Figure 4-5.** The screen of Figure 4-4 after copying row E to row F with the Copy command.

Notice that we have successfully copied the column. The formula at the active cell location

$$FORM=E7+5$$

has been copied with adjusted formulas. Also note that we'll need to edit the text at location F3 so that it contains FY+4 and not FY+3.

With the Copy command the TO and FROM areas are always the same size. We'll see, later in the chapter, that with the Replicate command this is not always true.

/D    THE DELETE COMMAND

The Delete command, /D, is used to delete a complete row or column of the sheet or to delete a file from a diskette. The action occurs when we type

/D

which places

R(OW), C(OLUMN), OR F(ILE)

on the prompt line. We then enter

R  to delete a row
C  to delete a column.
or F  to delete a file.

To cancel the delete action, we'll type CTRL-Z.

If we choose R or C, we then must enter the label for the row or column we want to delete or use RETURN for the active row or column. There is no restoring the row or column after deletion. Therefore, caution is necessary, and the need for backup of spreadsheets, emphasized in many other places of the book, is clear. A rippling may occur through the sheet as it is rewritten without the deleted row or column. With a large sheet this will require several seconds. The status line indicates this action by displaying

DELETING..

All rows below the deleted row (or to the right of the deleted column) are moved up one row (or one column to the left).

The action of deleting either a row or column will usually affect formulas on the sheet. Look at Figure 4-6 and notice that the formula for location B19 is

SUM(B10:B16)

Now let's delete row 12, by typing

/D R 12

look at the screen to verify that we've entered this correctly and then press

RETURN

This hesitation before pressing RETURN is important because it can prevent the unwanted deletion of a row or column. Notice in Figure 4-7

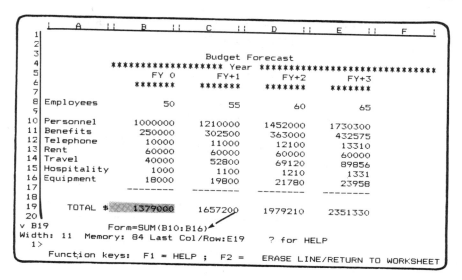

**Figure 4-6.** One entry of the sheet (B19) before deleting a row. Notice that the formula here is SUM(B10:B16).

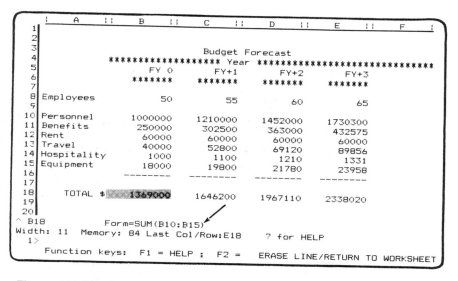

**Figure 4-7.** The formula in the total entry of column B is revised by SuperCalc to adjust for the deletion of row 12. Compare this to Figure 4-6.

that all entries below the old row 12 have moved up one row. Now let's look again at the total for this column.

Now the contents of the total entry are

SUM(B10:B15)    not    SUM(B10:B16)

and we see that SuperCalc has adjusted this formula, and all others, to reflect that a row has been deleted.

There are times when deleting a row or column can cause problems. Let's delete row 15 from Figure 4-7, and look at the results shown in Figure 4-8.

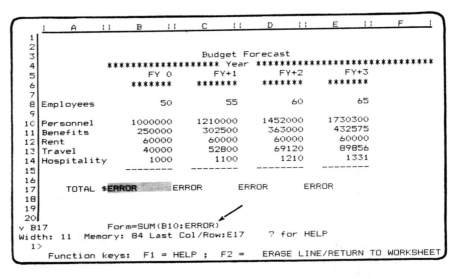

**Figure 4-8.** If we delete the row with the last element of the series, we cause ERROR entries in the sheet.

Notice that four entries show ERROR. The entry at location B17 shows a formula of

SUM(B10:ERROR)

SuperCalc has not replaced the old B15 in the sum with another coordinate but has instead replaced it with the ERROR function, indicating that no computation will be performed. (The ERROR function is discussed in Chapter 6, Built-in Functions.)

Notice that similar results have occurred in the other entries of row 17 of Figure 4-8. This problem is discussed again, and a solution suggested in the discussion of the SUM function.

For many users, the deletion of blank rows to improve the appearance of the sheet is a common activity. We need to be careful with this command so that we do not inadvertently delete a row when we really wanted to delete a column. We can prevent this by developing a hesitation before entering the RETURN.

This command is also used to delete a file from a diskette. We specify the desired file name, or retrieve it from the directory as described at the beginning of this chapter, and SuperCalc deletes the file. The file cannot be restored by SuperCalc after deletion so care must be used to ensure that the desired deletion occurs.

## /E    THE EDIT COMMAND

The Edit command, /E, provides a convenient method of changing the contents of an entry without requiring us to retype the complete entry, or of copying from one cell to the active cell with editing. It is initiated by moving the cursor to the location that we want to change and then typing

/E

at which time we indicate the current cell, by pressing RETURN, or a FROM cell by entering another cell coordinate then a RETURN. The entry then appears on the entry line.

Now the four arrow keys can be used in their editing functions.

CTRL-Z will cancel the editing activity and leaves the sheet unchanged.

/F    THE FORMAT COMMAND

The Format command, /F, is used to establish a format for a single cell or a group of cells on the sheet. It is initiated by typing

/F

at which time we are prompted for

G    Global, that is the full sheet.

C    Column, format a column. Then enter the column letter.

R    Row, format a row. Then enter the row number.

E    Entry, format a cell or group of cells. Then enter
      the range.

We select, and then must make an additional selection. The available formats are

| | |
|---|---|
| I | Integer |
| G | General |
| E | Exponential Notation |
| $ | Dollars and Cents |
| R | Right Justified, Numeric |
| L | Left Justified, Numeric |
| TR | Right Justified, Text |
| TL | Left Justified, Text |
| * | Graph |
| D | Default |
| Column Width | Change Column Width. (Available only for previous choice of Global or Column.) |

Format indicates the method that SuperCalc will use to display a value or text on the screen, or in a printed report when part or all of an electronic sheet is printed.

It is important to realize that this format affects the appearance of the entry and not the method of storage. For example, a number may have a decimal part that will not be displayed with the integer format; however, the integer format only affects the display. The decimal part of the number remains stored, and the full value is used in any references in formulas.

Each of the format options is discussed next.

I    Integer Format

This format indicates that the field will be presented as an integer value, although as with other values it may be stored as a noninteger. As with other formats this affects the way in which the number is presented, not the stored value. If the entry contains a number that is not an integer or a formula whose current value is not an integer, the value will be rounded and displayed as an integer. Rounding means that if the decimal portion of a positive value is greater than or equal to 0.5, then the next larger integer is displayed; otherwise the next smaller integer is displayed. With a negative value, if the decimal portion is greater than or equal to 0.5, then the next smaller integer is displayed; otherwise the next larger integer is displayed.

For example, four values are shown as they are stored and as they will be displayed with an integer format.

| Stored Value | Displayed Value, /F...I |
|:---:|:---:|
| 6.8 | 7 |
| 6.3 | 6 |
| −6.3 | −6 |
| −6.8 | −7 |

G    General Format

The G indicates the general format (not the global format obtained with the Default D option).

For numbers, this format will display values in either normal (as entered or computed) format or in scientific notation, depending on the column width. Numbers that are entered with leading or trailing zeros will be displayed without them. Leading and trailing zeros and scientific notation all are discussed in Chapter 5, Text, Numbers, and Formulas.

E    Exponential Notation Format

In this format, all numbers are displayed in scientific or exponential notation. Chapter 5, Text, Numbers, and Formulas, contains a full discussion of this in the Scientific Notation section.

**$    Dollar and Cents Format**

   This format displays numeric values with two decimal places. Entries evaluated with more than two decimal places will be rounded to two places. Entries evaluated with less than two decimal places will be shown with two places; for example, 16.5 will be shown as 16.50. Dollar signs ($) and commas (,) do not appear. This may be undesirable, depending upon the application. A $ may be right justified in the field immediately to the left of the value in order to give the desired appearance for some applications. If appearance is significant and the entry will not be used in computation, then it can be entered as text. For example, a price list could include an item description followed by the price included both as a label and as a value, such as

| Description: | Price (T) | Price (V): |
|---|---|---|
| MICROCOMPUTER | $2,867.00 | 2867.00 |

   In this example the middle column is text that could be used in printing reports, while the right column is a value that could be used in computation where the price is required. The middle column is right justified (/F...TR) and entered as

                    ”$2,867.00

Care is of course necessary to ensure that the two are the same and that if the price changes, both columns are changed.


**R and TR    Right Justified Format, R for Values, TR for Text**

   Values are right justified by default so that the R format is unnecessary for values or formulas unless a global left justification is in effect.
   The TR format means that all characters of a text entry will appear with the last character ending in the rightmost entry of the field.


**L and TL    Left Justified Format, L for Values, TL for Text**

   For SuperCalc, this format means that all characters of a text entry will appear, starting in the leftmost position of the field, and that all characters of a value displayed will appear, starting in the second left-most position of the field with a blank as the first character. For numbers, this blank prevents several fields from being run together when displayed. If we want to enter numeric characters that are fully left justified, they must be entered as text, for example, by entering

"50

in a field. When this is done, the characters 50 are a label and not a value, meaning that if it is referenced in a formula or other calculation it will be evaluated as 0 (zero) and not as the value 50.

With SuperCalc, all text is left justified by default, so that the /F...TL format is redundant when used with a label unless the global format is right justified.

\*    Graph Format

This format provides a simple bar graph capability. It left justifies asterisks in the field (starting at the second position of the entry). The number of asterisks placed is equal to the unrounded (truncated) integer portion of the value at the entry (with the exceptions that follow). When truncated both 9.1 and 9.8 become 9.

The exceptions are

• If a label is placed into a field with a /F...\* format, the graph format is ignored (although not destroyed) and the label is left justified.

• Values less than one, including negative values, or formulas evaluated in this range are displayed as a blank field.

• A value or formula whose truncated integer portion is equal to or greater than the width of the field will be displayed as the field filled with asterisks except for the blank in the leftmost character. Thus, a field of width 9 whose current value is 9 or greater (9.1, 10, 15.37, etc.), will be displayed as a space followed by eight asterisks. No error indication is given when this occurs, which is undesirable for many applications.

D    Default to Global Format

The D format indicates that this entry should be displayed with the global format. The entry line for a field with the D format indicates no format. Since an entry with no format defaults to the global format, this particular entry is used to erase an existing format within an entry or entries.

Column Width

This choice allows us to set the column width globally or for a selected column as we desire. To do so we enter a number, the width we want, followed by a RETURN when prompted under the Global or Column options of this command.

Considerations in Formatting

There are a number of important considerations in using the Format command.

• Every entry has a format even if one is not specified with this command. If no explicit format has been entered with the Format command, then the entry has the default format in effect at the time.

• Any rounding of values (for example, with /F...I or /F...$) affects only the display of the value and does not affect the way in which the number is stored or evaluated on the sheet.

• More than one format can apply to a single entry. It is possible to have a single entry in dollars and cents format (/F...$) and also left justified (/F...L). Multiple formats can be entered simultaneously.

• The formats established with this command for a range take precedence over those for a row. Row formats have precedence over column formats which in turn have precedence over Global formats.

• The column width significantly affects the display of values and labels; therefore, a combination of formats and column width determines how an item will be displayed. This will be discussed in Chapter 5, Text, Numbers, and Formulas.

• It is possible to use the Copy command (/C) or the Replicate command (/R) to replicate formats in the same way that other items are replicated. If there is a value, label, or formula in the entry or entries being replicated, then both will be replicated. Where this is undesirable, then either the format or the values, labels, or formulas must be entered separately.

• It is possible to generate formats in areas of the sheet that we expect to use, and then to leave them there in error when we do not use that part of the sheet. If it's desirable to remove these formats, then the default option of the Format command should be used (/F...D) as already described in this section.

• The formatting process in many data processing applications often requires more effort than the procedural aspects of the problem solving. This is true with many SuperCalc applications where correct placement of labels, setting of column widths, and formatting of individual entries may require significant activity on our part.

## /G    THE GLOBAL COMMAND

The Global command, /G, is used to control several options for the entire sheet. It is initiated by typing

/G

at which time we select from the options listed below.

F       Formulas. Display as text the contents of all
        cells. For items entered as formulas, we see
        the formulas and not the current values. Enter
        this again, and we return to a display of
        values, not formulas. Thus this works in on/off
        toggle fashion.

N       Next. Controls, in on/off toggle fashion, if
        the cursor advances automatically to the next
        cell when RETURN is pressed or if it does not
        advance.

B       Border. Controls, in on/off fashion, if
        the row and column labels appear on the
        screen or not.

T       Tab. Controls, in on/off fashion, if
        the cursor should skip all protected and
        blank cells when the RETURN is pressed
        or not.

R       Row. Indicates row order of recalculation.

C       Column. Indicates column order of recalculation.

M       Manual. Indicates manual calculation mode.

A       Automatic. Indicates automatic calculation mode.

Each of these is discussed below.


F    Formula


Figure 4-9 and Figure 4-10 illustrate this option. In the first we have a worksheet that is shown without formulas. This is the default with Super-Calc. In the second we have toggled this option by entering

/GF

and here we see the formulas for all of the sheet. This can be used in

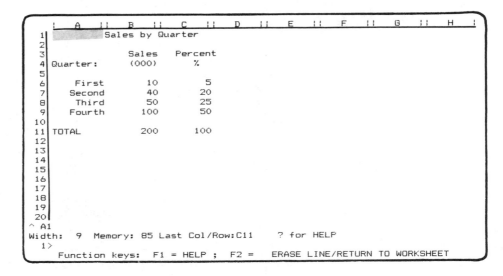

**Figure 4-9.** A worksheet displaying text plus values without displaying formulas.

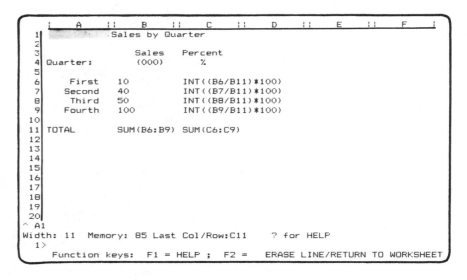

**Figure 4-10.** The worksheet of Figure 4-9 after entering /GF to toggle on the formula display.

conjunction with the Window command to display values in one window and formulas in the other. Formulas will spill into adjacent cells as other text does.

N    Next

This option controls the advancement of the cursor when RETURN is pressed. With this option toggled on, the cursor moves to the next entry in the "current" direction. When toggled off, the cursor does not advance automatically, and the arrow keys are used to advance the cursor as desired. The current direction is indicated by the first character of the status line ($\wedge$> $\vee$<), and is changed by pressing an arrow key while not in edit mode or cursor pointing mode.

B    Border

The border option controls whether the column and row labels appear on the screen. When printing with the Output command, this option is used to remove these labels if we do not wish them to print. This option can also be useful to remove the borders if they are confusing to the person using SuperCalc. There may be templates we create that others will be using, and for which we will want to eliminate the borders to simplify the appearance of the screen.

T    Tab

This is another option that can be very useful with templates. If we have many blank or protected entries on a template, we can use this option to have the cursor automatically jump over those two categories of entries. This is useful when we are entering data, and want to move quickly and accurately from cell to cell.

R and C    Row and Column, the Order of Recalculation

A recalculation of all entries of the sheet occurs, either by changing an entry or by entering an exclamation point (!) to initiate a recalculation. When we do so, the software can either perform the recalculation in column order, C, as indicated by the arrows in Figure 4-11, or in row order, R, as shown by the arrows in Figure 4-12. In both cases the action begins at entry A1. These figures contain a simple sales-by-quarter report

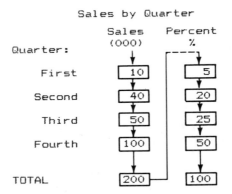

**Figure 4-11.** A sheet graphically indicating the meaning of columnwise recalculation order, C.

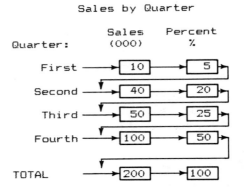

**Figure 4-12.** A sheet indicating rowwise recalculation order, R.

in which quarterly sales are totaled in the SALES column and then each of the four sales entries is divided by the total to determine the PERCENT for that quarter.

By default the recalculation order starts at entry A1 and proceeds down the A column, then continues at B1 and moves down the B column, etc. However, if we want to go across, we enter R, as described below, and we will start at A1 and go across row 1, return to A2, and then go across row 2, etc.

After entering

/G

we enter either R or C, indicating the desired reevaluation order. They mean

R       Rowwise recalculation
C       Columnwise recalculation

Let's look more closely at the last examples to demonstrate the difference between these two. Suppose that we begin with the example of Figure 4-12 with an R (rowwise) recalculation order. Look at Figure 4-13. It has been derived from Figure 4-12 by changing the entry for the FOURTH quarter from 100 to 0. Note that the SALES column now correctly totals 100. However, look at the PERCENT column. The individual percentages are all incorrect. The PERCENT total is 50% and not 100%. The formula for the percentage entry on the FIRST row has been computed by dividing FIRST by TOTAL and multiplying the result by 100, that is,

$$(B7/B12)*100$$

This is the correct formula but the wrong answer. The problem is that when this was computed, the value at B12 was still 200 and not the total of 100, which was correctly placed there later.

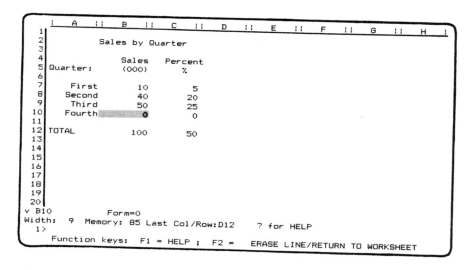

**Figure 4-13.** The rowwise order of recalculation has resulted in this incorrect sheet. Note that the percentages are all incorrect even though the formulas are correct.

Let's follow a simple trace through the reevaluation to emphasize how this occurred. To do so, we begin with the values shown in Figure 4-12. The trace is a step-by-step tracking of what occurs. Let's follow the action until we discover the cause:

| Entry Location | Entry Contents | Evaluation | Notes |
|---|---|---|---|
| B10 | 100 | 100 | We position the cursor to this location in order to change our FOURTH quarter value from 100 to 0. |
| B10 | 0 | 0 | We make the change, triggering the recalculation of the entire sheet, which occurs after the value here is changed. |
| | | | The reevaluation occurs, sweeping across the rows, from A1 to B1 to C1, then A2, B2, C2, etc. Nothing is in fact changed until the formula at C7 is encountered. |
| C7 | (B7/B12)*100 | (10/200)*100 <br> 5 | Here is the problem. Entry B12 still has the old total of 200. It is not updated until the other rows have been reevaluated. As a result, each percentage is wrong. |

At this point we see the value of the exclamation point. If we enter !, our sheet will be fully recalculated, providing the correct values as shown in Figure 4-14. We get correct results because the value at entry B12 is 100, and no longer the older value of 200.

Why use rowwise recalculation? For this sheet it was incorrect; however, its use can be demonstrated by a different presentation format of the same data. Suppose that we wanted to prepare this report in the format shown in Figure 4-15. For this report the correct order of reevaluation is rowwise. This is true because we must compute the value at location F8 before we compute any value in row 9.

With this understanding of the differences between row and column calculation order we can emphasize the need to develop models which do calculate correctly. We want to build our sheets so that each entry is a

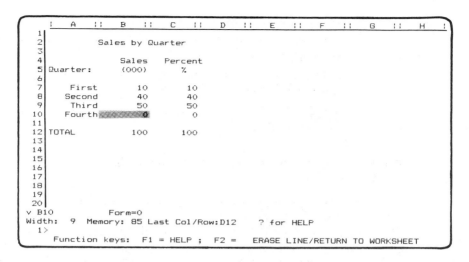

**Figure 4-14.** The sheet of Figure 4-13, now correct, after a recalculation initiated by entering an exclamation point (!).

```
   !   A   !!   B   !!   C   !!   D   !!   E   !!   F   !!   G   !!   H   !
 1 |
 2 |         Sales (000) by Quarter
 3 |
 4 |
 5 |            1st        2nd        3rd        4th      TOTAL
 6 |            ----       ----       ----       ----      -----
 7 |
 8 |Sales         10         40         50        100        200
 9 |Percent        5         20         25         50        100
10 |
11 |
12 |
13 |
14 |
15 |
16 |
17 |
18 |
19 |
20 |
 ^ F8            Form=SUM(B8:E8)
 Width:   9   Memory: 85 Last Col/Row:F9      ? for HELP
   1>
      Function keys:   F1 = HELP ;   F2 =    ERASE LINE/RETURN TO WORKSHEET
```

**Figure 4-15.** The same problem formatted in a way in which the correct order of recalculation is rowwise.

function of entries to its left and above its location. There is additional discussion of this concept in Chapter 7, Other Topics, under the discussion of Forward Reference.

Let's summarize:

- SuperCalc defaults to a columnwise order of recalculation.
- Users can change the recalculation order by use of the R and C options of the Global command.
- The correct choice (C or R) will depend on the requirements and layout of our solution to the problem.
- Entering an ! will usually eliminate any problems and is suggested before using the results.

M and A        Manual and Automatic Recalculation Mode

On large sheets, or on small sheets with lengthy or time-consuming formulas, the recalculation that automatically occurs when any value on the sheet is changed can take several seconds, or longer, to complete. Although not long, even this delay can be frustrating, especially when many changes are being made on the sheet. SuperCalc defaults to this automatic, instantaneous recalculation mode; however, it provides the capacity to shift to a mode in which a recalculation occurs only when we want it.

This is accomplished by entering

/G

and then selecting one of the two recalculation modes. The two recalculation modes are

A    Automatic
M    Manual

Automatic is the default and produces a recalculation wherever a value or formula is entered or revised. Manual postpones this recalculation until we initiate it by entering an exclamation point. Figure 4-16 contains a sheet on which the recalculation mode has been set to M, for manual. Notice that the TOTAL is shown as 0 (zero). At this point, assume that we want to see the total, which we can obtain by entering !. Figure 4-17 shows the result of entering the !.

Since a manual recalculation mode can temporarily leave the sheet with incorrect values, it's important to depress the ! before relying on values on the sheet.

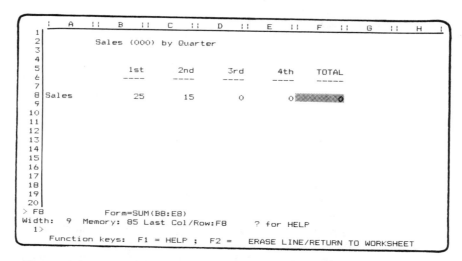

**Figure 4-16.** A spreadsheet on which the manual recalculation mode is in effect. Note that the total column is temporarily incorrect.

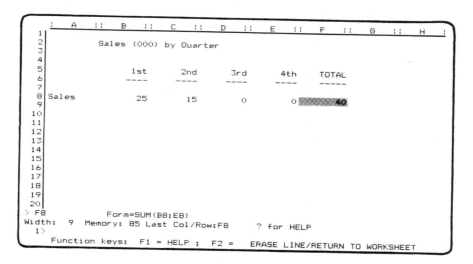

**Figure 4-17.** The sheet of Figure 4-16 after a recalculation (!). The total is computed and correctly displayed.

## /I    THE INSERT COMMAND

The Insert command, /I, is used to insert a complete row or column on the sheet. The action is initiated by typing

/I

which produces a prompt of

R(ow) or C(olumn)?

At this point, enter an R for a row to be added or C for a column to be added.

After entering an R we are prompted for the number of the row we want to insert; after a C we are prompted for the column letter. Enter the number or letter followed by RETURN, or alternately, enter RETURN alone to insert at the current row or column.

To cancel the action, depress the CTRL-Z or a function key if available.

No confirming action is required. The sheet ripples as the insertion occurs, which on a large sheet may require several seconds.

This command inserts a blank row or column. If we wish to have formulas, values, or labels in place on the newly inserted row or column, we can do so by writing on the newly expanded sheet.

As with the Delete command, formulas are automatically revised as necessary to accommodate the new row or column. When a row or column is added to the middle of a series, for example, with the SUM function, the values placed in the row or column will be included in the series. A review of the description for the Delete command will show what occurs. When a row or column is added at the start or end of a series—for example, a series that is an argument of the SUM function—the series is not revised to include the new values. The discussion of the SUM function in Chapter 6, Built-in Functions, presents one way of including this new row or column when it appears at an end of the series. The description of the Delete command earlier in this chapter also includes a discussion of the problems associated with deleting in series references.

Although it is sometimes desirable to have the capability to add more than a single row or column, only one row or column can be added at a time.

As suggested in Chapter 9, Creating Templates, blank rows or columns included for appearance should be inserted as the last step in developing a sheet. This will prevent undesired entries in the blank row or column, which can be generated when replicating down or across areas of the sheets that should be blank.

Although SuperCalc does not have a sorting capability, it is sometimes possible to perform a crude sort by inserting. If we have an unsorted list of items, for example, employee names, we can enter the names one after the other by inserting a blank row in the appropriate position and then entering the next name onto the blank row. Since this is being done "by eye," it is not a reliable sorting activity but can be helpful in some instances.

/L    THE LOAD COMMAND

The load command, /L, is used to load all or part of a file from a diskette into the memory of the computer. It is initiated by typing

/L

at which time we are prompted to enter the name of the file we want to load.

We can enter the filename at this point, or type RETURN as explained at the start of this chapter in the section entitled ''Working with Files on Diskettes,'' to obtain a directory of filenames. This can be helpful if we've forgotten the name of the file we want to load.

When a file is loaded from a diskette, it has the same characteristics (column width, cursor location, etc.) with which it was sorted.

We can use this command to load all or part of a file, and we can select the portion of the sheet where we want the file loaded. This can be very important when we have several files we want to combine. We can load them at desired locations so that we can use them in consolidated form.

If we do not wish to consolidate sheets, we should be careful to zap the sheet when we have finished with one sheet and wish to load a second from a diskette. If the first will be reused, it should be saved first before the Zap command is used.

The overlay/consolidation capability can also be important if we have data we wish to use in more than one sheet. If we receive monthly data on an activity and we use it in several reports, we can enter that data in column A (any location will be satisfactory) and then build several reports that use these data in this format in column A. We load a report format, then the data. Recalculate (!) and we have a report. Zap the sheet, load the second report, than the data again. Recalculate and we have the second report, etc.

## /M     THE MOVE COMMAND

The Move command, /M, is used to move either a full row or a full column to another location on the sheet. It is initiated by typing

/M

which places

R(OW) OR C(OLUMN)?

on the prompt line.

The same command is used to move either a column or a row. A starting FROM and an ending TO row or column are provided.

The Move command has an action similar to the action involved when we have a pile of 3×5 cards on the table and move a card from one position to another. If we move one card toward the front of the deck, all cards below its original position do not move, and all cards below its new position back to its old position are bumped down one relative position. It is a real move, which means that the card no longer exists at its old location.

Similarly, if we move a card toward the bottom of the deck, cards are shifted toward the top of the deck as the card is placed in its new position. In SuperCalc a move down for a row or to the right for a column—places the moved column (or row) at the TO location.

Let's look at the example in Figure 4-18, in which we have determined that we want to move the row with sales by NOAH to between MARTHA and TOMMY, its correct alphabetic position. We enter

/M R 5 RETURN 7 RETURN

which is what has occurred in Figure 4-19.

Notice that all subtotals and final totals are unchanged and still correct.

Now suppose that we realize that TOMMY is actually in DEPT. B and that we want to move him to that department and list him after JASON. Figure 4-20 shows the screen after completing this move.

Notice the two subtotals, both incorrect. The formula for the SUBTOTAL of department A shows

SUM(B3:B16)

at location B9 and for department B shows

SUM(B13:B15)

at location B18.

The formula at location B9 has been revised by SuperCalc to show the new location of TOMMY, now B16; the formula at B18 has not been revised to contain a new end entry for the series. In fact, repeated recalculation (!!...!!) will continually change the values. This is caused by the "forward reference," which is discussed in Chapter 7, Other Topics.

We'll need to use the Move command with care because of the type of problems already described. There is additional consideration of this problem and a partial solution suggested for the series problem in the discussion of the SUM function.

Moving only part of a row or column, instead of a complete row or column, cannot be accomplished with this command.

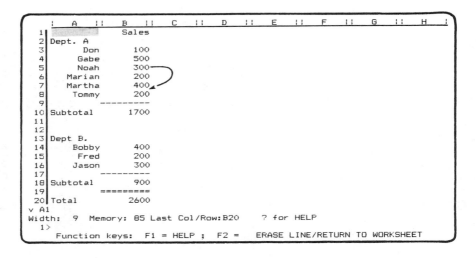

**Figure 4-18.** A screen before moving the row with NOAH to its correct alphabetical location in DEPT. A.

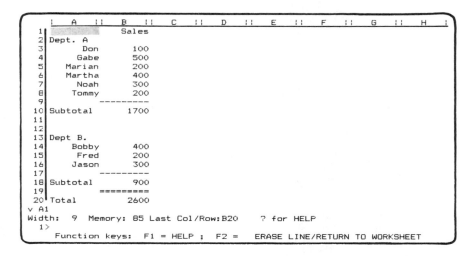

**Figure 4-19.** The screen after completing the move described in Figure 4-18.

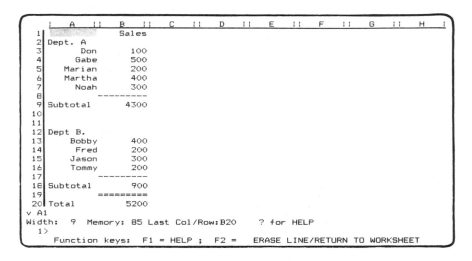

**Figure 4-20.** Errors introduced by moving TOMMY from the last position of DEPT. A to the last position of DEPT. B.  Neither SUBTOTAL is now correct.

## /O    THE OUTPUT COMMAND

The Output command, /O, is used to print all or part of a worksheet or to write a file to a diskette or console (screen) containing the current labels and values of the entries or formulas. It is initiated by typing

/O

at which time the prompt line reads

D(ISPLAY) OR C(ONTENTS) REPORT?

This prompts for one of two items:

D  meaning that we want to output information as shown on the screen.

C  meaning that we want to output the text and formats we entered to create the sheet.

The Output command is conceptually straightforward. We begin with information on an electronic sheet that we want to print. We will consider all printed reports as a rectangle. To print a report, we indicate the top left corner of the portion of the sheet that we want to print, and the lower right coordinate. Thus, on a grid system like the worksheets of Super-Calc, two coordinate points define the rectangle that we want to print.

Printers vary significantly in their capabilities and in the way in which we send information to them. To simplify this section, we will discuss printing with one of the very large number of printers available. For other printers the manual or our vendor can be helpful in supplying specific information.

Our example will be for the EPSON MX-100 printer on an IBM Personal Computer. Other printers may work differently. Let's look at the example in Figure 4-21 where we have on the screen a SIMPLE BUDGET report that we want to print. We initiate the Output command (by typing /O), receive the prompt line previously indicated and type

D

which places

ENTER RANGE

on the prompt line.

At this point we can enter

A1:B14

to indicate that we want this rectangle to be printed. We can also enter the word

ALL

which serves the same purpose, printing from A1 to the last column/row indicated. (However, the word ALL will not include any text that might be spilling over into cells beyond the last column, which is usually undesirable.)

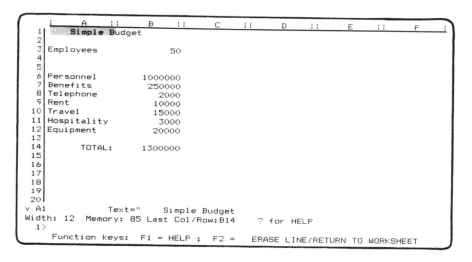

**Figure 4-21.** A screen displaying an electronic sheet that we want to print.

After entering one of these two options here, we are prompted again for another entry. This time we see

ENTER DEVICE: P(RINTER), S(ETUP), C(ONSOLE), OR D(ISK)

These options have the following meanings

P   Printer. Direct the output to the printer.

S   Setup. This option allows us to send a series of characters to the printer to establish settings for, or control, the carriage, line feed, and other features of individual printers, as illustrated below.

Under this option we are prompted again with

L(ENGTH), W(IDTH), S(ETUP), OR P(RINT)?

These options mean

L    Length. Change the length of the page, with 0 (zero) indicating continuous forms.

W    Width. Change the width of the output line.

S    Setup. Send special setup codes to the printer as demonstrated below.

P    Print. Print the data.

C    Console. Allows us to see the report on the display unit of our computer, as a preview of what will be printed.

D    Disk. This sends the output to a disk, instead of to the printer or display. This file will be a copy of what would normally be sent to the printer. It can then be printed later, or can become an input file to another program for later use. Since we do not "see" the file, the console option of the Output command described just above may be a good way of previewing the file before writing it with this option.

Figure 4-22 resulted from entering the following Output command.

/ O D A1:B14 RETURN P

Notice that the border printed along with the report. To remove it, as shown in Figure 4-23, we enter

/ G B  / O D A1:B14 RETURN P

Let's look at an example of a setup string. The output shown in Figure 4-24 results from entering the following (assuming that the borders are not present).

/ O D A1:B14 RETURN S S CTRL-O RETURN P

Here the CTRL-O combination signals this printer (EPSON MX-100) that condensed print is desired.

The Output command prints all columns with the column width in effect, and it uses existing formats from the sheet. Labels and current values of the entry are printed.

## Listing the "Contents" of a Worksheet

We can use the Output command to get a full listing of the formulas, text, and values that compose the sheet on which we are working. To do so we type

/ O C ALL RETURN P

```
   !       A    !!      B    !
 1!        Simple Budget
 2!
 3!Employees                 50
 4!
 5!
 6!Personnel          1000000
 7!Benefits            250000
 8!Telephone             2000
 9!Rent                 10000
10!Travel               15000
11!Hospitality           3000
12!Equipment            20000
13!
14!       TOTAL:       1300000
```

**Figure 4-22.** Our printed report, with borders.

```
   Simple Budget

Employees                 50


Personnel          1000000
Benefits            250000
Telephone             2000
Rent                 10000
Travel               15000
Hospitality           3000
Equipment            20000

      TOTAL:       1300000
```

**Figure 4-23.** The printed report, without borders.

```
      Simple Budget

Employees             50


Personnel        1000000
Benefits          250000
Telephone           2000
Rent               10000
Travel             15000
Hospitality         3000
Equipment          20000

   TOTAL:         1300000
```

**Figure 4-24.** A condensed printing of our report, resulting from the use of a SETUP string.

Figure 4-25 and Figure 4-26 illustrate this concept. For Figure 4-26 we have typed the line above, and we obtain this listing. The characters above have the following meanings.

| Keystrokes | Mean |
|---|---|
| / O | Enter the command structure and specify the Output command. |
| C | Request a listing of the contents. |
| ALL | Indicate that all of the sheet is to be listed. We could indicate the same thing by typing the full range of the sheet. We could also specify a portion of the sheet if that is what we wanted. |
| RETURN | This indicates the end of the range. A comma (,) serves the same purpose. |
| P | Specify that we want the printer as the output device. |

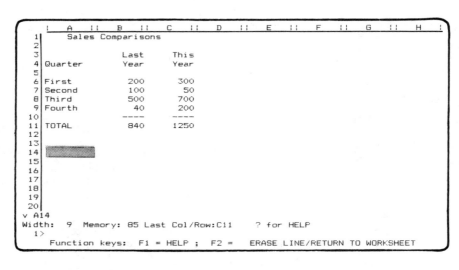

**Figure 4-25.** A report on the screen for which we'll obtain a "contents" listing.

```
SuperCalc ver.    1.10
     Sales Comparisons
A1        = "      Sales Comparisons
B3        = "Last
C3        = "This
A4        = "Quarter
B4        = "      Year      Year
A6        = "First
B6        = 200
C6        = 300
A7        = "Second
B7        = 100
C7        = 50
A8        = "Third
B8        = 500
C8        = 700
A9        = "Fourth
B9        = 40
C9        = 200
B10         = "----
C10         = "----
A11         = "TOTAL
B11         = SUM(B6:B9)
C11         = SUM(C6:C9)
```

**Figure 4-26.** A contents listing of the worksheet of Figure 4-25.

Considerations in Printing

There are a number of considerations in using the Output command to print a report to a printer.

• The capability for characters printed per line varies for different printers. There are printers available that will print several hundred characters per line.

• Each printer has a maximum number of characters per line that can be printed. If we attempt to print rows that are wider than the maximum, then the additional characters will be printed in a separate section below the first section of the report.

• Although the window may be split when printing, this is ignored when the sheet is printed. However, different sections of the sheet may be selected and sequentially printed for the desired format.

• Even though we may have titles fixed in place, the rectangle is printed ignoring the appearance of these titles on the screen, that is, as if there were no fixed titles.

• A method of simplifying the printing process is to include a row of directions like row 2 of the screen shown in Figure 4-27. Here we have a direction to enter

/ G B / O D A1:B16 RETURN P

Following these directions will produce our report. This row has been entered as text, beginning with the double quote ("). This serves as a reminder for us of the necessary steps to print our report. This can be especially helpful with setup strings.

• If a report is to be prepared on special preprinted forms, then an alignment check may be necessary. To do so, we can place a rectangle of "dummy" data on the top of the sheet and then print from this area above the desired report. This can be used to test that the paper has been properly loaded into the printer.

Chapter 8, Recognizing, Preventing and Correcting Errors, and Chapter 9, Creating Templates, also contain considerable information and suggestions regarding printing.

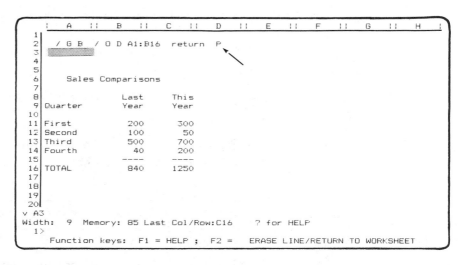

**Figure 4-27.** This spreadsheet contains directions included as a row of the sheet.

## /P     PROTECT COMMAND

The Protect command, /P, is used to protect a range of cells from later change. This is an important command, for it provides us with a level of security against the accidental destruction of text, values, or formulas we have placed in cells of the worksheet.

After we have entered the information we wish into the desired locations of the worksheet, we protect the area by entering

/P

and then the range of cells we want to protect.

Entries that have been protected will have a "P" on the status line.

After cells have been protected, we will receive an error if we try to edit the cells, or if we try to enter text, values, or formulas over the protected cells. The Delete command will not delete a row or column with a protected cell. If the Blank, Copy, Load, or Replicate command is used, and the range includes protected entries, those protected areas will not be destroyed, although other nonprotected entries will be.

To change cells that are protected, we must first unprotect them using the Unprotect command described later in this chapter.

This is an extremely important capability in building templates that others may use. This topic will be discussed in Chapter 9, Creating Templates.

## /Q    QUIT COMMAND

The Quit command, /Q, is used when we want to quit using SuperCalc. It is initiated by typing

/Q

at which time we receive the prompt line

EXIT SUPERCALC? Y(ES) OR N(O)

Now we must respond with a "Y" if we wish to leave SuperCalc, or with an "N" if we do not wish to quit. This request for confirmation from the SuperCalc program is very important. Any sheet that is in memory when we quit is destroyed. It is our responsibility to save it before quitting. The Y/N confirmation can prevent us from accidentally quitting when that is not the action that we want to take. We should be careful to develop a hesitation after typing the "Q" of this command so that we ensure that this action is the desired one.

/R    THE REPLICATE COMMAND

The Replicate command, /R, is used to replicate text, values, or formulas from one section of the sheet to another. The examples in this section will explain the meaning of replicate as used in this context. The command is initiated by typing

/R

at which time a series of prompts asks us in turn for a FROM and TO range, and other information. The two required ranges are:

FROM range—the coordinates of the items which are already entered on the sheet and which we want to reproduce elsewhere.

TO range—the coordinates of the locations into which we want our items replicated.

The Replicate command was introduced in some detail in Chapter 3, Getting Started; a rereading of that section may be helpful before continuing.

Let's look in detail at some examples of replication processes, beginning with text and studying what we want to do, why we want to do it, and then how we do it with SuperCalc. In each case refer to Figure 4-28.

Replicating Labels

**Example 1.**

*What we want done:* Copy the contents of one entry to another location, for example, from B2 to D2.

*Why we might want to do this:* We may have entered a lengthy label that we want to enter again completely at another location. Instead of typing it fully, we can use the Replicate command (or the Copy command) to do this for us.

*How we do this:* Let's assume we have the word YEAR at B2. We type

/R B2 RETURN D2 RETURN

**Example 2:**

*What we want done:* Replicate a label from a single entry to a series of entries on the same row. Now we see the difference between the Replicate and Copy command. With Copy we cannot expand the original cells as we can here.

*Why we might want this done:* Suppose that we have entered a title at B5 and want to replicate it from C5 through F5.

*How we do this:* We type

/R B5 RETURN C5:F5 RETURN

We can also use the arrow keys to enter the coordinates.

**Example 3:**

*What we want done:* Replicate a single entry across a row, as shown in Example 3 of Figure 4-28.

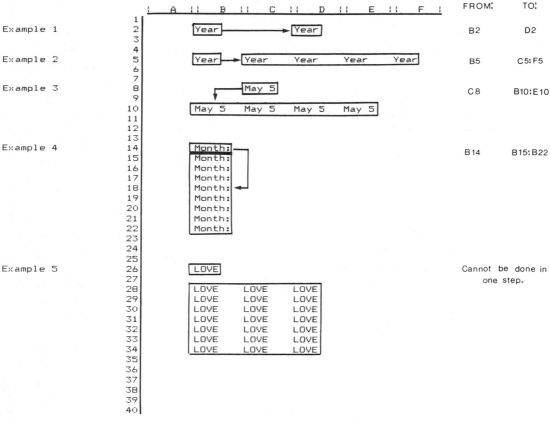

**Figure 4-28.** Examples of the process of replicating a single entry onto other areas of the sheet.

*Why we might want to do this:* We may have entered a date at the top of the sheet that we want to repeat at the top of each column.

*How we do this:* Type

/R C8 RETURN B10:E10 RETURN

**Example 4:**

*What we want done:* Replicate a single label entry down a column.

*Why we might want to do this:* We want to repeat a label, as shown in Example 4.

*How we do this:* As in the previous examples, we type

/R B14 RETURN B15:B22 RETURN

**Example 5:**

*What we want to do:* Replicate a single label entry into a two-dimensional shape.

*How we do this:* This cannot be done with one Replicate command. To accomplish this, we'll need several Replicate commands.

In all these examples, we began with a single entry. Now let's begin with a row and replicate a row, also of text. Refer to Figure 4-29 for these examples.

**Example 6:**

*What we want to do:* Copy a row into another row.

*How we do this:* The command to do this is

/R B3:E3 RETURN B5 RETURN

This is tricky, and the cause of errors. When replicating a row (or column) into another row (or column), only the starting coordinate of the TO range is provided. SuperCalc does the replicating with only this information. In the next example we'll see what happens if we give both the start and end of the TO range.

**Example 7:**

*What we want to do:* Same as example 6.

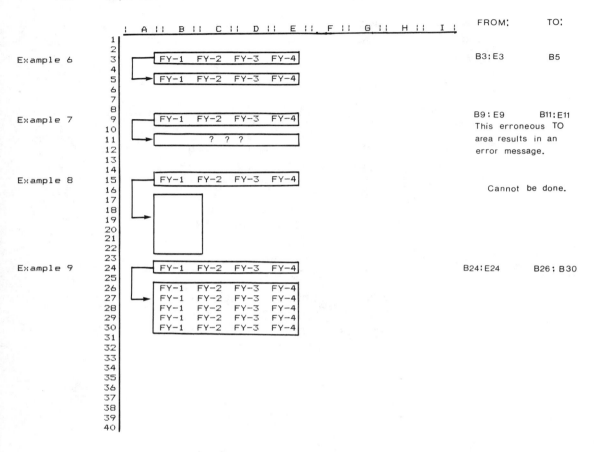

**Figure 4-29.** Examples of the process of replicating a row onto other areas of the sheet. The same principles apply to replicating a column.

*How we do this:* Now let's enter

/R B9:E9 RETURN B11:E11 RETURN

Our result is an error message. This kind of specification is used only to replicate a row (or column) into a two-dimensional area as we'll see below.

## Example 8:

*What we want to do:* Replicate a row down a column.

*How we do this:* This cannot be done with this command. We'll see next that a horizontal source range with a vertical target range results in a two-dimensional area, not in perpendicular areas.

**Example 9:**

*What we want to do:* Replicate a row into a two-dimensional area.
*How we do this:* We enter

/R B24:E24 RETURN B26:B30 RETURN

In this example we get the row successfully repeated over several rows.

These concepts for replicating a row apply similarly to replicating a column.

Finally let's discuss replicating a two-dimensional area of labels. This cannot be done in one step with the Replicate command although the Copy command can do this.

Replicating Formulas With Adjusted Coordinates

When formulas including coordinate references are replicated, one step may be added to the process of replicating. Let's follow this processing, beginning with the screen shown in Figure 4-30. Here we have entered numbers for our sales for each quarter of last year and this year. We've

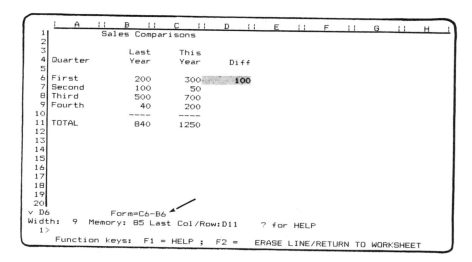

**Figure 4-30.** We'll replicate the formula at D6 down column D.

placed a total at the bottom of each of these two columns and we're beginning the process of finding the difference between sales this year and last year.

Notice that at D6 we have the formula

$$C6-B6$$

We want similar, but not identical, formulas all the way down that column. What we want is

| Location | Formula |
| --- | --- |
| D7 | C7-B7 |
| D8 | C8-B8 |
| D9 | C9-B9 |
| D11 | C11-B11 |

The similarity between these formulas occurs because each performs a computation like the one at D6 but with coordinates adjusted to location.

The power of the Replicate command allows the replication process to occur while accommodating these changing relationships. Let's see how.

We'll begin the process by typing

$$\text{/R D6 RETURN D7:D11}$$

Now we'll press RETURN, producing Figure 4-31.

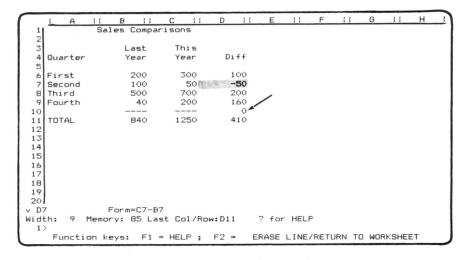

Figure 4-31. We have successfully replicated our formula with the exception of entry D10, where we'll need to correct the entry.

Everything is correct, with the exception of D10, where 0 (zero) has occurred as the difference between the two labels at C10 and B10. This illustrates the desirability of postponing parts of the labeling process until the last steps of preparing electronic sheets. We'll discuss this again at several points in later chapters.

Replicating Formulas With Unadjusted Coordinates

Let's continue with a similar example and explain how the NO AD-JUST option is used. We've simplified our report and have one column for sales THIS YEAR and another column started in column D in which we want to determine the percentage of our sales in each quarter of the year, as shown in Figure 4-32. At location D5 we've placed the formula

$$(B5/B9)*100$$

that is, divide the sales for the first quarter by the total and multiply by 100. Notice that an integer format (/F...I) has been placed at the entry, as indicated by the I on the status line.

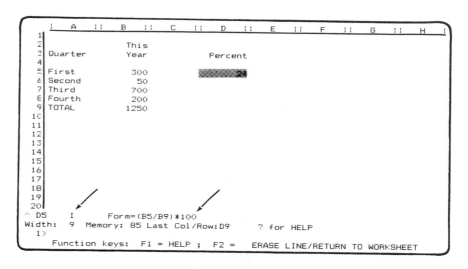

**Figure 4-32.** We'll replicate this formula, using both the ADJUST and NO AD-JUST options.

Now consider the formulas that we want at the other locations. What we want is

| Location | Formula |
|----------|---------|
| D6 | (B6/B9)*100 |
| D7 | (B7/B9)*100 |
| D8 | (B8/B9)*100 |

In studying the formulas, notice that the first coordinate adjusts relatively as we go down the column; however, B9 is absolute, it does not change; that is, it is NO ADJUST.

Let's replicate.

| We type | Meaning |
|---------|---------|
| /R | Initiate the Replicate command. |
| D5 RETURN | Establish this as the replication of the single cell D5. |
| D6 | Type this as shown or move the cursor to this location. |
| : | Signals the middle of the series. |
| D8 | Enter the end of the series. |
| , | We enter the comma (,) *not* RETURN to obtain the "options" for this command. |

At this point, we receive the prompt line below

N(O) ADJUST, A(SK FOR ADJUST), V(ALUES)

The three options available to us now are:

N   No adjust. This is the same as pressing the RETURN key to automatically adjust each entry. However, we will see that N below has another meaning.

A   Ask for adjust. This allows us to indicate, coordinate by coordinate, if we want to adjust a coordinate or not. It is the option we will select for our example.

V   Values. This option copies the current values associated with entries being replicated, and not their formulas.

Here we've decided that we want to adjust one coordinate and not adjust another. Therefore we will continue our replication process as below.

| We type | Meaning |
|---------|---------|
| A | Ask for adjustment. |
| Y | When we ask for adjustment, we are presented with a prompt asking us if we should adjust B5 or not (Y means adjust, N means do not adjust). In our example we want to adjust B5 so we enter Y. |
| N | We are then asked if we want to adjust B9. Since we do not, we enter N. |

Now we have successfully replicated our formula. If we were replicating from more than a single source cell, then we would use the information provided on the prompt line that indicates exactly which coordinate of which source (FROM) cell we were deciding to adjust or not.

Our formulas are replicated as required on the screen of Figure 4-33. We can include the total at the bottom of column D and complete the sheet. (*A word of caution:* In Chapter 5, Text, Numbers, and Formulas, the topic of computing percentages and accurately totaling them is discussed. Values have been chosen here so that rounding occurs with a total of 100%. With different quarterly sales values, this might not occur.)

Here we also replicated the format by including it with the formula that

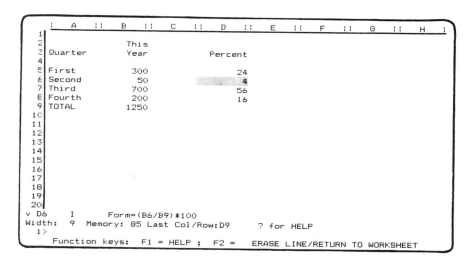

**Figure 4-33.** We have replicated D5 (including the format) down column D as planned.

we reproduced. If we hadn't done that we could enter it separately for the range with the Format command.

Additional Considerations

This command is the most complex of the SuperCalc commands and can easily lead to significant problems in developing a sheet. For this reason, when using this command experimentally, it's important to copy the current sheet to backup so that if replicating causes problems, the previous sheet can be retrieved. Backup is discussed in the next section of this chapter and in Chapter 7, Other Topics.

/S   THE SAVE COMMAND

The Save command, /S, provides the capability to save files on diskettes. It is initiated by typing

/S

at which time we are prompted to enter the file name or RETURN for a directory as explained in the section entitled ''Working with Files on Diskettes'' at the start of this chapter.

This command can save all or part of the worksheet, and for each of these two options can save either ALL of the sheet, or the VALUES from the sheet. ALL indicates that text, formulas, and constant values should be saved for the sheet. VALUES indicates that only the text and current values, and not the formulas should be saved.

If only part of the sheet is to be saved, we are prompted to enter the desired range.

When the sheet is saved and then loaded, it is reloaded with the same characteristics that it had when saved. For example, it will have the same active cell as when stored; it will display the same rows and columns on the screen; global characteristics will be the same, etc.

If we try to save a file with the name of an existing file, SuperCalc informs us of that and offers us these choices:

C   Change name. We return to the edit line and change the name.

B   Backup. The file from memory is stored with a suffix indicating it is a backup copy.

O   Overwrite. Write this file over the existing file on the diskette, destroying the existing file.

## /T    THE TITLE LOCK COMMAND

The Title Lock command, /T, is used to fix column or row titles in place above or at the left of the screen. The command is initiated by typing

/T

at which time we are prompted as follows.

| Option | Means |
|--------|-------|
| H | Horizontal title only. |
| V | Vertical title only. |
| B | Both horizontal and vertical titles. |
| C | Clear (remove) existing titles. |

The value of this command can be seen in Figure 4-34, where the large budget in the background is one electronic sheet. Two screens have been imposed upon this background. The top screen simply shows a section of the screen without any identification labeling the rows or columns displayed. In the bottom screen, however, we have used the Title Lock command to display the row labels (columns A and B) on the left of the screen. This command allows us to freeze columns, as in the bottom screen of Figure 4-34, where titles are frozen vertically.

In Figure 4-35 the same budget is displayed with titles frozen both vertically and horizontally (B).

Some general considerations in using this command are

• The location of the cursor when the command is executed is important. With the H option the current row and all above it are frozen. With the V option the current column and all to the left of it are frozen. With the B option the rows and columns above, to the left, and including the cursor location are frozen.

• Frozen titles are released by entering the C option.

• Once locked, the rows or columns become the new edge of the sheet.

• To move into a frozen area, the GO TO command must be used.

• The status of any frozen titles is maintained with the sheet if the sheet is saved.

• Titles can be frozen separately in split screens. This can be an important capability since it allows us to display four separate areas of the sheet at once.

- Areas frozen into titles can include values and formulas as well as labels.

- Using titles reduces the area of the screen that can be used to scroll the spreadsheet.

- This command only affects the display and not the contents of the sheet.

- If the sheet is printed, titles that have been frozen are ignored.

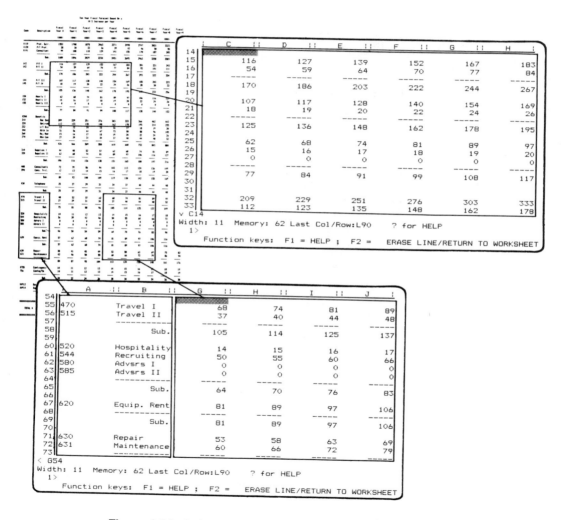

**Figure 4-34.** A demonstration of a screen without titles (at the top) and another in which frozen titles improve the readability of the screen.

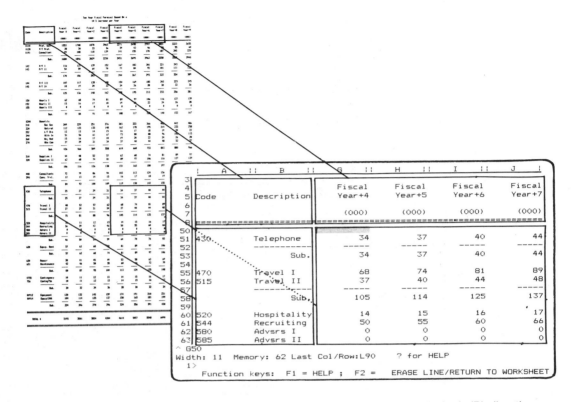

**Figure 4-35.** A screen in which titles have been frozen in both (B) directions.

/U    UNPROTECT COMMAND

The Unprotect command is used to remove protection from cells that we have previously "locked" with the Protect command. The command is initiated by entering

/U

followed by the range that we want to unprotect.

If we wish the Blank, Copy, Delete, Load, or Replicate command to have an effect on entries that are protected, we must unprotect those cells first with this command before using any of those other commands. Similarly, if we want to enter new text, values, or formulas at protected cells, the cells must first be unprotected with this command.

By default all cells are unprotected when we begin with a clear worksheet.

/W    THE WINDOW COMMAND

The Window command, /W, is used to split the screen either horizontally or vertically into two windows that can be scrolled separately. It is initiated by typing

/W

at which time the available options are

| Option | Means |
| --- | --- |
| H | Split the screen horizontally. |
| V | Split the screen vertically. |
| C | Return from a split screen to a single screen (clear). |
| S | Scroll both windows simultaneously (synchronized). |
| U | Discontinue synchronized scrolling, that is, unsynchronize the scrolling action. |

Some general considerations when using this command are

- The command affects the display and not the contents of the sheet.

- There continues to be only one sheet, not two separate sheets, so that changing an entry in one window affects both windows.

- With the H option, a single row of column labels is included in the display above the current cursor location. One row is removed from the bottom screen.

- With the V option, a new set of row labels is included in the three character positions to the left of the current cursor location.

- With a split screen, it's possible to have separate global formats and column widths in each window.

- It's possible to freeze titles separately in each window, providing an opportunity to see four separate areas of the sheet at once.

- The semicolon (;) causes the cursor to jump from screen to screen, landing at its most recent position on the screen to which it moves.

- If a sheet is stored while split, it will be reloaded in the same state.

- If the sheet is printed, the split screen is ignored.

- Unsynchronized scrolling is used by default unless the Synchronized (S) option is selected.

- Once the S option has been chosen, enter U to turn it off and return to unsynchronized scrolling.

Figure 4-36 contains an example of a screen superimposed on a larger sheet in which the screen has been split and windows scrolled separately in each. This allows us to visualize simultaneously the effect of changes in the items at the top upon the totals at the bottom of the sheet.

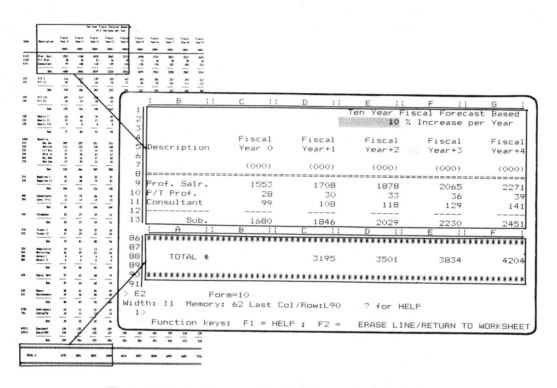

**Figure 4-36.** A split screen in which the two windows allow us to display the effect on the totals of changing values at the top of the sheet.

## /X    THE EXECUTE COMMAND

The eXecute command, /X, allows us to "run" a file that we have previously created which contains SuperCalc commands. This means that we can store a series of steps that we create, and then have SuperCalc perform those steps automatically for us, in the order in which they were specified.

We initiate the command by typing

/X

followed by the name of the file in which we have previously placed the steps.

Let's look at an example involving Figure 4-37. To print that figure, we would follow the steps below. The column labeled keystrokes contains the exact keys we press for the desired action.

| Keystrokes | Explanation |
| --- | --- |
| /GB | Remove borders. |
| /ODALL,P | Output (O) in display (D) form all (ALL) of the worksheet to the printer (P). |
| RETURN | This returns us to the worksheet after the report is printed. |
| /GB | Restore the borders. |

Suppose we want to "automate" this procedure with the eXecute command. To do so we enter all of the "Keystrokes" column onto the worksheet, and then output it to a diskette as a text file. The details of this are below. The file is called a command file.

First with a clear sheet, we enter the following (at A1)

''/GB/ODALL,P
''/GB

Here each of the quotes means that the command will not occur when we type it, but rather it will be stored as text on the worksheet. The first line combines two commands because the Global border command is not followed by a RETURN. If we separate this into two lines, the cursor will move when we 'execute,' and our commands will not work correctly.

Now clear the border from this 2-cell sheet (a requirement when creat-

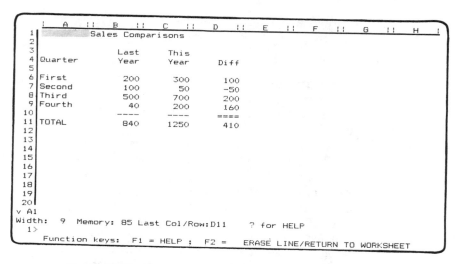

```
     !   A   !!   B   !!   C   !!   D   !!   E   !!   F   !!   G   !!   H   !
  1 |         Sales Comparisons
  2 |
  3 |             Last      This
  4 |Quarter      Year      Year      Diff
  5 |
  6 |First         200       300       100
  7 |Second        100        50       -50
  8 |Third         500       700       200
  9 |Fourth         40       200       160
 10 |             ----      ----      ====
 11 |TOTAL         840      1250       410
 12 |
 13 |
 14 |
 15 |
 16 |
 17 |
 18 |
 19 |
 20 |
v A1
Width:   9  Memory: 85 Last Col/Row:D11      ? for HELP
    1>
     Function keys:  F1 = HELP ;   F2 =    ERASE LINE/RETURN TO WORKSHEET
```

**Figure 4-37.** A report we will print with the eXecute command.

ing command files), and then save the two cells by entering the command below:

/ODA1:A2,DB:OUTSALES,

Let's explain each keystroke here:

| Keystrokes | Explanation |
| --- | --- |
| /O | Use the Output command. |
| D | Output in display format. |
| A1:A2 | Output these two cells. We could also type ALL. |
| , | Indicate the end of the range. |
| D | Send the output to a disk, not the printer. |
| B:OUTSALES | Indicate the desired disk drive (here B:), and the desired filename (here OUTSALES). |
| , | Signal the end of the file name. |

Now, with the screen of Figure 4-37, we eXecute the file that we have just created by typing the following

/XB:OUTSALES.PRN RETURN

Notice that we must add the suffix .PRN to our file, since it was added by SuperCalc in creating the file with the Disk option of the Output command. As the file executes, the border disappears, the report is printed, and then there is a pause at which time we must enter any key to return to the worksheet and then the borders are restored.

PRN files cannot be edited by SuperCalc, therefore it may be a good habit to use the Save command to save the command file worksheet, as well as using the Output command to create the command file. Since development of lengthy command files may require a series of trial and error attempts, creating the file with the Save command makes revision a simpler task. Also, developing a command file may be a complicated task, with potential for error, so it may be a good idea to ensure that backup copies exist for all files used, so that no important data are lost.

If an error occurs, or CTRL-Z is pressed, the execution of the command file is terminated. The documentation for this command indicates that all commands can be included, but that if the Edit command is used, it should only be used as the last command of the file.

This is a very powerful capability that allows us to create complicated streams of processing, ranging from simple command files such as one we could name INSERT10, which contains ten Insert commands (to insert 10 blank rows at the current row), to a series of commands to combine sheets and print the results.

In addition to creating command files with the SuperCalc Output command, we can also use a word processor or other text processor to create these files.

/Z     THE ZAP COMMAND

The Zap command, /Z, is used to clear the electronic sheet. Its action is final, and for this reason there is a built-in requirement that you verify your desire to destroy the existing contents of the sheet. The command is initiated by typing

/Z

at which time the entry line reads

/ZAP−ENTIRE−WORKSHEET?

and the prompt line reads

Y(ES) TO CLEAR EVERY EVERYTHING, ELSE N(O)

If you want to complete the action, type

Y

at this point. The screen is blank for several seconds and then reappears with a clear sheet.

To cancel the command, type CTRL-Z or use the function key if available.

Clearing the sheet means that

- All entries are set to blank.
- The global parameters are set to general:
  The column width is set to 9.
  The order of calculation is columnwise (explained earlier in this chapter).
  The recalculation mode is automatic (explained earlier in this chapter).
  The format is general, indicating no particular global format.
  The window is cleared (a single window appears).
  The cursor is positioned to entry A1, and advances automatically.
  There are no fixed titles.
  The border is displayed.
  Numeric values, and not formulas, are displayed.
  The tab mode is not active.

Clearing affects the sheet currently stored in memory but does not affect this or any other sheet stored on a diskette. If we zap a sheet in memory that we want to restore, we can do so only if we have saved it. This emphasizes the importance of creating backup copies of valued spreadsheets.

The Zap command should be used between finishing work on one sheet and before starting on another at the same sitting. If the first sheet is to be saved, do so before issuing the Zap command. Then clear the sheet. If a second sheet is to be loaded from diskette, do so after clearing memory with this command. If one sheet is loaded on top of the other without issuing the Zap command, an incorrect combination of the two sheets may result. However, this action can be used constructively as an overlay technique or to combine several sheets.

We should never think of this command as a continuous three keystroke /ZY command. Instead, it's important to consider this command as a three-step process:

Step 1. Type /Z.
Step 2. Hesitate to be certain that we want to zap the sheet.
Step 3. Type Y.

This will ensure that we use the confirmation action of this command appropriately.

# CHAPTER 5

# Text, Numbers, and Formulas

## INTRODUCTION

This chapter provides information on entering and using text, numbers, and formulas. In each case the capabilities, limitations, and cautions are presented. We'll start by discussing text.

## TEXT

The variety of SuperCalc data appearing in the window of Figure 5-1 illustrates a number of the considerations involved in using labels. This entire window is composed of two lines of report titles at the top and then the row and column labels.

Let's start at entry A5, where the letters QTR appear at the left of the column. To enter them, we simply type a double quote ("), and then the three letters followed by a RETURN. When we're done the status line shows

TEXT="QTR

indicating that text has been entered. Notice that the label is at the left of the column. This is called left justification.

The top row of the screen illustrates several additional topics in dealing with labels. At location B1 we have the full first line of titles. SuperCalc spills text from a cell into cells to the right as long as the cells to the right have no entries in them. This is a very convenient feature for entering text.

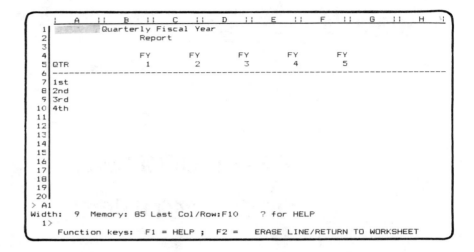

**Figure 5-1.** An illustration of a variety of labels on a SuperCalc window.

Also, notice at B2 that RE appear at the right of the cell. This was done by including spaces after the double quote and before beginning this line.

SuperCalc limits text to 116 characters.

The text FY in B4 was right justified, and then the format and the label (FY) were replicated together across the row by placing the cursor at B4 and typing

/R RETURN C4:F4 RETURN

The Replicate command is explained in Chapter 3, Getting Started, and in the Replicate section of Chapter 4, Commands.

On row 5 the characters 1, 2, 3, 4, and 5 were entered as values, and as such are right justified by SuperCalc. Here SuperCalc values are used as report column headings. Occasionally this can simplify title entry, as here. For instance, we may want to enter years as labels; for example, we may want to use the years 1900, 1901, 1902, ... 1950 as titles. They can be conveniently entered as SuperCalc values.

Finally the characters 1ST, 2ND, 3RD, and 4TH down column A were entered by first entering a double quote. This was necessary since the numbers 1, 2, 3, etc., if used as the first character of an entry, cause the cell to be a value and not text.

The Repeating Text feature was used to create the simulated underline across row 6. This feature causes entered text to be repeated across a cell, and spilled into adjacent cells to the right until a non-empty cell is encountered. It is initiated by typing a single quote

,

followed by the characters we want to repeat, and then a RETURN. For example, on row 6 we typed

'- RETURN

and the full line shown was generated.


## Using Text as Documentation

Text can be used within the sheets to provide helpful directions to users of the sheet, including ourselves, as we'll see in Chapter 9, Creating Templates, and Chapter 10, Documentation. For example, we can place the label

" =A25 RETURN

onto row A starting at A1 (or any other location).  In this example we've placed a GO TO prompt on the sheet as a reminder of the steps necessary for a user of the sheet.  Additional examples are provided in the two chapters mentioned.

This line serves only as a reminder and can't be executed automatically by SuperCalc.


## Evaluating Text When Used in Formulas

Text is evaluated as zero (0) when referenced in a formula.  This can be either an advantage or disadvantage, depending on the usage. It's an advantage when used in electronic sheets in problems such as the examples in the SUM section of Chapter 6, Built-in Functions. There we specify a range of a series including the element above and below the numbers to be totaled.  This allows for rows to be added or deleted within the series without changing the formula. However, zero evaluation is a disadvantage in examples such as the replication of a formula involving subtraction of elements of one column from another. If some elements are blanks, or underlines, their difference will be zero.

This is demonstrated in Figure 5-2 and Figure 5-3, where we've placed some values down columns A and B with an underline at row 4. C1 contains the formula A1-B1. When we replicate this formula down column C, we get the zero (0) shown at C4 in Figure 5-3, not an underline. This illustrates a reason for postponing the labeling process until other parts of the sheet have been completed. If row 4 is added after replicating, then we won't need to "clean up" the sheet as is now necessary with Figure 5-3.

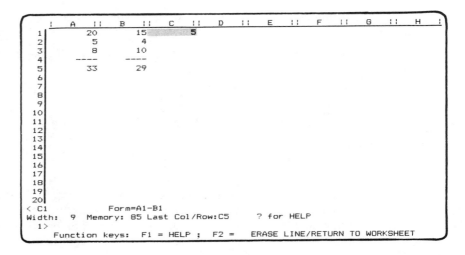

**Figure 5-2.** This figure shows our screen before we replicate the formula at C1 down column C.

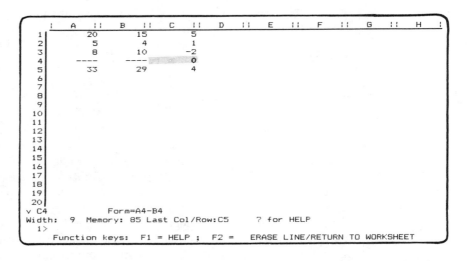

**Figure 5-3.** After replicating C1 from C2 through C5, we see that C4 has been given a value of zero because each underline is valued at zero, and their difference is therefore also zero.

INTRODUCING NUMBERS

Numeric values include data such as 1 or 3.14159 or −356, etc. Numbers in SuperCalc begin with one of the digits 0 to 9, with the positive or negative sign, or with a decimal point.

Numbers are not allowed to have commas, dollar signs, or other non-numeric characters (with the exception of E as will be explained). Let's look at some valid and invalid numbers:

Valid
Numbers

1000

−247.56

+197.000

0002

| Number | Invalid<br>Reason why invalid |
|---|---|
| 1,100 | No commas allowed. SuperCalc will not accept the comma. |
| $312.13 | No $ allowed. SuperCalc will not accept an entry with this character. |
| 42.00CR | No letters allowed (except E as explained later). |
| TEN | No letters allowed; however, SuperCalc will accept this as a label if entered as<br>"TEN<br>and as such it will be evaluated as zero (0), not 10. |

SuperCalc accepts extra zeros before the number, called leading zeros, and extra zeros to the right of the decimal point, called trailing zeros but does not normally display the extra zeros. If we enter 15.2 or 0015.2 or 15.20000, all are displayed as 15.2.

Significant Digits: Values Stored versus Values Displayed

SuperCalc stores up to sixteen significant digits for a value stored. Let's see what we mean with the following numbers.

| | | SuperCalc displays | |
|---|---|---|---|
| We type | SuperCalc stores | (Column width 9) | (Column width 18) |
| 1 | 1 | 1 | 1 |
| 75 | 75 | 75 | 75 |
| .0173 | .0173 | .0173 | .0173 |
| 745.896 | 745.896 | 745.896 | 745.896 |

In each of these examples, SuperCalc acts as we expect. Values are stored and displayed as entered.

Now let's look at the same set of numbers typed and stored but displayed with various formats and a narrower column width.

| | | SuperCalc displays (Column width 5) | | | |
|---|---|---|---|---|---|
| We type | SuperCalc stores | /FG...D | /FG...G | /FG...I | /FG...$ |
| 1 | .1 | 1 | 1 | 1 | 1.00 |
| 75 | 75 | 75 | 75 | 75 | >>>> |
| .0173 | .0173 | .017 | .017 | 0 | 0.02 |
| 745.896 | 745.896 | 746. | 746. | 746 | >>>> |

In these examples there are several things to notice. First, numbers are always displayed with at least one blank at the left of the column. This is done to prevent the confusion that would result if numbers from one column ran together with numbers in an adjacent column. Second, numbers are not always displayed the same way that they are stored. This is very significant.

Third, at times it may not be possible to display the value stored with the column width and format specified. For example, look at the stored value of 75, which we have tried to display with a column width of 5 and a dollar and cents format of two decimal places. This displayed value becomes 75.00 with that format. This has five characters; since SuperCalc leaves one blank at the left of the field, this cannot be displayed in a column five characters wide. When this occurs, SuperCalc fills the field with the greater-than symbol (>) except for one blank at the left. The other examples are explained in the Format command section of Chapter 4, Commands.

Let's look at additional examples.

| We type | SuperCalc stores |
|---|---|
| 987654321 | 987654321 |
| 4000000000000 | 4000000000000 |
| 1234567890123456 | 1234567890123456 |
| 12345678901234567 | nothing, we see FORMULA ERROR |

When we look at the first three examples, it seems that SuperCalc can accurately store extremely large numbers. However, look at the fourth value. Here an error is displayed. SuperCalc is limited to storing sixteen significant digits.

## Scientific Notation

Scientific users often work with numbers of very large or very small magnitude. SuperCalc provides scientific notation, common in computer languages, to aid in storing and displaying large and small values. Let's look at some numbers written in scientific notation and explain their meaning.

| Number | Means |
|---|---|
| 1.4E4 | In this "number," and in all numbers written in scientific notation, the letter E means, and is read as |

_____ times 10 raised to the _____ power

where the blanks are replaced by the values to the left and right of the E.

If we do that with the number shown here, we have the value

1.4 times 10 raised to the 4th power
or 1.4 times 10000
or 14000.

Therefore, 1.4E4 is equal to 14000.

| | |
|---|---|
| 1.4E+4 | This is identical to the preceding example. Here the plus sign (+) is redundant. |

1.4E-4    This is evaluated by raising 10 to a negative value, meaning that we are multiplying the initial value by a small number. We evaluate this as

> 1.4 times 10 raised to the −4th power
> or 1.4 times .0001
> or .00014

From these few examples we have the concepts of scientific notation without realizing their real impact in terms of SuperCalc and other computer languages. Let's examine additional examples.

| Number | Means |
|---|---|
| 6.21597E20 | When we convert this number from scientific notation to "normal" decimal notation, we have |

> 6.21597 times 10 to the 20th power
> or 6.21597 times 100000000000000000000
> or 621597000000000000000

6.21597E-20    Again we'll convert to decimal notation

> 6.21597 times 10 to the -20th power
> or 6.21597 times .00000000000000000001
> or .000000000000000000621597

From these two examples we can observe several things. First, it's possible to express numbers with extremely large or small magnitudes in a simple abbreviated notation. Second, the notation itself can require fewer characters to display and store than the full decimal equivalent. For example

$$6.21597E-20$$

requires twelve characters to display (including a blank at the left), while

$$.000000000000000000621597$$

requires 27 characters to display.

It's for this reason that scientific notation is used by SuperCalc. SuperCalc will revert to scientific notation for display (and storage as we'll see) of values that could not otherwise be shown.

Look at the items in Figure 5-4 for some additional information about scientific notation and the magnitude of values permitted in SuperCalc. This spreadsheet was created by placing the value 1 into location A1 and

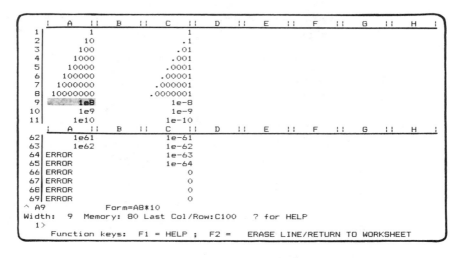

**Figure 5-4.** This demonstrates in scientific notation, the magnitude of the largest and smallest numbers that can be stored with SuperCalc.

then multiplying that value by 10 relatively down column A. Similarly the value 1 at C1 was multiplied by 0.1 relatively down column C.

At location A9 we see that SuperCalc begins to display the value in scientific notation, for it is at this location that the value cannot be fully displayed with at least one blank to the left.

Notice in the lower portion of the screen that we begin to display an ERROR value in column A between 1E62 and 1E63 and a zero value in column C after 1E-64. These values thus provide a relative range (and not exact values) of the largest and smallest numbers that SuperCalc can store.

We can also enter values in scientific notation, with some limitations. Following are some acceptable values that we can type as shown and, which will place the value shown in the entry. The first item, 12E30, will be accepted and then displayed as 1.2E31.

12E30

9.8734E-15

1.8E41

However, we should not enter items such as E20 or +E61 or E-12 since the first two will be accepted as formulas, with E20 and E61 accepted as entry coordinates rather than scientific notation, and the third will result in a FORMULA ERROR.

A final important concept in working with this notation is the combination of the magnitude of the number with the number of significant digits stored by SuperCalc. Suppose we type

1234567890123456 + 5.0E20

as the entry value at a location. When we press RETURN, the entry shows

500001234567890100000

when displayed with a column width of 25. Let's closely compare these values and subtract the result from the entered value:

entered:    500001234567890123456
minus calculated:    500001234567890100000
difference:                        23456

For these values the difference illustrates the significant compromise that we must accept with scientific notation in SuperCalc. We give up accuracy beyond 16 significant digits in order to obtain a value that is approximately correct when considered relative to the magnitude of the values involved.

In this example, with the global column width set at 9, this value will be displayed as

5.000E20

illustrating that SuperCalc will display the value as closely as possible to the stored value within the specified column width and format.

The meaning of significant digits is illustrated with this example. The decimal place has been accurately preserved, but digits after the sixteenth digit have been lost and zeros stored instead. The magnitude, or size, of the number has been roughly preserved but the accuracy has been sacrificed. For some electronic sheets, particularly in the scientific area, being close is sufficient. For others, it's insufficient. SuperCalc users need to recognize this limitation on accuracy and use caution as appropriate in preparing spreadsheets. We'll see additional examples in the next section.

## FORMULAS

Formulas usually involve a relationship between items where the items may be numbers, coordinate references, or built-in functions. Some examples follow:

| Formula | Comments |
|---|---|
| 18000+21000 | This is the simple relationship of addition between two constant numbers. We might type such a formula if we're using SuperCalc as a calculator or if we're entering values from several budget worksheets and want to preserve the separate numbers as well as use their sum. |
| 12+B3 | Our formula adds 12 and the value at B3 and places the result at the location of this formula. |
| B3+12 | This is equivalent to the previous example. |
| (B3+12) | This is again equivalent to the previous example. |

In the last three examples we see three ways to enter the same formula. Let's look at additional formulas.

| Formula | Comments |
|---|---|
| SUM(A1:A8) | A built-in function is a formula. |
| 230+2*PI | This formula also uses a built-in function. |
| PI*R1∧2 | This formula demonstrates the use of the exponentiation symbol (∧). In SuperCalc five mathematical operators are permitted. They are |

| Operator | Indicates |
|---|---|
| + | Addition |
| − | Subtraction |
| / | Division |
| * | Multiplication |
| ∧ | Exponentiation (raise to a power) |

However, this example raises a more important question. When more than one operation occurs in a formula, which is evaluated first? This topic, called the order of computation, is discussed next.

SuperCalc's Order of Computation

That last formula above is the familiar formula for the area of a circle. SuperCalc, in the absence of parentheses, performs computations from left to right. *However,* exponentiation ($\wedge$) is performed before multiplication (*) and division (/), and multiplication and division are performed before addition (+) and subtraction (−). This is very important to remember.

Let's look at additional examples. In each case the underline indicates the current computation.

Formula

| | |
|---|---|
| $16+\underline{4/2}$ | $= \underline{16+2} = 18$ |
| $16+(\underline{4/5})$ | $= \underline{16+0.8} = 16.8$ |
| $21+\underline{14/7}*2*6$ | $= 21+\underline{2*2}*6 = 21+\underline{4*6} = \underline{21+24} = 45$ |
| $21+(\underline{14/7}*2)*6$ | $= 21+(\underline{2*2})*6 = 21+\underline{4*6} = \underline{21+24} = 45$ |
| $5*\underline{3\wedge2}/3$ | $= \underline{5*9}/3 = \underline{45/3} = \underline{15}$ |
| $21+(14/(\underline{7*2}))*6$ | $= 21+(\underline{14/14})*6 = 21+\underline{1*6} = \underline{21+6} = 27$ |

In the last example we see that sets of computations ''nested'' within parentheses (that is, one within another) are evaluated from the inside out.

Efficiencies in Preparing Formulas

Although many electronic sheets require merely seconds, or less, to recalculate an entire sheet, some sheets may require a significant amount of time. For some sheets the manual recalculation initiated by an exclamation mark (!) and discussed under the Global command in Chapter 4, Commands, will minimize overall waiting time. However, for other sheets that require regular recalculation we may find ourselves with a longer wait for the sheet to be recalculated.

Let's look at an example in which the way that we write a formula influences the length of time necessary to calculate all entries of the sheet. In Figure 5-5 a formula commonly used for tests of this kind has been entered. It is

$$A(X)^3 + B(X)^2 + C(X) + D$$

The constant values of A, B, C, and D in the formula are 12, 6, 3, and 5. The value of X is stored in entry A1. We'll place this formula at A2

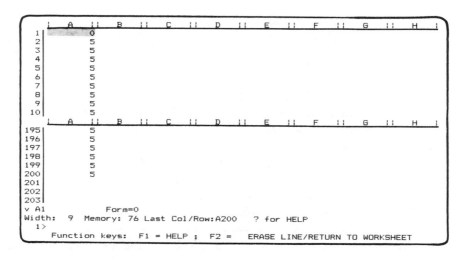

**Figure 5-5.** A sheet where the manner in which we enter the formula affects the recalculation time.

and replicate it through A200. Then we'll change the value at A1 and record the time necessary for the full calculation of the sheet.

If we enter the formula below, SuperCalc gives us the value that we wish. We'll carefully place the formula

$$12*A1\wedge3+6*A1\wedge2+3*A1+5$$

in locations A2 through A200. When the value at A1 is changed from 0 to 10, the full recalculation of the sheet on one system requires almost 3 minutes (168 seconds).

We'll rewrite the formula, without exponentiation, and try again. Our formula, arithmetically identical, will now be written as

$$12*A1*A1*A1+6*A1*A1+3*A1+5$$

This revision reduces the time required from 168 seconds to about 10 seconds.

Finally, let's try with a third version of the same formula. This time we'll write

$$5+(A1*(3+(A1*(6+(12*A1)))))$$

at A2 through A200. This recalculation required 8 seconds.

The purpose of these examples is to demonstrate that the way in which we write formulas can significantly affect timing on some sheets. On most sheets involving addition, subtraction, multiplication, and division, timing may not be a problem. But on sheets with many built-in functions or with exponentiation, we can sometimes reduce the time required, as shown.

Let's list some efficiencies that can reduce calculation time. Using these suggestions may make sense only if we are working on a sheet that is used often and recalculated often. That is, use the suggestions if the time that we save by following them is greater than the time required to implement them.

- If one computed value is used at many locations, compute it one time at one location (not repeatedly at each occurrence) and refer to its value.

- Trigonometric functions are slow. If we calculate the same function for an angle in many places, establish a single entry in which that function is calculated and reference it elsewhere as needed.

- Exponentiation is a slow operation; avoid it if repeated multiplication can be used.

In general if we have several ways to perform a calculation, we can establish a worksheet like that used in Figure 5-5 and actually time each method to determine which is faster.

# CHAPTER 6

# Built-In Functions

## INTRODUCTION

This chapter discusses the built-in functions provided by SuperCalc. Most of these functions perform a numerical computation for us, using values that we supply or reference. For example, there is a built-in function to find the sum of specified entries, another to find the average of selected values, others to find the sine, the cosine, or the tangent of angles, others for logarithms, etc. In this chapter, we'll discuss each of these in alphabetic order by the name of the function.

Some general considerations apply to all functions:

- We initiate a function by typing the name of the function.

- Functions may appear other than at the beginning of a line, and more than one function may be used in a formula.

- The left parenthesis terminates naming the function and indicates that we are ready to enter the function "arguments" if required (some functions have no arguments).

- The arguments of a function are the values on which we want the function to operate. Arguments may have several forms. For example, we can write

| Function | Explanation |
|---|---|
| SUM(A1,A12,B13) | This will provide the sum of the three items listed. Here we have three arguments separated by commas. |
| SUM(A1:A8) | This will calculate the sum of all entries from A1 through A8. This example has one argument, here a series. Even though there are eight entries here, there is only a single argument. |
| SUM(A1:A8,A12,A16) | Here three arguments occur, the series A1:A8, then A12, and then A16. Again the sum is computed. Not all functions can have more than one argument. For example, we can only request the sine for a single argument and that must be one value, not a series. This will be discussed for each function described next. |
| SUM(A1:A8,SIN(A32)) | This demonstrates the use of one function as an argument of another function. |
| (A7-SUM(A18:A30)) | A function can also be used as part of a formula or expression, as shown here. |
| SUM(A1:A8,A12*3) | The second argument in this example is an expression, the product of A12 and 3. |

• In many cases the entire function becomes one numeric value. This is not true for the NA or ERROR functions.

• The arguments, if present, and the function itself are terminated by a right parenthesis ) except for those functions without arguments.

In the following discussion we'll describe each built-in function separately and, where appropriate, suggest possible uses of the function. Where the term ''argument'' or the terms ''argument1, argument2, ... '' appear, substitute values or references as discussed.

## ABS(ARGUMENT)      THE ABSOLUTE VALUE

The absolute value of a number is its numeric value, ignoring the sign. For example, the absolute value of 5 is 5, of −5 is 5 (the sign is ignored), and of 0 is 0. The argument must evaluate to a single value. For example, an argument like B3 or B3*(A12-C14) is acceptable, while arguments of A16:A30 or A7,A12,3*A18 are not and will result in a FORMULA ERROR.

## ACOS(ARGUMENT)      THE ARCCOSINE

The arccosine is the angle, in radians, with a cosine equal to the value of the argument. In requesting the arccosine we are asking for the angle whose cosine has the value that we provide as the argument. Refer to angle $A$ in Figure 6-1; the cosine of angle $A$ is the ratio of the length of side $b$ to side $c$, that is, the COS $A = b/c$. This ratio will always have a value between −1 and +1, and in the function an ERROR will result in the field if the argument is not evaluated within this range. The argument must evaluate as a single numeric value and can't be a series.

A radian is the angle formed at the center of a circle, subtending an arc on the circle equal to the length of a radius. In Figure 6-2, the radius ($r$) has been measured along the circumference of the circle, and the resultant

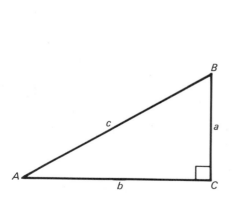

**Figure 6-1.** A triangle that will be referenced in discussions of the trigonometric functions.

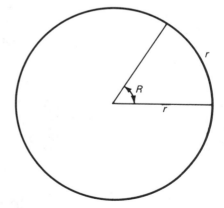

**Figure 6-2.** A visual representation of one radian, the angle R, formed at the center of a circle by an arc the length of the radius.

angle *R* at the center is one radian. Since the total length of the circumferance is the product of $2\pi r$ this means that there are $2\pi$ radians in the circle of 360 degrees. Therefore one radian is approximately 57.2958 degrees (360 degrees divided by $2\pi$). This explanation is intended only as a very brief introduction to these topics.

With this function, angles are returned as values from 0 (for a cosine of 1) to $\pi$ (for a cosine of $-1$).

Refer to the ERROR section of this chapter for a discussion of the ERROR value.

## AND(ARGUMENT1,ARGUMENT2)    LOGICAL AND

The logical AND function, which takes any two expressions as arguments, returns a value of 1 (meaning TRUE) in some circumstances and 0 (meaning FALSE) in others. The following table summarizes the way in which the function is evaluated.

| AND function value is | When: |
|---|---|
| 1 (TRUE) | Both arguments have the value 1 (TRUE). |
| 0 (FALSE) | Both arguments are Boolean (have value 0 or 1) and one or both of them have the value 0 (FALSE). |
| ERROR | One or both arguments are not Boolean and do not have the value NA. The value NA means not available. |
| N/A | One or both arguments have the value NA (not available). |

Refer to the IF, NA, NOT, OR, and the TRUE sections of this chapter for additional related discussions. Also refer to Chapter 7, Other Topics, for a discussion, with examples, of all these built-in functions; for those unfamiliar with these concepts that chapter contains an explanation of the importance of these capabilities.

## ASIN(ARGUMENT)    THE ARCSINE

The arcsine is the angle, in radians, with a sine equal to the value of the argument. We are asking for an angle whose sine has the value that we provide as the argument. Referring to angle $A$ of Figure 6-1, the sine of angle $A$ is the ratio of the length of side $a$ to side $c$, that is the SIN $A$ = $a/c$. This ratio will always have a value between $-1$ and $+1$, and the value ERROR will result in the entry if the argument does not evaluate within this range.

> Refer to the ACOS section of this chapter for a brief discussion of radians, and to the ERROR section for a discussion of the ER-ROR value.

## ATAN(ARGUMENT)     THE ARCTANGENT

The arctangent is the angle, in radians, with a tangent equal to the value of the argument. We are asking for an angle whose tangent has the value that we provide as the argument. Referring to angle $A$ of Figure 6-1, the tangent of angle $A$ is the ratio of the length of side $a$ to side $b$, that is the TAN $A$ = $a/b$. Since there are no numeric limits on this ratio, the limitation becomes the capability of SuperCalc. Here the arctangent of $-1E31$ is $-1.570796326794897$ radians ($-90°$) and the arctangent of $+1E31$ is $+1.570796326794897$ ($+90°$). Arguments of $-1E32$ or smaller, or of $1E32$ or larger, result in an ERROR.

> Refer to the ACOS section of this chapter for a brief discussion of radians, and also to the COS and ERROR sections. Refer to Chapter 5, Labels, Numbers, and Formulas, for a discussion of scientific notation (that is, to review the meaning of the values $-1E31$ and $+1E31$).

## AVERAGE(ARGUMENT1,ARGUMENT2,...)     THE AVERAGE

The average is the single value that results when quantities are summed and that sum is then divided by the number of quantities. For an example of the functioning of AVERAGE, refer to Figure 6-3 in which we have recorded test scores for several students and used the AVERAGE function to compute their averages. Let's look at each carefully to understand fully how blank entries affect the computations; see the table on the following page.

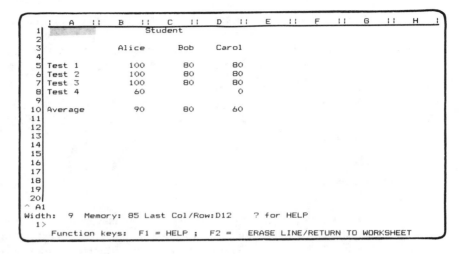

**Figure 6-3.** Examples of the effect of blank entries when used with the AVERAGE function.

| Student | Explanation of the AVERAGE function |
|---------|-------------------------------------|
| ALICE | The function at location B10 is |

$$AVERAGE(B5:B8)$$

and the average is 90 as expected.

| BOB | The same function is used here as with ALICE, and the result is 80, the sum 80+80+80 (or 240) divided by 3, giving 80. The last entry C8, which is blank, is ignored in the count of the items in the column. This is desirable if we are waiting for BOB to take the last examination and want to have his average "to date" for the three exams taken; however, if Bob did not take the last test, and the blank entry really means that he has received a 0, then we will have to enter a 0, which will produce an average of 60 as discussed for CAROL. |
|---------|--|

| CAROL | The function used here is |
|--------|---------------------------|

$$AVERAGE(D5:D8)$$

which produces an average of 60.

The AVERAGE function must be used with care if blank entries are expected in any of the references of the arguments. Since the AVERAGE function is equivalent to the SUM function divided by the COUNT function, a thorough understanding of how both of them function is necessary.

Refer to the COUNT and SUM sections of this chapter for additional relevant discussion.

## COS(ARGUMENT)    THE COSINE

The cosine of an angle, for example, angle $A$ of Figure 6-1, is the ratio of the length of side $b$ to the hypotenuse, side $c$; that is, COS $A = b/c$. In this function the argument is an angle provided in radians. The cosine is returned with the appropriate sign (positive or negative), depending on the quadrant in which the angle falls.

Refer to the ACOS section of this chapter for a brief discussion of radians.

## COUNT(ARGUMENT1,ARGUMENT2,...)    COUNT HOW MANY

The COUNT function provides a single value, the number of nonblank nontext entries in the arguments referenced.

For example, Figure 6-4 contains information received from the reader response cards common in magazines. Suppose this service limits people to choosing up to five items about which they wish to receive product information. Here TOM has asked for information on advertisements 32, 58, and 104. We'll assume the addresses and actual mailing appear in a different system and that we have created this data from that system.

This figure uses the COUNT function in column I to count how many requests each person has made. The formula at I5 is

COUNT(C5:G5)

and results in a value of 3. This indicates that the person has requested information for three items. The formula in location I8 of Figure 6-5 shows

COUNT(C8:G8)

and gives the value 0 as expected at location I8.

In our example we cannot use the function to count how many of the people requested one mailing, how many requested two, etc.

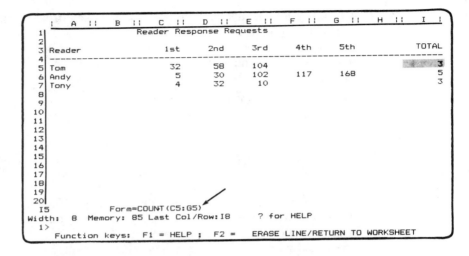

**Figure 6-4.** An example of the COUNT function.

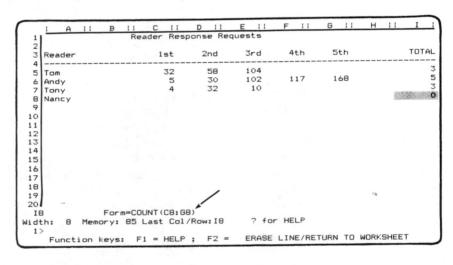

**Figure 6-5** A second example of the COUNT function.

A zero entry will be counted as 1, which we can see in the row for STEVE in Figure 6-6.

This function, although it only counts nonblank entries, can also be used to obtain the number of blank entries by using it in a formula that subtracts the value counted from the total entries. For example, in another problem, if we wanted to know the number of blank entries in the 15 entries from G1 through G15, we could obtain this value with the formula

$$15-COUNT(G1:G15)$$

The functioning of the COUNT is equivalent to the computation of the denominator in the AVERAGE function.

Refer also to the AVERAGE section of this chapter.

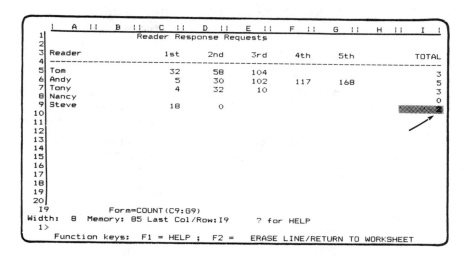

**Figure 6-6.** An additional example of the COUNT function where a zero value is counted.

ERROR      THE ERROR FUNCTION AND VALUE

This function requires no argument and is used by deliberately typing

ERROR

This function may appear wherever functions are permitted (i.e. within a formula, within another function, in an expression, alone).

The value ERROR can occur at an entry for many different reasons. When it does, all other entries referencing it will have value ERROR. For example,

| Entry contains | Explanation |
|---|---|
| 16*ERROR/81 | This formula will be evaluated as ERROR. The formula is not destroyed, but the value is displayed as ERROR on the sheet. |
| ERROR | The same results are obtained as in the preceding formula, that is, the value ERROR is displayed here. |
| TAN(1.570796326794897) | This function, the tangent of 90 degrees, will generate an ERROR value, as will other trignometric functions when the function has no value at the given argument. |
| A1/C3 | If C3 is evaluated as zero, then the attempt to divide by zero will place the value ERROR at this entry. |
| AVERAGE(A1:A4) | If all entries from A1 to A4 are blank, then the average is computed as ERROR. This is true since this function only counts nonblank entries, and the number of entries will therefore be zero, resulting in an attempted division by zero. |
| SQRT(B3) | If B3 is a negative value, the square root (refer to the SQRT function later in this chapter) will be the value ERROR. |

These examples are representative of the type of activity that will display the value ERROR on our sheets. This can be a common occurrence in creating templates (refer to Chapter 9, Creating Templates) when we have entries that either are blank or contain labels while awaiting data entry activity.

## EXP(ARGUMENT)    *E* TO A POWER

This function provides the value of the mathematical constant $e$ raised to the power of the included argument. If a value for $e$ itself is required, using the function with an argument of 1 will provide a value of 2.718281828459045 for $e$.

IF(ARGUMENT1,ARGUMENT2,ARGUMENT3)      LOGICAL IF

This function must have an expression as argument1 and then any values as argument2 and argument3. The following table summarizes the way in which the function is evaluated. This very important function is discussed in detail in Chapter 7, Other Topics.

| IF function evaluates as | When |
| --- | --- |
| Argument2 | Argument1 has the value 1 (Boolean value TRUE). |
| Argument3 | Argument1 has the value 0 (Boolean value FALSE). |
| ERROR | Argument1 is not 0, 1, or NA. |
| N/A | Argument1 is NA. |

Refer to the AND, NOT, and OR sections of this chapter for additional related discussions.  Also refer to Chapter 7, Other Topics, for a discussion, with examples of all these built-in functions; for those unfamiliar with these concepts, that chapter contains an explanation of the importance of these capabilities.

INT(ARGUMENT)      INTEGER

This function removes any fractional part of the argument, leaving only the integer portion. Let's look at some examples:

| When | And A1 contains | |
| --- | --- | --- |
| B1 contains | Formula | Evaluates as |
| 6 | INT(B1) | 6 |
| 0 | INT(B1) | 0 |
| −3 | INT(B1) | −3 |
| 6.4 | INT(B1) | 6 |
| 6.8 | INT(B1) | 6 |
| −3.4 | INT(B1) | −3 |
| −3.8 | INT(B1) | −3 |

In these examples, all entries at A1 not only are displayed as integer values but also are stored as integers.

This operates differently from the integer formats (/F...I or /FG...I) in several ways. First, the integer *format* (not the INT *function*) affects only the display on the screen and not the entry value. Second, the displayed value with the integer format will be rounded; this is different from the action of the INT function. With the integer format (not function) the following occurs:

| Entry value at B1 | Format at B1 | Screen display of B1 |
|---|---|---|
| 6.4 | /F...I | 6 |
| 6.8 | /F...I | 7 |
| −3.4 | /F...I | −3 |
| −3.8 | /F...I | −4 |

These two capabilities must be used with care to ensure that desired results are achieved. For example, with a global integer format it's possible to have the following occur:

$$
\begin{array}{r}
1 \\
1 \\
\underline{1} \\
\text{TOTAL} \quad 4
\end{array}
$$

What's happened is that the three individual entries listed as 1 above are actually each 1.3. Their total, which is 3.9, becomes the integer 4 in the TOTAL entry. To avoid this, if desired, each entry forming a part of the total should be computed within the integer function INT.

Let's demonstrate this with a dollar and cents example where exact totaling is usually very important. Here we may not wish to display a total that is not the apparent column total. Look at the column at the right:

| Entry coordinate | Entry value | Value displayed /FG$ |
|---|---|---|
| A3 | 1.3333... | 1.33 |
| A4 | 1.3333... | 1.33 |
| A5 (total) | 2.6666... | 2.67 |

When this is unacceptable it is possible to ignore decimal places of each entry, without rounding, beyond two decimal places by multiplying the entry contents by 100 (effectively shifting the decimal place two places to the right), taking the integer value of the result with the INT function, then dividing the results by 100 (to shift the decimal place back). A formula to do this is

$$INT(\textit{entry}*100)/100$$

where *entry* is the value or formula at the entry.

If rounding of entries is desired (rather than ignoring the decimal places to the right of two places), then the formula

$$INT((entry+0.005)*100)/100$$

can be used. This provides a value rounded to two decimal places. This should be done for each separate entry before totaling and will then produce a correct total. If this formula is used at entries A3 and A4 in the preceding example, we have

| Entry coordinate | Entry value | Value displayed with /FG$ |
|---|---|---|
| A3 | 1.33 | 1.33 |
| A4 | 1.33 | 1.33 |
| A5 (total) | 2.66 | 2.66 |

We'll need to decide when this is necessary.


## LN(ARGUMENT)    NATURAL LOGARITHM

This function returns the natural logarithm of the argument, that is, the value to which *e* must be raised to produce the argument. A single positive argument will return a value; arguments that evaluate to zero or to a negative number produce a value of ERROR.

Refer to the ERROR and EXP sections of this chapter.


## LOG10(ARGUMENT)    LOGARITHM, BASE 10

This function operates similarly to the LN function just described with the exception that the base is 10, not *e*. The second character of this entry is the letter O and the fifth character is the digit zero.


## LOOKUP(ARGUMENT1,ARGUMENT2)    LOOK UP A VALUE IN A TABLE

This function performs a simple search, or lookup, of a value that we provide (argument1) in a table that we place on the sheet (argument2). The example of Figure 6-7 illustrates how this operates. This sheet has been set up with a simple energy-related table containing the R-values of insulation blown in at depths varying from 3 inches, at which the R-value is 11, to 10.5 inches, at which the R-value is 38. For our problem we have used location B2 to hold the number of inches for which we want to look up the R-value in the table of columns D and E. The R-value that is found will be placed in entry B3 in which we have placed

LOOKUP(B2,D7:D11)

This can be read: Look up the value currently in location B2 in column D from D7 through D11. When there is a match, put the corresponding relative entry from column E into location B3 (the entry with the LOOKUP function).

Argument2 may be either a column series or a row series, and the entries corresponding to these must be in the column to the right, or the row below, argument2.

The values in argument2 should be sorted in ascending order, or incorrect values may result.

It's important to understand what occurs when argument1 is not in the table. The following examples clarify this, again using Figure 6-7. Let's place other values at B2, examine the results in B3, and explain what occurs.

| B2 contains | Results at B3 | Explanation |
|---|---|---|
| −2 | N/A | Not available. The lookup begins with the first entry of the series of argument2. If that entry is greater than argument1, the function returns the value NA. |
| 0 | N/A | Same as the preceding −2. |
| 3 | 11 | The item is found, with the function returning 11. |
| 7 | 22 | The table (D7:D11) is searched. After proceeding to an entry where a value larger than argument1 is encountered, the function is given the value corresponding to the previous entry of the table. Here, as value 8 is reached, (8 being larger than 7), the returned value is 22, which is the value associated with the next smaller entry of the table. |
| 10 | 30 | Same as the preceding 7. |
| 10.5 | 38 | The item is found, returning 38. |
| 15 | 38 | Same as the preceding 7. |

Also refer to the NA section of this chapter.

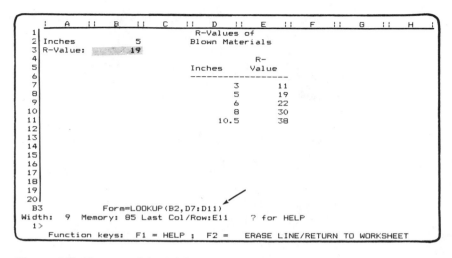

```
 !   A   !!   B   !!   C   !!   D   !!   E   !!   F   !!   G   !!   H   !
 1|                              R-Values of
 2|Inches           5       Blown Materials
 3|R-Value:        19
 4|                                       R-
 5|                              Inches    Value
 6|                              ------------------
 7|                                 3        11
 8|                                 5        19
 9|                                 6        22
10|                                 8        30
11|                              10.5       38
12|
13|
14|
15|
16|
17|
18|
19|
20|
 B3              Form=LOOKUP(B2,D7:D11)
Width:   9  Memory: 85 Last Col/Row:E11     ? for HELP
  1>
       Function keys:   F1 = HELP ;   F2 =    ERASE LINE/RETURN TO WORKSHEET
```

**Figure 6-7.** The use of the LOOKUP function in an energy-related example.

MAX(ARGUMENT1,ARGUMENT2,...)      THE MAXIMUM VALUE

MIN(ARGUMENT1,ARGUMENT2,...)      THE MINIMUM VALUE

We'll consider these two functions together. The maximum and minimum functions, MAX and MIN respectively, accept arguments as just shown and return one value.

Figure 6-8 contains the golf scores of the members of a league for the three rounds played to date. Notice that column F contains the individual best score to date (the low score) and column G contains the individual worst score to date. In the LOW column we have placed a formula that states

MIN(C10:E10)

for player GABE and in the high column for him we've placed

MAX(C10:E10)

His best and worst scores are provided by these functions.

In the same figure notice the bottom of columns F and G where the formulas

MIN(F7:F18)     and     MAX(G7:G18)

have been written. These are similar to the usage in the rows for each player.

These two functions are simple in concept but can be powerful in a wide range of applications. For example, we can find the high and low test score of students in a class. High and low sales values can be selected. Even beyond these uses, a series of additional problems can be solved with this function.

For example, suppose that we have the total number of hours that an individual worked during the week and we want to determine how many hours were regular time and how many were overtime. A solution to this problem is shown in Figure 6-9. Data are entered for each person's name and total hours worked. Then formulas are used to determine the number of regular hours (REG) and overtime hours (O/T) worked.

The formulas in columns D and E follow the example presented next for the entries for ROZZIE at location D4 and E4. They are as follows:

| Location | Formula | Explanation |
|----------|---------|-------------|
| D4 | MIN(40,B4) | The value of the function will be the lower of either 40 or B4. Thus, if the person worked over 40 hours, as ROZZIE did, we display 40, the regular hours. |
| D5 | MIN(40,B5) | For an individual such as TOM, who worked a total of 25 hours, the function is evaluated as the lower of 40 or 25, here 25. |
| E4 | B4-D4 | Here if the total hours is over 40, as with ROZZIE, then this formula is evaluated as (55−40), which is 15.<br><br>Therefore, we list ROZZIE's overtime hours correctly. |
| E5 | B5-D5 | Now for Tom the formula becomes (25−25), which is 0. Again we have the correct overtime. |

An argument with an entry coordinate that refers to an entry that is blank or contains a label will be evaluated as zero.

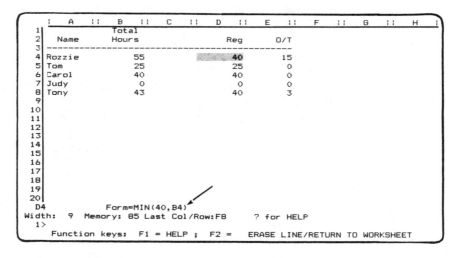

```
      ! A !! B !!  C !! D  !! E !! F !! G !! H !! I !! J !
    1 !         Golf League Scores
    2 !
    3 !                 Round
    4 !           ---------------------
    5 !  Name           1      2      3  Low   High
    6 !---------------------------------------------------
    7 !Lil            44     39     47     39     47
    8 !Joe            47     39     44     39     47
    9 !Noah           50     44     40     40     50
   10 !Gabe           45     38     39     38     45
   11 !Marian         39     46     42     39     46
   12 !Don            50     55     50     50     55
   13 !Roz            52     39     44     39     52
   14 !Martha         61     42     55     42     61
   15 !Tommy          39     40     39     39     40
   16 !Marian         49     50     52     49     52
   17 !Melroy         50     49     52     49     52
   18 !Tinka          39     44     55     39     55
   19 !
   20 !      League low high                38     61
  > F10          Form=MIN(C10:E10)
  Width:  7  Memory: 84 Last Col/Row:H20     ? for HELP
     1>
      Function keys:  F1 = HELP ;  F2 =   ERASE LINE/RETURN TO WORKSHEET
```

**Figure 6-8.** Examples of the use of the MAX and MIN built-in functions.

```
      ! A !! B !!  C !!  D  !! E !! F !! G !! H !
    1 !        Total
    2 !  Name  Hours              Reg    O/T
    3 !-------------------------------------------
    4 !Rozzie    55               40     15
    5 !Tom       25               25      0
    6 !Carol     40               40      0
    7 !Judy       0                0      0
    8 !Tony      43               40      3
    9 !
   10 !
   11 !
   12 !
   13 !
   14 !
   15 !
   16 !
   17 !
   18 !
   19 !
   20 !
   D4          Form=MIN(40,B4)
  Width:  9  Memory: 85 Last Col/Row:F8    ? for HELP
     1>
      Function keys:  F1 = HELP ;  F2 =   ERASE LINE/RETURN TO WORKSHEET
```

**Figure 6-9.** Additional examples of the capabilities of the MAX and MIN built-in functions.

Refer to the section "Detecting and Preventing Errors" in Chapter 8, Recognizing, Preventing, and Correcting Errors, where an additional similar use of the MAX function is presented.

## NA    NOT AVAILABLE

The NA function, which requires no arguments, stands for not available, and returns a constant, like the built-in function PI. When it is written into an entry of the sheet several things occur. First, the value N/A appears in the entry. Second, all entries that reference this entry are also calculated at the value N/A.

This is useful in instances where we do not have values available and where if we left blanks, or the value 0, we would have undesirable results on the sheet. An example is shown in Figure 6-10 and Figure 6-11. In Figure 6-10 we have columns for the MONTH, QUOTA, ACTUAL SALES, and the DIFFERENCE (ACTUAL SALES minus QUOTA). Suppose that we are updating this sheet monthly as we receive sales figures. It is now JUNE. In the figure some of the ACTUAL SALES values have been left blank, and for illustration some of them have been valued at 0. Notice that the difference in both cases is shown as −1000. This is misleading since the sales figures for the month are not available yet.

In Figure 6-11 the ACTUAL SALES for JUNE through DECEMBER have been changed and entered as NA. We do not change the formulas in column D. Notice that all the differences now also show the value N/A. As we enter a numeric value for each month, our difference will be computed for that month.

The cursor at location C9 displays N/A as the value.

The NA value can be useful on occasion to determine every entry on the sheet that refers to a specific entry. With no NAs on the sheet, place NA at the desired entry, and print the full sheet; a visual cross reference of this particular entry appears.

The effect of this value is described in the discussions of many other functions.

NA appears left justified by default. In the figures here it has been right justified.

## NOT(ARGUMENT)    THE LOGICAL NOT

This function returns a value as described next:

| NOT function evaluates as | When |
| --- | --- |
| 1 (TRUE) | Argument evaluates to 0 (FALSE). |
| 0 (FALSE) | Argument is a value other than 0. |
| N/A | Argument is NA. |
| ERROR | Argument has value ERROR. |

Refer to the AND, IF, and OR sections of this chapter for addi-

```
 !   A   !!   B   !!    C    !!   D   !!  E   !!   F  !!   G   !!   H   !
 1 |                        Actual
 2 |Month        Quota      Sales      Diff
 3 |-----------------------------------------
 4 |January      1000       1200        200
 5 |February     1000        700       -300
 6 |March        1000       1100        100
 7 |April        1000       1500        500
 8 |May          1000       1400        400
 9 |June         1000                 -1000
10 |July         1000                 -1000
11 |August       1000                 -1000
12 |September    1000          0      -1000
13 |October      1000          0      -1000
14 |November     1000          0      -1000
15 |December     1000          0      -1000
16 |
17 |
18 |
19 |
20 |
 A1
Width:   9   Memory: 85 Last Col/Row:E15      ? for HELP
   1>
      Function keys:  F1 = HELP ;   F2 =    ERASE LINE/RETURN TO WORKSHEET
```

**Figure 6-10.** A sheet before using the NA function. Misleading information is displayed in entries D9 through D15.

```
 !   A   !!   B   !!    C    !!   D   !!  E   !!   F  !!   G   !!   H   !
 1 |                        Actual
 2 |Month        Quota      Sales      Diff
 3 |-----------------------------------------
 4 |January      1000       1200        200
 5 |February     1000        700       -300
 6 |March        1000       1100        100
 7 |April        1000       1500        500
 8 |May          1000       1400        400
 9 |June         1000         N/A       N/A
10 |July         1000         N/A       N/A
11 |August       1000         N/A       N/A
12 |September    1000         N/A       N/A
13 |October      1000         N/A       N/A
14 |November     1000         N/A       N/A
15 |December     1000         N/A       N/A
16 |
17 |
18 |
19 |
20 |
 C9      TR      Form=NA
Width:   9   Memory: 84 Last Col/Row:E15      ? for HELP
   1>
      Function keys:  F1 = HELP ;   F2 =    ERASE LINE/RETURN TO WORKSHEET
```

**Figure 6-11.** After entering NA in entries C9 through C15, we have replaced the misleading information in column D of Figure 6-10 with the value N/A, for not available.

tional related discussions. Also refer to Chapter 7, Other Topics, for a discussion, with examples, of all these built-in functions; for those unfamiliar with the concepts of logical values that chapter contains an explanation of the importance of the capabilities of these functions.

NPV(ARGUMENT1,ARGUMENT2)    THE NET PRESENT VALUE

This function gives us the value today of money that we will receive. Let's look at an example that will explain the elements of this concept. Suppose that today we invest $100 at a prevailing simple interest rate of 15% for a year. At the end of the year we will have $115. Now if we ask what is the value today of $115 one year from now when the current interest rate is 15%, the answer is $100. To have $115 in a year, we must invest $100 now.

With this function, argument1 must be a single value, which is the interest rate, here called the discount, and entered as a decimal (that is 15% is entered as .15). Argument2 must be a series, the money available at the end of each time period.

Look at Figure 6-12 where two rows are entered as examples of the NPV function. At location A3

$$NPV(B3,C3:C3)$$

has been entered. This is the example with which we began this discussion. We're asking for the net present value of $115 one year from now if the interest rate is 15%. Our result, displayed at A3, is $100, as expected. (The sheet has a global format of dollars and cents.)

Look at row 4. Here we have the formula

$$NPV(B4,C4:E4)$$

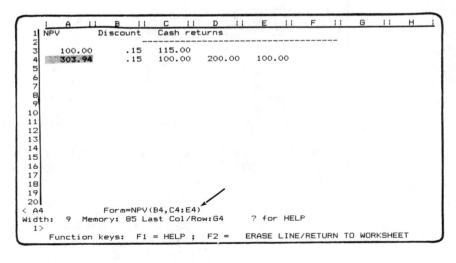

Figure 6-12. Two examples of the NPV function.

which is asking what is the value today at 15% of $100 in one year, plus $200 in two years, plus $100 in three years. Our NPV function says that it is worth $303.94 today.

Let's verify that result by working forward from the $303.94 as shown next.

| Amount | Explanation |
| --- | --- |
| $303.94 | We begin today with this amount. |
| +45.59 | At the end of one year, our money has earned interest at 15%, returning us $45.59. |
| $349.53 | The total of our principal plus interest at the end of year one. |
| −100.00 | We remove $100 at the end of the year. This is an amount that we've specified (location C4) that we expect to receive at that time. |
| $249.53 | At the beginning of the second year we start with only $249.53. |
| +37.43 | Our interest at 15% for the money for the second year. |
| $286.96 | Our principal plus interest at the end of the second year. |
| −200.00 | Here we remove $200, as we've specified at location D4. |
| $86.96 | We enter the third year with this amount. |
| +13.04 | Our interest is $86.96 for the third year at 15%. |
| $100.00 | Our total at the end of the third year. |
| −100.00 | As specified at E4, we remove another $100. |
| $0.00 | We're at zero. |

These calculations indicate that the net present value of $100 at the end of year one, plus $200 at the end of year two, plus $100 at the end of year three, all at an interest rate of 15%, is indeed $303.94.

Initial investments with cash outflows can be obtained by adding the initial investment to the value obtained from the NPV function.

## OR(ARGUMENT1,ARGUMENT2)    THE LOGICAL OR

The logical OR function takes two expressions as arguments and returns values as follows.

| OR function value is | When |
| --- | --- |
| 1 (TRUE) | One or both arguments have the value 1 (TRUE). |
| 0 (FALSE) | Both arguments have the value 0 (FALSE). |
| ERROR | One or both arguments are ERROR. |
| N/A | One or both arguments have the value N/A. |

Refer to the AND, IF, and NOT sections of this chapter for additional related discussions. Also refer to Chapter 7, Other Topics, for a discussion, with examples, of all these built-in functions; for those unfamiliar with the concepts of Boolean values, that chapter contains an explanation of the importance of the capabilities of the functions.

## PI    VALUE OF $\pi$

This function, which has no argument, provides a value of $\pi$ equal to 3.141592653589793. It is used directly in formulas requiring this value; for example, in finding the circumference of a circle whose radius is at location B7, the formula would be

$$2*PI*B7$$

## SIN(ARGUMENT)    THE SINE

The sine of an angle, for example, angle $A$ of Figure 6-1, is the ratio of the length of side $a$ to the hypotenuse, side $c$, that is, SIN $A = a/c$.

The argument is provided in radians, and the sine value will have the appropriate sign (positive or negative), depending on the quadrant in which the angle falls.

Refer to the ACOS section of this chapter for a brief discussion of radians.

## SQRT(ARGUMENT)     THE SQUARE ROOT

This function returns the square root of the argument for an argument equal to or greater than zero, and a value of ERROR for negative arguments.

Refer to the ERROR section of this chapter.

## SUM(ARGUMENT1,ARGUMENT2,...)     SUM THE VALUES

The SUM built-in function returns one value, the sum of all entries referenced in the arguments. Let's look at a simple example in Figure 6-13 where two columns of numbers are totaled with slightly different formulas at A9 and B9 as follows.

| Location | Formula | Explanation |
|---|---|---|
| A9 | SUM(A2:A7) | This is a straightforward example of the use of the SUM function. |
| B9 | SUM(B1:B8) | In this function the series begins and ends one row beyond the actual values that we want to sum.  Here one of those entries is blank (location B1), and the other has a label that evaluates to zero (the ---- at location B8). Therefore, neither affects the result. |
| | | The advantage of this usage occurs if we want to add or delete a full row. With the formula at B9 we can add or delete rows without the need to revise the formula. We can do the same at A9 unless we want to add or delete the first or last entry of the series. When we want that to occur we must revise the series reference of the function at A9. |

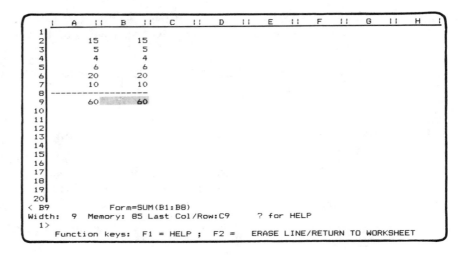

**Figure 6-13.** Two examples of the SUM function.

Refer to the "Introduction" section of this chapter, where a number of examples of arguments are included. In addition, in Chapter 3, Getting Started, the SUM function is described in the section "Using one of the Built-in Functions." Chapter 8, Recognizing, Preventing, and Correcting Errors, contains a discussion of some possible problems with this function.

TAN(argument)    THE TANGENT

The tangent of an angle, for example, angle $A$ of Figure 6-1, is the ratio of the length of side $a$ to side $b$, that is, TAN $A = a/b$. The argument is provided in radians, and the tangent returned will have the appropriate sign (positive or negative), depending on the quadrant in which the angle falls. Angles for which the tangent is not defined, for example $\pi/2$, return the value ERROR.

Refer to the ACOS section of this chapter for a brief discussion of radians.

# CHAPTER 7

# Other Topics

INTRODUCTION

This chapter contains information on a number of additional features or concepts to be considered when using a SuperCalc system. These topics are

- Backup
- Memory
- Accessing worksheets from other software
- Circular references
- Forward references
- Using Boolean variables
- Color

We'll discuss each of these topics and illustrate their importance to using SuperCalc successfully.

BACKUP

Backup is the concept of providing an alternate course of action if some problem appears in the original. For our purposes, we need to consider a relatively wide, systems-oriented variety of problems. Any one of them can halt our successful operation of SuperCalc. If we use a Super-Calc system in areas where its use is crucial, then we need to provide for alternates when problems occur.

Let's look at the components of our system, the potential problems that can develop with them, and methods of backup for each.

| System Component | Potential Problem | Backup Procedure |
|---|---|---|
| SuperCalc | Our copy of SuperCalc may not work properly, may be misplaced or otherwise lost, or may have been damaged, for example, through mishandling of the diskette. | Study the warranty accompanying the SuperCalc diskette, and as appropriate create backup copies of SuperCalc. |
| Hardware | Part or all of our hardware may not work properly. | Complete appropriate service agreements and potentially arrange with another user of similar hardware to support each other in an emergency. |
| Worksheets | The diskettes on which we have saved worksheets may not function appropriately, may be lost, or may have been inadvertently destroyed. | Use SuperCalc to save sheets to more than one diskette, or use software of the computer system to copy one complete diskette from another. These procedures will provide multiple backup copies of each sheet. |
| | | Then store the backup copies separately from the original copy. If and when the backup copies are needed, copy them before use so that at least two copies always exist. |
| Documentation | The printed information we prepare to accompany our spreadsheets may be lost or destroyed. | Prepare photocopies and store them separately from the originals. |

| Users | If our system depends upon a trained user to enter data or otherwise use the sheet, that person may not be available when needed for a variety of reasons. | Train backup personnel who will be able to use the full system should it become necessary. |

What's important is to be prepared for a wide variety of problems that may cause a disruption in the use of our SuperCalc system.

## MEMORY

Parts of the SuperCalc program and the single sheet on which we are working are both in memory of the hardware at the same time. SuperCalc leaves us with a fixed area that becomes the maximum size of a sheet that we can enter. As we write on the sheet, the information is stored in memory, reducing the amount available for us to continue writing.

The memory indicator on the prompt line provides information for us on the amount of memory remaining for our use. In Figure 7-1 notice that the indicator shows 62. On this system, which began with 128 of these units of memory, called kilobytes, SuperCalc itself required 42, leaving a balance of 86, which is the maximum that we can use for each sheet. This

```
     |   A   !!   B    !!    C   !!   D   !!    E   !!    F    |
   6 |
   7 |                                            Ten Year Fiscal Fore
   8 |                                               14 % Increase
   9 |
  10 |                              Fiscal     Fiscal    Fiscal     Fiscal
  11 | Code      Description        Year 0     Year+1    Year+2     Year+3
  12 |
  13 |                              (000)      (000)     (000)      (000)
  14 |===========================================================================
  15 | *110      Prof. Salr.         1553       1770      2017       2299
  16 | *120      P/T Prof.             28         31        35         39
  17 | *141      Consultant            99        112       127        144
  18 |           -----------         -----      -----     -----      -----
  19 |               Sub.           1680       1913      2179       2482
  20 |
  21 | 142       P/T I                116        132       150        171
  22 | 143       P/T II                54         61        69         78
  23 |           -----------         -----      -----     -----      -----
  24 |               Sub.            170        193       219        249
  25 |
 ^ E8            Form=14
Width: 11   Memory: 62 Last Col/Row:L96      ? for HELP
   1>
     Function keys:  F1 = HELP ;   F2 =   ERASE LINE/RETURN TO WORKSHEET
```

**Figure 7-1.** The memory indicator shows 62.

particular spreadsheet therefore required 24 of these, leaving 62 for our use.

As we continue to build on this sheet, we may exhaust the remaining memory. If this occurs, the memory indicator will change from a number to a zero (0), we will get an error message indicating that memory is full, and no additional entries will be accepted.

We can control the amount of memory in several ways. On most systems, we have a choice of the amount of memory purchased for the hardware. Some systems have a memory expansion capability, which allows for additional memory.

SuperCalc manages memory differently in versions for different machines. On some, we can control in some ways the required memory of the sheets that we build. For example, if we build sheets beginning at the top left of the sheet, we'll use less memory than if we begin in the middle of the sheet.

The major action that we can take when we need additional memory is to take steps to make the sheet smaller. This can include removing blank lines or underlines, breaking the sheet into parts, and eliminating some labels. Documentation on the sheet can be placed on a separate sheet. It may be desirable to reorganize the sheet completely so that the problem is solved in smaller parts.

After removing any "extra" data as suggested, it may be necessary to store and then reload the sheet to notice the effect of reducing the memory used. Before reloading, memory should be cleared to prevent overlapping of the smaller and larger sheets.

It's crucial to recognize the difference between SuperCalc sheets in memory and these sheets on an external storage device (diskette). When we have a sheet on a diskette, we must load it into memory to use it in any way. If we change it while it's in memory, we have not altered the data on the diskette. The copy on the diskette is not changed until we take a deliberate action with the Save command.

This has both advantages and disadvantages. If we load a sheet and inadvertently destroy part or all of it, the original is still safe on the diskette. At the same time, if we load a sheet, and work to refine it in some way, and then forget to store it, the refinements are lost. We must understand that external storage and memory are different.

Most diskettes have the capability to store more than one sheet, which can be a timesaver for us in terms of exchanging, or swapping, diskettes as needed. It also means that backup becomes more important since loss of one diskette may mean that many spreadsheets are lost.

## ACCESSING WORKSHEETS FROM OTHER SOFTWARE

Sorcim has announced Super Data Interchange, which will allow users to convert from CAL files to a format usable by other programs and the reverse. A utility program will perform the conversions. In addition, files generated through sending data to diskettes with the Output command can then be accessed as a text file from other software.

## CIRCULAR REFERENCES

With SuperCalc it is possible to write an entry that refers to itself.  For example, at location B3 it is possible to write the formula

$$B2+B3$$

This is referred to as a circular reference. Let's demonstrate.

| We type | Means |
| --- | --- |
| /Z | Begin the action to zap the sheet. |
| Y | Hesitate to be sure that we want to clear the sheet, then type Y. |
| =B3 RETURN | GO TO B3. |
| B2+B3 RETURN | Place this formula at location B3. After entering RETURN, the number 0 appears as the value at this location on the sheet. |
| =B2 RETURN | GO TO B2. |
| 5 RETURN | Enter a value of 5 for B2. At this point, both B2 and B3 have the value of 5. |
| ! | Recalculate. B2 continues to show 5, but B3 shows 10. |
| ! | Recalculate. B2 remains 5; B3 becomes 15. |

Repeated recalculation results in increasing the value at location B3 by 5 for each ! entered.

Usually this is undesirable and can be avoided by using care and not entering a formula at a location that refers to the location.

On occasion, this capability may be of value. For example, let's begin again with a clear sheet and develop a problem that makes use of a circular reference. We'll begin with the sheet of Figure 7-2, in which the global column width has been set at 12 and the dollar and cents format has been set globally. Column A contains values 100.00, etc., entered from A9 through A13. Column B has had the formula

$$A9*B3$$

replicated from location B9 through B13 with A9 adjusted and B3 with no adjustment.

We're computing interest at a rate of B3 (not yet entered) on principal in positions A9 through A13.

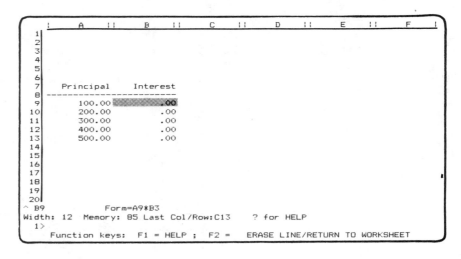

**Figure 7-2.** A sheet on which we'll demonstrate a possible use for a circular reference.

Now let's move to B2, enter .01, then move to B3, and enter .08. We now have the screen in Figure 7-3.

Now, at location B3, let's enter

$$B2+B3$$

Our value at B3 becomes 0.10. B2 (value .01) was added to B3 (value .08), which changed the value at B3 to 0.09, which caused a recalculation resulting in another increment of 0.01 to B3. The results are in the screen of Figure 7-4. Repeated recalculation, by pressing the exclamation point repeatedly, will cause the regular incrementing of location B3 by

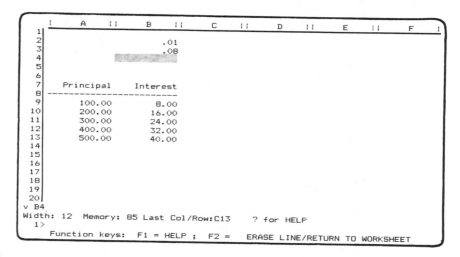

**Figure 7-3.** A starting value of .08 is placed at location B3.

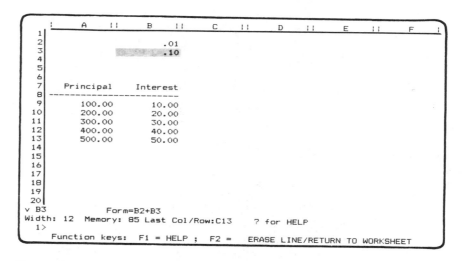

**Figure 7-4.** The formula at B3 refers to itself and is therefore a circular reference.

.01, and the resulting recomputation of all the INTEREST values dependent on it. After pressing ! several times, the screen in Figure 7-5 was obtained for an interest rate of 14%.

In these examples, we see the hazards as well as the potential for using circular references productively. We see the need for caution since inad-

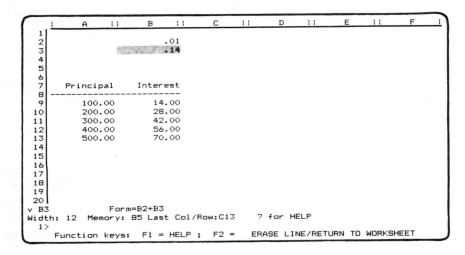

**Figure 7-5.** At each recalculation (!), the full sheet is recomputed.

vertent circular references can easily lead to erroneous results. We have also seen how we can use the technique to generate a series of sheets, each of which may be printed as a table, then recalculated to obtain new values, printed, recalculated, etc. We can similarly use a circular reference to determine quickly the results of changes or to zero in on a value that we're searching for without using a large portion of the sheet.

## FORWARD REFERENCES

The topic "forward references" was introduced in Chapter 4, Commands, under the Row-wise and Column-wise recalculation sections of the Global command. Recall that a forward reference occurs when a formula refers to a value that has not yet been computed. For example, consider entry F8 in Figure 7-6. Intersecting lines have divided the sheet into four sections—I, II, III, and IV—in the figure. If a formula at F8 refers to any location in section I, then F8 should be computed correctly, independent of the global order of recalculation.

If an entry at F8 refers to an entry in section II, then F8 will be computed correctly if the order of recalculation is rowwise. Similarly, a reference to an entry in section III will be computed correctly for a column-wise order of recalculation. In both cases, with the order of recalculation reversed, the entry at F8 may be incorrect unless a recalculation (!) is performed. Finally, a reference to a value in section IV is a forward reference independent of the order of recalculation and may result in an erroneous value at F8 unless a recalculation is performed.

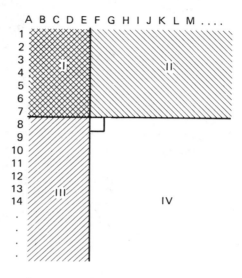

**Figure 7-6.** We'll study what occurs if a formula at location F8 references entries in each of the four areas marked.

## BOOLEAN VARIABLES

A Boolean, or logical, variable in SuperCalc has a value of either 1, meaning TRUE or 0, meaning FALSE. Although scientific users may recognize and be familiar with these ideas, the business user may not immediately realize how frequently we also work with these concepts without labeling them as Boolean, or logical, operations. For that reason, let's look at a nonscientific example.

Suppose that we have columns of information that record age and income for individuals as follows.

| Name | Age | Income |
|---|---|---|
| GABE | 65 | 3000 |
| NOAH | 85 | 45000 |
| DON | 62 | 1200 |
| MARIAN | 40 | 500 |
| MARTHA | 81 | 1900 |
| TOMMY | 60 | 1000 |

We want to know who is over 60 years of age. In logical terms, this becomes TRUE or FALSE for each individual, depending on whether the age is over 60 or not. Here

| It's TRUE for | It's FALSE for |
| --- | --- |
| GABE | MARIAN |
| NOAH | TOMMY |
| DON | |
| MARTHA | |

We might want to know who is under 50 or has an income of over 40000. For these conditions

| It's TRUE for | It's FALSE for |
| --- | --- |
| NOAH | GABE |
| MARIAN | DON |
| | MARTHA |
| | TOMMY |

We can ask who is over 60 and has an income of less than 2000. In this example,

| It's TRUE for | It's FALSE for |
| --- | --- |
| DON | GABE |
| MARTHA | NOAH |
| | MARIAN |
| | TOMMY |

As a final example, we can ask for anyone who is not over 50 years old. Here

| It's TRUE for | It's FALSE for |
| --- | --- |
| MARIAN | GABE |
| | NOAH |
| | DON |
| | MARTHA |
| | TOMMY |

In these examples, we've written narrative descriptions of a number of the logical operations available in SuperCalc. Let's list them explicitly.

| We wrote | SuperCalc logical operation |
|---|---|
| Is age over 60 | Logical IF |
| Is age under 50 or income over 40000 | Logical OR |
| Is age over 60 and income less than 2000 | Logical AND |
| Not over 50 years old | Logical NOT |

Let's look at a specific implementation of the third item on a SuperCalc electronic sheet. That is, is the age over 60 and the income less than 2000?

Suppose we simply want to know for each person whether these conditions are met (1=TRUE) or not (0=FALSE). Figure 7-7 shows a sheet on which this AND operation has been implemented. Notice the formula at location D5 contains

$$AND(B5>60,C5<2000)$$

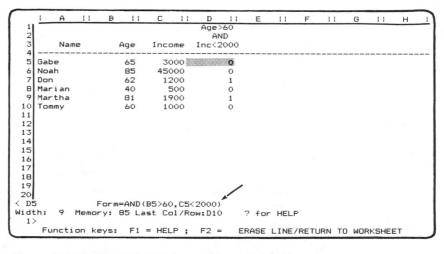

**Figure 7-7.** The logical AND function is used here in a nonscientific example.

The built-in AND function, which accepts two arguments, has value 1 only when all arguments are TRUE. In Figure 7-7, this is TRUE only for DON (age 62, income 1200) and for MARTHA (age 81, income 1900).

In determining Boolean values, we can make comparisons that involve a number of operators in addition to the AND, OR, and NOT. We can also use the equal operator (=), the greater than (>), the less than (<), greater than or equal to (>=), less than or equal to (<=), or the not equal to (<>).

We can write

$$A2=12$$

at an entry, which will result in a logical value of 1 or 0 being placed at the entry, depending upon the result of this comparison.

We learned in Chapter 5, Text, Numbers, and Formulas, the order in which arithmetic operations in SuperCalc are evaluated. Let's examine a series of such comparisons and explain their results.

| We write | Display value is | Explanation |
|----------|------------------|-------------|
| 12=4 | 0 | As expected, they are not equal. |
| 8+4=12 | 1 | Again, as expected. |
| 12=8+4 | 1 | We see that SuperCalc does arithmetic operations before logical operations. |

We can write lengthy comparisons from these simple relationships, and because the result is numeric, we can use the resultant value in computations.

## AND, OR, NOT

Figure 7-8 contains what is commonly called a truth table for the AND, OR, and NOT functions of SuperCalc. In columns A and B, the four possible combinations for A and B have been included, beginning with both FALSE, then one TRUE and the other FALSE, the reverse, and finally both TRUE.

Let's list the formulas at locations D8, E8, and F8 (other entries in each column are relative replications of these rows).

| Entry | Contains |
|-------|----------|
| D8 | OR(A8,B8) |
| E8 | AND(A8,B8) |
| F8 | NOT(B8) |

In these examples, the constant values of 1 and 0 for TRUE and FALSE have been entered into columns A and B.

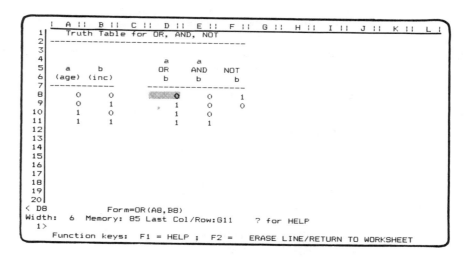

**Figure 7-8.** Truth tables for the SuperCalc AND, OR, and NOT.

Notice that column A is marked for age (AGE) and column B is marked for income (INC). You may then wish to think of column D, the OR column, as asking if an individual meets age OR income requirements. For row 8, the answer is FALSE since both age and income are FALSE. However, for row 9, 10, and 11, the OR column is TRUE since one or the other or both are TRUE.

Similarly, column E, the AND column, can be thought of as asking if both the age and income requirement are met. This is TRUE only for row 11 and FALSE for the other rows.

Finally, column F, the NOT column, gives the opposite logical value of what is stored in column B. That is, at F8 it is TRUE that the person does not meet the income requirement.

## IF

Recall from Chapter 6, Built-in Functions, that the IF function has the form

$$IF(argument1, argument2, argument3)$$

where argument1 must become nonzero (TRUE) or zero (FALSE) and where the whole function has the value of argument2 when argument1 is TRUE and the value of argument3 when argument1 is FALSE.

In building argument1, we can include the relational operators that we just used (=, >, <, >=, <=, <>).

This is a powerful function that can be used in a wide variety of problems. Let's look at some examples.

### Example 1

**Problem:** If the extended price (at B10) is less than or equal to $1000, there is no discount; otherwise, the discount is 10%.

**Solution 1:** IF(B10<=1000,B10,.9*B10)

**Solution 2:** IF(B10>1000,.9*B10,B10)

**Explanation:** Both preceding solutions determine if argument1 is TRUE or FALSE. Then either the full value B10 (with no discount) or 90% of B10 (a 10% discount) is placed at this location.

### Example 2

**Problem:** For a budget problem, we perform a division for which the denominator is E12. If the value there is 0, SuperCalc would normally show the value ERROR; however, we want the value 0 to show instead of ERROR.

**Solution:** IF(E12=0,0,E11/E12)

**Explanation:** Here, if E12 is 0, we place the value 0 at this location; however, if it's not equal to 0, we perform the indicated division and the quotient is placed here.

### Example 3

**Problem:** At this location, list the larger of C8 or C9.

**Solution:** IF(C8>C9,C8,C9)

**Explanation:** If C8 is greater than C9, we place C8 here; otherwise, C9 is placed here. (When they are equal, C9 is placed here.)

### Example 4

**Problem:** We want to know (TRUE/FALSE) if a student has passed a course where passing means the average is over 65%.

**Solution 1:** IF(AVERAGE(B12:B16)>65,1,0)

**Solution 2:** AVERAGE(B12:B16)>65

**Explanation** Both solutions leave the value 1 here if the average is over 65 and 0 otherwise.

## COLOR

Some versions of SuperCalc are available that use color in the worksheet display. For example, positive and negative numbers appear in different colors, as do protected and nonprotected cells, and other elements of the worksheet. Hardware to support color must of course be available on the system, and the user must follow procedures as specified, when the version is installed.

# CHAPTER 8

# Recognizing, Preventing, and Correcting Errors

---

## INTRODUCTION

With SuperCalc, as with other computer software, we must continually be certain that the results we produce are correct. We must ask ourselves if our spreadsheet is working properly and if it will continue to work properly. We must work with an attitude that mistakes are common in working with computer systems, and we must accept responsibility for ensuring that steps are taken to reduce the possibility of errors.

To do so we must understand how errors are made with a SuperCalc system. The system from this perspective involves the computer hardware, SuperCalc, the spreadsheets we prepare, the data we provide, the way the sheet is used (by ourselves or others we train), and the final results produced.

We will discuss the types of errors commonly made with SuperCalc, and then the process of locating and changing errors which are discovered through our use of this computer system.

Our approach will be to build spreadsheets that are designed to prevent errors and are self-testing to assure correctness. If we are to depend on the results, we must be certain they are accurate. It doesn't matter if we are working on a one-time problem or on template preparation (Chapter 9) of a sheet that will be used repeatedly.

## SUPERCALC FEATURES DESIGNED TO PREVENT ERRORS

SuperCalc itself contains a number of devices designed to prevent us from making errors. Several common ones are the prompts appearing on the screen. As an example, if we enter a slash to initiate a command, SuperCalc produces a prompt line. This prompt line is designed to help us by providing the valid character choices available. At this point if we press almost any key other than those listed, we are prevented by SuperCalc from making an error.

A second built-in error prevention device of SuperCalc is the requirement of commands such as the Zap command that we confirm our action, here our desire to clear the sheet, by entering the Y key. Similar actions are required at other times by various commands or functions of SuperCalc.

A third important feature of SuperCalc is the appearance of an error message on the screen when we enter information which SuperCalc determines to be incorrect. The SuperCalc documentation explains these error messages.

We need to be particularly alert to each signal that SuperCalc issues, whether it is a prompt, a request to confirm an action, or an error message. These are designed to help prevent an error on our part.

If and when unusual things occur, we need to understand them so that we learn from them, and can use them it to our advantage.

In the remainder of this chapter we will look at some common problems possible with SuperCalc, discuss methods of preventing them, and finally present ideas for how to track and correct errors.

## COMMON ERRORS WITH SUPERCALC

Look carefully at Figure 8-1, in which we are trying to produce a sum (TOTAL) at the bottom of each column. The sheet contains a number of errors, in fact, only one of the totals appears to be correct. Let's work through each of the columns and explain the cause of the error.

**Column B:** The formula at location B8 contains

$$B5+B5+B5$$

It is simply the wrong formula for computing the total. With SuperCalc the ease with which we can enter formulas can also cause problems since it is easy to include the wrong reference.

**Column C:** Again the formula is incorrect; here it was entered as

$$C6+C7$$

In this example, it is possible that at some time during the development of this sheet we were only totaling what is now row 6 and row 7. Then we may have decided to add what shows as row 5. We inserted the new

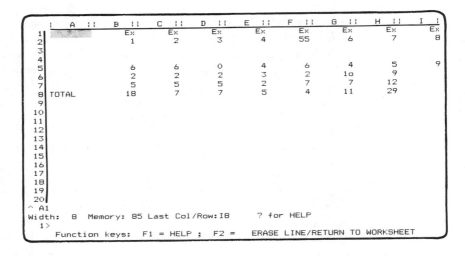

**Figure 8-1.** A number of examples of errors that can occur with SuperCalc.

row (row 5) but never revised the formula at C8, causing the incorrect result.

**Column D:** Finally, a correct result. However, if we looked at the formula at D8, we would see

$$D6+D7$$

This is "correct" only because entry D5 happens to contain a value of 0. For this reason we do not even know we have an error waiting for us when (and if) we change the value at D5.

This example illustrates clearly the need to be certain that our sheets are functioning correctly. Hopefully, a test of this column with other values would reveal the error. This is particularly important if we depend on this sheet to produce results for a wide range of values over a long period of time.

**Column E:** Entry E8 contains

$$SUM(E6:E7)$$

and may have occurred for the same reason as the error of column C. An incorrect range appears within the built-in SUM function.

**Column F:** A look at the contents of location F8 reveals

4

Strange. Suppose that we had carefully placed in that location a SUM function that we are sure had a range of F5:F7, but that is gone and the value 4 appears.

Retracing our steps, we can remember going down the column entering values followed by the arrow keys. We entered 6, then 2, then 7, then 4. At this point we realized the 4 should have gone at the top of column G in location G5. We then moved the cursor to position G5 and correctly entered values down that column.

However, when we entered the value at F8 (incorrectly) we destroyed the formula and replaced it with the value 4.

We see that we must use extreme care in entering values with Super-Calc to ensure that we avoid destroying the formula relationships as we have just done. Because there is a way of "protecting" an entry to prevent this, we will need to use this device, the Protect command, to reduce the possibility of this occurring.

Also notice entry F2, which shows 55, a typing error, for it should have shown only a single 5.

**Column G:** This is a tricky example since the formula at location G8 correctly shows

$$SUM(G5:G7)$$

The error is the data at G6. It looks like the number 10, but in fact it is the digit 1 followed by the letter O not the digit 0. Although contrived for this example, it can happen with SuperCalc because no direct editing capability exists.

**Column H:** Again we have the correct formula at location H8. It contains

$$SUM(H5:H7)$$

Here the recalculation mode was set at manual, and we simply have forgotten to enter !, which when depressed will cause a recalculation with the resultant correct sum placed at location H8.

**Column I:** This unwanted 9 was incorrectly left when we thought that we were moving vertically from location H5 to H6 but instead moved horizontally. We realized the error, moved to H6, correctly placed a 9, but forgot to blank location I5.

These examples demonstrate clearly the need for care in the use of a SuperCalc computer system. Our conclusion is to use the power of Super-Calc, while remaining aware of its limitations.

In a number of these examples we solved the problem incorrectly. This was clear in columns B, C, D, and E, where the wrong formula was used. In general, this is an error on our part rather than a hardware, SuperCalc-related, or data problem. We must understand clearly what we're doing and then convert our solution correctly into a spreadsheet.

Additional errors may have occurred because of "forgetfulness" on our part. For example, in the errors of column C and column E we may have forgotten to revise the formula when a row was added to the spreadsheet. In column E the range of the SUM function may be wrong because we read the column location incorrectly from the row and column labels, or we may have moved the cursor to the wrong location.

Column F reveals a different type of error, another human error. Here we destroyed a formula by incorrectly typing a value over it. We have a way of locking an entry so that it cannot be inadvertently destroyed, but we did not use it.

## ADDITIONAL EXAMPLES OF COMMON ERRORS

Let's look at additional examples of errors common with SuperCalc systems. Again each will require a thorough understanding of the limitations of SuperCalc, of our spreadsheets, of the hardware, of the human users of the system, and of the data.

First, if we have a cell whose true value is 123456789012345678012 in a location on the spreadsheet, it is stored as 123456789012345600-0000. Those who work with computers regularly accept this, with the acceptance based usually on an understanding of the hardware or software limitations of the system in use. What is significant (in addition to the number of digits stored here), is the fact that the wrong value is stored. Thus, the number of digits stored can clearly affect results. Chapter 5, Text, Numbers, and Formulas, discusses this problem.

Another example is shown next. We may have a column that shows

$$\begin{array}{r} 1 \\ 1 \\ \underline{1} \\ \text{TOTAL} \quad 4 \end{array}$$

This can occur because of the way in which we use the integer format (/F...I or /FGI) and the integer function as discussed for the INT (integer) function in Chapter 6, Built-In Functions.

The next few figures illustrate some other common errors that can occur with SuperCalc. In Figure 8-2 look closely at entry B7. These are intended to be dollar ($) values, but we have forgotten to use the appropriate format here, resulting in a value displayed as 18.6 instead of the desired 18.60.

Also look at entry E6. It shows a value of 0 when it should show a series of hyphens. The problem was our use of the Replicate command. We established a formula in entry E4, which was the sum of the entries

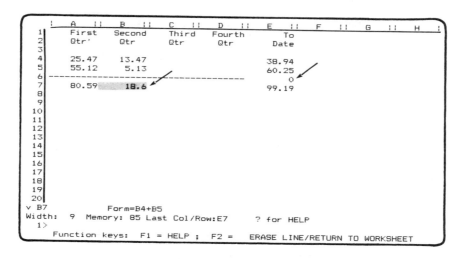

**Figure 8-2.** A window showing two common errors with SuperCalc usage.

on the row. When replicated down Column E, the sum was included for row 6, incorrectly placing the value 0 at E6.

Another common problem occurs with formatting of row and column headings. In Figure 8-3 and Figure 8-4 we have two reports; one printed after the sheet of Figure 8-2 has had the column width reduced and the other after widening the columns. Notice how the headings over the rows are now distorted and misplaced. Also notice in Figure 8-3 that the unformatted entries are displayed with inconsistent, misaligned decimal places.

The lesson of these examples is to postpone some labeling activity until the last steps of spreadsheet preparation. Doing so allows us to prepare correct column and row identification the first time. We should determine our formats early in the process so that they can be replicated as needed.

In Figure 8-5 we have printed a report on which the bottom has been omitted by improperly specifying the range of the report during an Output command. Also notice that the word FOURTH has been improperly spelled (FORTH).

Let's briefly mention additional problems that can occur with Super-Calc.

• We can misuse the commands. The Replicate command, probably the most complicated and powerful of SuperCalc, can cause a number of problems that we discussed in Chapter 4, Commands. Misuse of prompts of that command can easily cause problems, as can incorrectly specifying "from" and "to" locations.

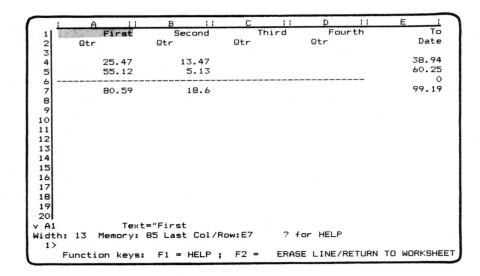

```
 | A || B || C || D ||  E || F || G || H || I || J || K || L || M || N || O |
 1|FirstecondThirdourth    To
 2|   Q    Q    Q    Q Date
 3|
 4| 25.5 13.5           38.9
 5| 55.1 5.13           60.3
 6|--------------------  0
 7| 80.6 18.6           99.2
 8|
 9|
10|
11|
12|
13|
14|
15|
16|
17|
18|
19|
20|
v B7            Form=B4+B5
Width:  5  Memory: 85 Last Col/Row:E7       ? for HELP
   1>
      Function keys:  F1 = HELP ;  F2 =    ERASE LINE/RETURN TO WORKSHEET
```

**Figure 8-3.** Our report after reducing the column width (resulting in incorrect, incomprehensible column titles). The report also displays inconsistent decimal places because of erroneous formatting.

```
 |     A    ||    B    ||   C   ||   D   ||   E   |
 1|    First     Second     Third    Fourth      To
 2|  Qtr        Qtr        Qtr       Qtr        Date
 3|
 4|       25.47      13.47                    38.94
 5|       55.12       5.13                    60.25
 6|------------------------------------------------  0
 7|       80.59      18.6                     99.19
 8|
 9|
10|
11|
12|
13|
14|
15|
16|
17|
18|
19|
20|
v A1            Text="First
Width: 13  Memory: 85 Last Col/Row:E7       ? for HELP
   1>
      Function keys:  F1 = HELP ;  F2 =    ERASE LINE/RETURN TO WORKSHEET
```

**Figure 8-4.** The same results as Figure 8-3, but here the column width has been increased.

| FIRST QTR | SECOND QTR | THIRD QTR | FORTH QTR | TO DATE |
|-----------|------------|-----------|-----------|---------|
| 25.47 | 13.47 | | | 38.94 |
| 55.12 | 5.13 | | | 60.25 |

**Figure 8-5.** A printed report in which the bottom has been omitted by improperly specifying the range of the sheet in the Output command. We also have a misspelling (FORTH).

• Because we cannot see the full sheet on the screen, there may be unusual erroneous entries that we are not aware of and cannot easily detect.

• It's easy to point to the wrong entry in completing a formula. If we replicate from this initial incorrect value, we are replicating an error.

• If we unintentionally load one sheet onto another without clearing the screen, we will end up with a spreadsheet that is usually an erroneous combination of the two.

• Circular or forward references (refer to Chapter 7, Other Topics) may cause undesired results as may an incorrect order of computation (refer to the /G section of Chapter 4, Commands).

Throughout this chapter we have illustrated problems that can cause errors for us. Now let's move to a discussion of detecting, correcting, and, even more important, preventing errors.

## DETECTING AND PREVENTING ERRORS

Our goal should be to produce accurate information. Although we want to take advantage of the speed of spreadsheet preparation, we do not want to do so at the cost of accuracy. What we have seen is the extreme need for caution. For example, it's very easy to destroy a formula by writing a value over it and not even realize that this has occurred.

In writing programs or in using software other than SuperCalc, a major portion of the program may be devoted to checking input data to make sure that they are valid. For example, if we are preparing a payroll report, we want to be certain that the input field containing the number of hours the employee worked, in fact contains a number. If it does not, we probably have an error. If it has a number, we may want to check on its reasonableness in some way. For example, if the number is generated from a weekly employee, we may not want to process it if it's greater than 70 hours without independent verification.

Even though we will suggest a solution for this particular problem later in the chapter, we must recognize that this editing and checking process is not conveniently available with SuperCalc. We must be especially alert during the data entry activity with the sheet; that is, the user provides this validation function, not the spreadsheet.

In Chapter 9, Creating Templates, we'll develop a series of guidelines to help us include steps that can be taken with SuperCalc to avoid these problems. In the remainder of this chapter we'll look at some examples of actions that we can take to prevent and detect errors that could occur with our sheets.

The QUARTERLY REPORT of Figure 8-6 is a common type of report for which SuperCalc can be used. We show four columns of information with subtotals (SUB) included for each and a grand total (TOTAL) at the bottom of each column. Notice that we've filled the sheet with numbers for which it is easy to determine if the sheet is working correctly. This is certainly not an exhaustive test, for we have seen earlier in the chapter that a large number of things could go wrong.

Let's demonstrate a simple way of providing one check on the accuracy of our work. In Figure 8-6 the TOTAL was computed by adding together the SUB totals of rows 8 and 13. Thus, the formula at entry B16 contains

$$B8+B13$$

As a double check, look at Figure 8-7. Two rows have been added to the report, rows 19 and 20. The formula at entry B19 is

$$B3+B4+B5+B6+B10+B11$$

We have separately added all the entries used to compute the SUB totals. Finally row 20 contains the difference between row 16 and row 19; that is, entry B20 contains

$$B16-B19$$

As we manipulate the values in this sheet, we will watch row 20 carefully to be certain that it contains zero values across the row.

Another simple way to do this is to place the formula

$$SUM(B3:B15)/2$$

at location B19. All non-numeric values are ignored (since they have value 0), and since each value is included twice, division by 2 gives a sum of the column.

If we print a report from this sheet, these last two rows can be omitted if desired.

We have built a simple check into our sheet. It is redundant and can be

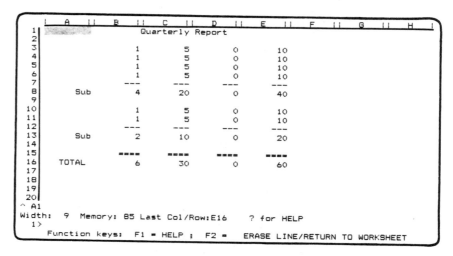

```
     A      B      C      D      E      F      G      H
 1               Quarterly Report
 2
 3               1      5      0      10
 4               1      5      0      10
 5               1      5      0      10
 6               1      5      0      10
 7               ---    ---    ---    ---
 8      Sub      4      20     0      40
 9
10               1      5      0      10
11               1      5      0      10
12               ---    ---    ---    ---
13      Sub      2      10     0      20
14
15               ====   ====   ====   ====
16      TOTAL    6      30     0      60
17
18
19
20
^ A1
Width:   9   Memory: 85 Last Col/Row:E16      ? for HELP
   1>
        Function keys:  F1 = HELP ;  F2 =    ERASE LINE/RETURN TO WORKSHEET
```

**Figure 8-6.** A typical SuperCalc sheet with test data but no double-checking of the totals.

```
     A      B      C      D      E      F      G      H
 1               Quarterly Report
 2
 3               1      5      0      10
 4               1      5      0      10
 5               1      5      0      10
 6               1      5      0      10
 7               ---    ---    ---    ---
 8      Sub      4      20     0      40
 9
10               1      5      0      10
11               1      5      0      10
12               ---    ---    ---    ---
13      Sub      2      10     0      20
14
15               ====   ====   ====   ====
16      TOTAL    6      30     0      60
17
18
19                      6      30     0      60
20               0      0      0      0
v B19            Form=B3+B4+B5+B6+B10+B11
Width:   9   Memory: 84 Last Col/Row:E20      ? for HELP
   1>
        Function keys:  F1 = HELP ;  F2 =    ERASE LINE/RETURN TO WORKSHEET
```

**Figure 8-7.** The sheet of Figure 8-6 after revision to perform a double check on the totals.

time-consuming on a large sheet, but techniques like this are extremely important in order to detect and prevent errors.

Let's look at another technique that can be helpful as a testing device. We can create temporary rows or columns that can help us determine if information is entered correctly.

For example, if we have one column for each of the 40 people in one department, we can quickly insert a row above the names and place the values 1, 2, 3, ... 39, 40 across this new row. If 40 appears over the last name, we know that we have 40 columns (although we may have a duplicate among them). If 40 does not fall over the last name, then this testing device has been helpful in identifying an error that we can find and correct. The new row can be deleted, if desired, after serving this testing function.

For a second example, let's return to our payroll problem. In Figure 8-8 we've shown part of a spreadsheet including employee names, the number of hours each worked this week, and a column labeled CHECK (column C). The formula at the highlighted cell, C4, contains

$$MAX(B4-70,0)$$

A similar relative formula exists at C5 and C6. Let's follow the action for the entries shown. Remember our purpose: we want to know any employees for whom our data shows more than 70 hours worked. On the screen, MARIAN shows 80 hours in entry B4, that is, above the exception level of 70. For her the formula evaluates as

$$MAX(B4-70,0)$$
or $MAX(80-70,0)$
or $MAX(10,0)$
or 10

For NOAH, who worked 40 hours, it evaluates as

$$MAX(B5-70,0)$$
or $MAX(40-70,0)$
or $MAX(-30,0)$
or 0

GABRIEL is evaluated similarly, to value zero (0).

Thus, we have created, in the C column, an exception report, that can be scanned for nonzero entries, each of which indicates an individual who worked for over 70 hours this week.

It is important to recognize that although we have automated this calculation, the exception recognition shown in column C is still dependent upon an individual scanning that column for nonzero entries. Thus, the process of identifying possible errors is still heavily dependent upon the user of the system. Although this is ultimately true of most computer systems, other systems provide the capability for exception reporting, etc., which is not available with SuperCalc.

In this chapter we've seen several concepts in testing, including checking with simple numbers, and built-in checking. The latter indicates the important concept of considering testing when the sheet is constructed.

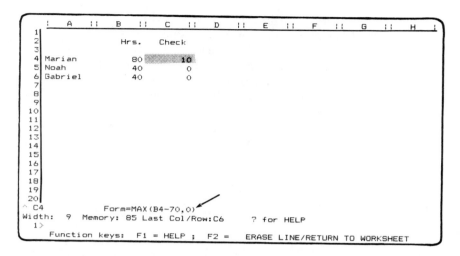

**Figure 8-8.** An example in which a CHECK column has been added to check on the validity of the input data.

Let's list a number of other concepts that can help produce correct results.

• Create templates using the concepts in Chapter 9, Creating Templates, and use these techniques even for one-time use. That chapter contains suggestions for avoiding some of the problems discussed in this chapter.

• If the same spreadsheet is used repeatedly for different test values, consider clearing and then reloading the sheet for each new group of values. If we have inadvertently destroyed part of the sheet when entering one set of data, this action will limit the damage to that one set rather than that set plus all that follow.

• In addition to testing the sheet with these simple values, also test with ''large'' numbers to ensure that column widths for all entries are wide enough to display expected values in an appropriate format.

• Test our results against results that we have computed by hand or with other programs that can serve as controlled comparisons. Do this for test data and for real data alike.

• Follow the cursor movement carefully and be certain that we are at the correct location before entering a value.

• Use the Replicate command to help fill entries with test data.

• Have someone else test our system. This might include working with the person while he or she begins with our documentation (refer to Chapter 10, Documentation) and works through to the final steps of report preparation. We'll need to be alert to parts of the system that cause problems and then revise them to produce a better system. If others will regularly use our work, this training step is very important for both ourselves and the user (refer to Chapter 11, What Our Client, Secretary, or Supervisor Needs to Know).

- Recognize the limits of SuperCalc. As we have seen, it may not be appropriate for all problems that we wish to solve with a computer system.

## CORRECTING ERRORS

Once our testing reveals an error, we need to locate and correct the problem. We should be delighted that the error has been found during testing and not later, after we acted on what we believed to be accurate information. We will need to be careful that in locating and correcting an error we don't inadvertently create additional errors. When we believe that we've corrected an error, we'll need to begin our testing again.

Debugging, the process of locating and correcting known errors in a spreadsheet, will usually begin with an examination of the entry at the locations known to be incorrect. If these entries appear to be correct, we can examine entries that are referenced in formulas contained at the locations known to be incorrect. This step-by-step process will hopefully reveal the problem. If it is an error detected at a location created by a replication process, then all corresponding entries may need to be replicated again with the correction.

## SUMMARY

SuperCalc itself provides limited assistance in the processes discussed in this chapter. We are limited to examining contents of entries one by one. We do not have cross reference listing facilities; that is, we cannot determine all entries that reference a particular entry. We cannot tell which entries of the sheet are blank and which have contents without moving over the entire sheet entry by entry.

This chapter has listed a broad range of possible errors, ranging from incorrect expressions, to destruction of formulas, to solving the wrong problem, and has provided modest suggestions for avoiding errors.

# CHAPTER 9

# Creating Templates

## INTRODUCTION

One of the most powerful features of SuperCalc is the ability it provides to create templates. Templates are patterns or models that guide a person in entering data onto the electronic sheet. A template is an electronic sheet on which we've written text, formulas, and possibly some, but not all, of the values needed to evaluate the sheet fully. We'll store this sheet and later, when we need to get information involving this sheet, we'll load it, enter the missing values, and instantly have our information.

Templates also allow for the separation of the data entry function from the steps involved in defining the relationships between the entries. This is extremely important, as we'll see.

Let's look at the simplified expense budget in Figure 9-1. In looking at this report we can't tell if relationships exist between the entries. How are PERSONNEL dollars computed? Are they a function of EMPLOYEES (the number of people working for us)? Are BENEFITS related to PERSONNEL costs, EMPLOYEES, both, or neither? Was TRAVEL computed as $300 per person?

It's clear that the report reveals nothing of the functional relationships between the entries. If we intend to use this spreadsheet for new calculations we can do so only if we are intimately familiar with which entries we can change. We need to know which hold values that we are to enter and which hold formulas that we do not want to change. If we prepared the report three months ago, it's possible that the details may now be hazy. What if we ask an employee to work with the sheet and the individual is not familiar with it? What if our manager wants to use this sheet?

187

What if the sheet has hundreds of entries instead of the few of the example?

Creating a template as the first step of solving a problem can alleviate many of these potential difficulties. Let's follow a number of iterations in the process of creating a template for the example of Figure 9-1. As we do so, we'll develop a series of template guidelines. These guidelines will consist of a mixture of common sense, an understanding of the capabilities and limitations of SuperCalc, and a knowledge of what computer programmers and users have learned (primarily the hard way) about interacting with a computer system. This last category will be extremely important to SuperCalc users who do not have previous experience in writing and regularly using computer systems.

Let's start. We will built templates for several different examples, starting with the problem of Figure 9-1.

## GUIDELINES FOR CREATING TEMPLATES:   EXAMPLE 1

**Template Guideline 1:**   Understand the problem thoroughly.

The ease of using SuperCalc can tempt us to start filling the blank sheet without a complete understanding of the problem to be solved. In general it's a mistake, but not always, as we'll see. The new computer user is probably developing an understanding of the explicit nature of the directions that must be provided to a computer to receive the results desired. This is as true with SuperCalc as with any other method of programming or communicating instructions to a computer.

On the other hand there are often problems that we try to solve but

```
                      Simple Budget

            Employees                  50


            Personnel             1000000
            Benefits               250000
            Telephone               10000
            Rent                    10000
            Travel                  15000
            Hospitality              1000
            Equipment               18000

                 TOTAL:           1304000
```

**Figure 9-1.** A simple expense budget example for which we'll create a template.

which we know we do not understand well. Tools like SuperCalc can be helpful for this type of problem since they permit, or even encourage, experimentation with different model solutions. For this type of problem SuperCalc can become a working tool to help us develop a thorough understanding of the problem.

What's important is that we be able to distinguish between the problems that we do understand (or should understand) and those we know we don't understand.

Let's apply this guideline to our sample budget problem. Our budgeting assumptions here will be simple and straightforward, and we'll assume that we thoroughly understand our problem. Each of the fields is briefly explained as follows:

| Field | Formula, variable, or constant | Notes |
|---|---|---|
| EMPLOYEES | variable | We'll enter this field. Figure 9-1 shows 50 people working for us. This is a variable, meaning that we'll enter a numeric value for this field. When we develop our template we'll leave a "place-holder" for it, as we'll see. |
| PERSONNEL | formula | We compute this as $20,000 times the number of EMPLOYEES. We'll place the formula in our template. |
| BENEFITS | formula | Compute as 25% of PERSONNEL costs. |
| TELEPHONE | variable | We'll enter this value. |
| RENT | constant | Although SuperCalc doesn't distinguish between variables and constants, the distinction can be important in templates. A constant is a value that will be entered by the person who creates the template and not by the person who later uses this template. |
| | | For our problem we know that RENT will be a fixed cost and we'll place the $10,000 directly into the template. |

| | | |
|---|---|---|
| TRAVEL | formula | Compute as $300 per person. |
| HOSPITALITY | variable | We'll enter this. |
| EQUIPMENT | variable | We'll enter this. |
| TOTAL | formula | The sum of the seven expense fields. |

Let's create a template for this problem. For each of the four variables to be entered, we'll place a series of periods (.......) in the entry. This field is the "place holder" that we mentioned. We'll do this here by typing

"...........

This fills the field with periods. In a later section of this chapter we'll discuss other ways of identifying such a field as one in which a variable should be entered. The use of repeated periods is only a convenient, visual way of marking the field and is not related to any SuperCalc operational requirement. Let's identify this concept as our second guideline.

**Template Guideline 2:**   Clearly identify all fields for which data is to be provided.

In creating our template, the formulas, labels, and constants (such as RENT here) are entered normally on the sheet. Figure 9-2 shows our template. Let's call it a template-in-process, because we'll be revising it significantly.

Notice that a number of entries in which we have placed formulas show 0. As we know, when SuperCalc encounters text in the field of a formula the text is treated as a zero value. Here, for example, PERSONNEL has been entered as a formula (20000 multiplied by the number of EMPLOYEES), and the EMPLOYEES field contains ........... Therefore, PERSONNEL is evaluated as

$$20000 * 0$$

or 0, the value shown in Figure 9-2.

The zero-evaluation of text by SuperCalc will be very useful in our work on templates.

We are beginning to see the power of a template. The variables that need to be entered are clearly identified (here by periods).

In Figure 9-3 we have entered the four values and have our new budget. We've done this by

- Loading the template.
- Positioning the cursor in turn over the four locations requiring an entry (indicated by a series of periods).

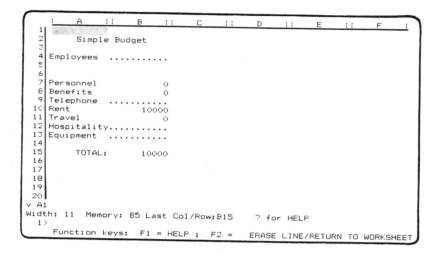

**Figure 9-2.** Our template-in-process for our budget example.

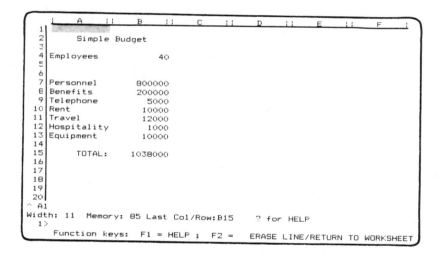

**Figure 9-3.** A new budget after entering four values on the template that we've created.

- Entering the values:

  EMPLOYEES    =      40
  TELEPHONE    =    5000
  HOSPITALITY  =    1000
  EQUIPMENT    =   10000

After following these few steps, we can view our new budget as a function of these four new values.

Let's continue to develop this same template and introduce some additional guidelines.

**Template Guideline 3:** Include documentation within the template.

Documentation is a broad term in the computer field encompassing a wide variety of written materials intended to be helpful to a user of all or part of a computer system. It may be program documentation, operating documentation, system documentation, user documentation, etc. Chapter 10, Documentation, discusses the topic more fully from a SuperCalc perspective. In our example we'll start by discussing documentation for a person using the templates we'll create.

Our environment and intended use of a template should provide guidance for the appropriate level of documentation. If we use this template several times within a short period and then discard it, we may need little documentation. However, if our template is used by a large number of people over a long period of time, we need to provide more extensive documentation. If we use the template infrequently, then we need to provide enough documentation for ourselves to ensure that we can successfully use or revise this template when we need it next. Figure 9-4 suggests the beginning of modest documentation, which here has been placed in the top left corner of the sheet. Included are the file name

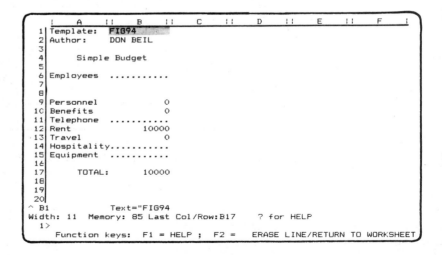

**Figure 9-4.** Minimal documentation has been included in the first entries of the template.

under which the template has been stored, here FIG94, and the name of the author of the template, here DON BEIL. As we proceed, we'll add additional documentation to our templates.

Let's use our template again. Assume that we need revised budget information because of potential changes in the number of EMPLOYEES and other expenses. Suppose the projected values are

$$
\begin{aligned}
\text{EMPLOYEES} &= 50 \\
\text{TELEPHONE} &= 9000 \\
\text{HOSPITALITY} &= 1000 \\
\text{EQUIPMENT} &= 30000
\end{aligned}
$$

Figure 9-5 shows our template after we've partially entered the data. In the figure we've entered the number of EMPLOYEES (note the cursor position) and can see that PERSONNEL, BENEFITS, and TRAVEL all have been computed as a function of EMPLOYEES. Then, in Figure 9-6 we enter the $9000 TELEPHONE expense; however, look carefully at the cursor location. In error the number has been entered in the BENEFITS location, destroying the correct value.

Not only have we destroyed the value at the BENEFITS entry, but we have also destroyed the formula that created the relationship between BENEFITS and PERSONNEL. This error leads us to our next two guidelines.

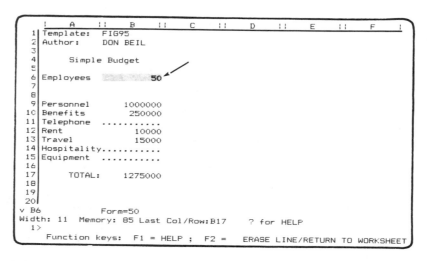

**Figure 9-5.** Our template after partially entering values. The EMPLOYEES value has been entered.

**Template Guideline 4:**    Back up templates on diskettes.

As templates are developed, they should be saved periodically to ensure that work is not destroyed. It's a point that's been made several times and that will be made again later in this book.

The example of Figure 9-6 demonstrates clearly the need to have backup of files. In this case we've destroyed the formula for BENEFITS by placing a value incorrectly in its entry location. If we know the relationship, we can reenter the formula. But if we're entering data on a template that someone else has written, or someone else is using our template, there are problems.

The backup is crucial. If we inadvertently destroy a template, we can reload it from the last backup if it has been saved. In fact, this is one of the values of templates; they can be saved and loaded as necessary to obtain desired results.

This example also leads to the next two guidelines.

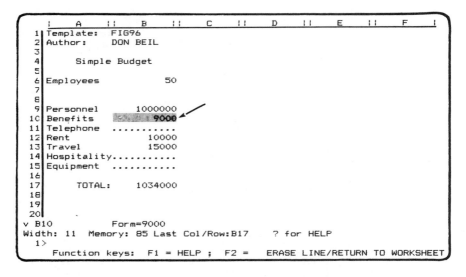

**Figure 9-6.** Our template after inadvertently destroying the BENEFITS entry by writing our TELEPHONE entry there incorrectly.

**Template Guideline 5:**    Separate the data entry process from the calculations.

In Figure 9-6 we destroyed a formula by replacing it with a value in a single potentially devastating move. Such an action can easily go undetected with SuperCalc. It requires extreme care in entering data, a point we'll return to later.

It is important in considering template creation to understand the difference between the processes performed to generate a template and the processes followed to use a template. In discussing data entry, we're discussing using an existing template (not generating a new template). With SuperCalc, data entry is the process of placing values onto predetermined locations of the electronic sheet. As designers it's our responsibility to create templates that make this second process as easy and foolproof as possible.

The last guideline suggests that we can take actions in the design of our template to reduce the likelihood of such a destructive action. Figure 9-7 shows the same template on which we have created a separate area for data entry located below the report. We'll enter values in a separate section of the sheet that functions only as the data entry area. To add this area to the sheet, we must change our formulas.

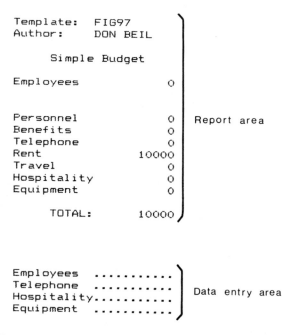

**Figure 9-7.** The budget template in which we've separated the data entry area from the calculation report area.

The changes in formulas have occurred as follows:

| Entry | Figure 9-4 entry contained | Figure 9-7 entry contains this formula |
|---|---|---|
| B6  (EMPLOYEES) | ........... | B22 |
| B11 (TELEPHONE) | ........... | B23 |
| B14 (HOSPITALITY) | ........... | B24 |
| B15 (EQUIPMENT) | ........... | B25 |

We can see that we've replaced our series of periods (...........) with a simple formula reference to the data entry area of the template. These formulas are essentially four "copy" instructions. SuperCalc copies the data entered in the lower portion of the screen to the desired report format area at the top of the screen.

This action alone can reduce the possibility of destruction of the formulas forming the relationships in our budget template, and as such is a valuable addition to the template.

Additional steps can be taken to isolate the data entry function, as we'll discuss.

**Template Guideline 6:**   "Write protect" the report area.

There may be no concept more important than this one in creating a template. The ease with which values, text, or formulas can be entered onto the sheet is both an advantage and a disadvantage in using SuperCalc.

Use the Protect command when creating templates. It provides protection against accidentally moving into, and subsequently writing on, the report portion of the template. We'll demonstrate this and combine it with the two following guidelines.

**Template Guideline 7:**   Build redundancy into the template.

**Template Guideline 8:**   Store the templates so that when reloaded the cursor is positioned to the first value entered.

Figures 9-8 and 9-9 summarize the last several guidelines. Notice in Figure 9-8 that two rows have been inserted above the data entry section. These lines, which are redundant, are

TEMPLATE: FIG98
AUTHOR:    DON BEIL

They are the same as the top two rows of this template but serve to provide information in the window that the person entering data will see, as we'll discuss.

Figure 9-8 has been shaded on the area of the worksheet which has

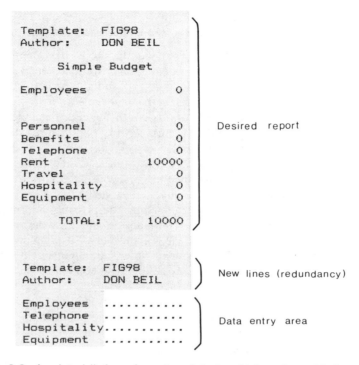

```
Template:   FIG98
Author:     DON BEIL

      Simple Budget

Employees              0


Personnel              0        Desired  report
Benefits               0
Telephone              0
Rent                10000
Travel                 0
Hospitality            0
Equipment              0


      TOTAL:        10000



Template:   FIG98                 New lines (redundancy)
Author:     DON BEIL

Employees    ...........
Telephone    ...........          Data entry  area
Hospitality...........
Equipment    ...........
```

**Figure 9-8.** A printed listing of our template to which we've added protection (the shaded area), and two redundant lines of documentation.

been protected with the Protect command. This will prevent inadvertant destruction of any of the shaded entries.

Figure 9-9 shows the value of this redundancy. It is the image that will appear when an individual issues a Load command to load the file FIG99. In this way we have built redundancy into our template and have stored the template so that when reloaded, the cursor is positioned at the first value entered. The redundancy is an extra effort but provides additional information and documentation for the user. We have another example of redundancy with our four variables entered in one location and copied automatically into another. We'll see other examples later in the chapter.

The cells have been protected as marked in Figure 9-9, and the cursor comes up on the screen as shown, ready to accept the first value to be entered. If the person entering data accidentally moves up the screen or to the left, the user will be prevented from destroying cells.

With this technique it's possible to achieve success in "write protecting" our sheet. Another technique is demonstrated later in the chapter.

The screen of Figure 9-9 also demonstrates another guideline.

**Template Guideline 9:**   For data entry, reveal only as much of the sheet on the screen as necessary for this process.

Compare Figure 9-9 with Figure 9-10. The first is a simple screen containing only the area needed for data entry. Much of the screen is blank and easy to understand and to use. Borders have been omitted. Figure 9-10 on the other hand reveals a larger number of entries (almost the full sheet here) and is confusing. For example, a number of the fields occur twice on the same screen. For this reason, the simple screen of Figure 9-9 is preferable.

This last guideline works counter to one of the strengths of SuperCalc, that of observing the instantaneous effect of a change in one field on another entry. Because of that, this particular guideline will be meaningful for some templates but possibly not others.

What's important is to design the data entry function to be simple, direct, and easy to use for the person (including ourselves) entering the data. SuperCalc demands the full attention of the user entering data; therefore templates should be designed not to distract from this process in any way.

Let's think again of the person entering the data, and assume that we have a printer available. Since we've isolated the values to be entered, we could get printed copies of this blank data entry section of the sheet and follow the next guideline.

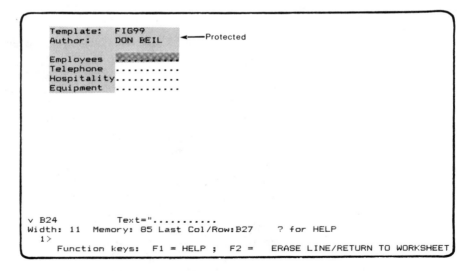

**Figure 9-9.** The window that appears when loading the budget template. This is the data entry area of the sheet on which the shaded cells have been protected.

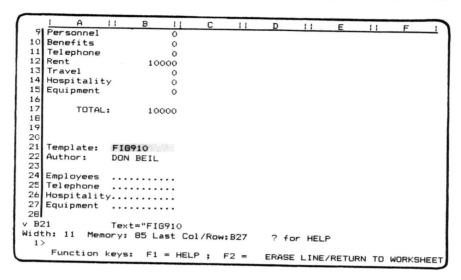

**Figure 9-10.** An example of a window that may be confusing to a person entering data on the sheet.

**Template Guideline 10:**   Use the data entry layout of the sheet for the external data collection.

This is demonstrated in Figure 9-11. Suppose that we want to prepare printed reports for several budget options and that another person will be preparing these reports for us. To communicate our wishes to the person doing the data entry, we can simply write the values we want onto "input" forms printed from the data entry portion of the template as shown in Figure 9-11 on the left. On the right are our finished reports.

We can think of this as using a portion of the template in printed form to prepare "input" for a report generated by SuperCalc.

To assist further in this process, and to build on the report preparation activities of Figure 9-11, let's introduce several more guidelines.

**Template Guideline 11:**   Include instructions in the template.

In Figure 9-12 we've done that. Notice the new last row. It directs the person to GO TO A3 after the data entry function for the four values has been completed. A person entering values vertically down the template will encounter the last row and can follow the directions included there in the form of a SuperCalc command.

This label was placed at this entry by entering the double quote key (to indicate that a label is being entered), followed by the characters shown in the entry. That is, we entered

" =A3 RETURN

"INPUT"                                "OUTPUT"

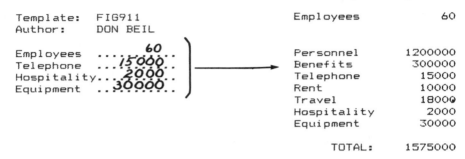

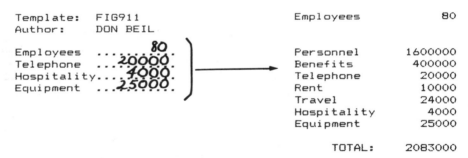

**Figure 9-11.** A demonstration of recording variables on preprinted "input" forms prepared by printing the data entry segment of the template and then using these forms as a reference for entering data onto the sheet to obtain the reports shown as "output."

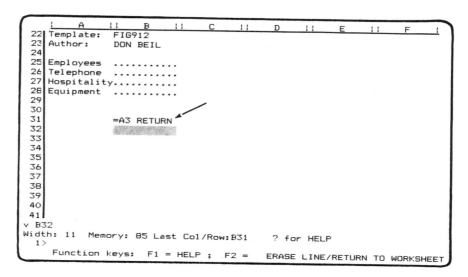

**Figure 9-12.** Our template with instructions (=A3 RETURN) included.

In this example, assume we have entered the four required values, as shown in Figure 9-13. We then execute the GO TO A3 as directed. Following this command, the screen appears as in Figure 9-14.

Here a line of additional instructions is included, directing us to remove the borders,

/ G B

and then print the report

/ O D A4:B23 RETURN P

This is the series of keystrokes for a printer on one computer system to print a report from location A4 (the desired top left corner of the report) to location B23 (the bottom right corner desired).

When the instructions of row 3 are followed, the report of Figure 9-15 is produced. Notice the line

TEMPLATE: FIG915

printed near the bottom. This line serves as excellent documentation for the printed report itself. It should be circulated with the report since it can be a needed reference to the particular template used. Let's produce a guideline from this concept.

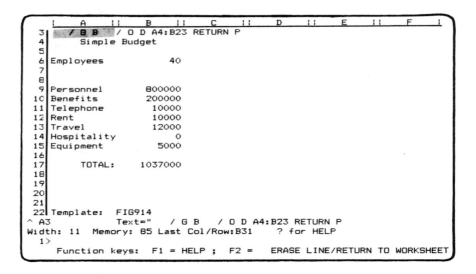

```
      |    A    ||    B    ||    C    ||    D    ||    E    ||    F    |
  22| Template:   FIG913
  23| Author:     DON BEIL
  24|
  25| Employees           40
  26| Telephone        10000
  27| Hospitality         0
  28| Equipment        5000
  29|
  30|
  31|             =A3  RETURN
  32|
  33|
  34|
  35|
  36|
  37|
  38|
  39|
  40|
  41|
  v B29
  Width: 11   Memory: 85 Last Col/Row:B31    ? for HELP
    1>
       Function keys:  F1 = HELP ;  F2 =    ERASE LINE/RETURN TO WORKSHEET
```

**Figure 9-13.** Our template after entering the four values and before following the instructions of the last row.

```
      |    A    ||    B    ||    C    ||    D    ||    E    ||    F    |
   3|   / B B    / O D A4:B23 RETURN P
   4|      Simple Budget
   5|
   6| Employees           40
   7|
   8|
   9| Personnel       800000
  10| Benefits        200000
  11| Telephone        10000
  12| Rent             10000
  13| Travel           12000
  14| Hospitality         0
  15| Equipment        5000
  16|
  17|     TOTAL:     1037000
  18|
  19|
  20|
  21|
  22| Template:   FIG914
  ^ A3              Text="   / G B    / O D A4:B23 RETURN P
  Width: 11   Memory: 85 Last Col/Row:B31    ? for HELP
    1>
       Function keys:  F1 = HELP ;  F2 =    ERASE LINE/RETURN TO WORKSHEET
```

**Figure 9-14.** Our screen after executing a GO TO A3. We are given additional instructions.

```
                    Simple Budget

        Employees              40


        Personnel         800000
        Benefits          200000
        Telephone          10000
        Rent               10000
        Travel             12000
        Hospitality            0
        Equipment           5000

            TOTAL:        1037000




        Template:    FIG915
        Author:      DON BEIL
```

**Figure 9-15.** The report printed by following the instructions in the top line of Figure 9-14.


**Template Guideline 12:** Label all printed reports with identification of the template used to produce it.

In addition, it's often desirable to know the ''assumptions'' from which our report has been prepared. With the layout of the sheet that we've developed, it's easy to add this to any printed reports by simply printing a larger part of the full sheet. This has been done in Figure 9-16 after adding one row with the word ASSUMPTIONS. The variable values used to create this report are clearly indicated at the bottom of the report.

A summary of our final template for this example is shown in Figure 9-17. A number of things have been marked including

- Several areas of documentation.
- Several lines of instructions.
- The format of the first printed report including the template identification (printed report 1).
- The format of a second report, which includes the printed ''assumptions'' used to create the spreadsheet (printed report 2).
- The data entry window, which appears when the template is first loaded and which in printed form can be used for external data collection.
- The protected area of the sheet.

An additional important concept follows:

```
                    Simple Budget

        Employees                40


        Personnel           800000
        Benefits            200000
        Telephone            10000
        Rent                 10000
        Travel               12000
        Hospitality              0
        Equipment             5000

            TOTAL:         1037000




        Template:   FIG916
        Author:     DON BEIL
             "Assumptions"

        Employees                40
        Telephone            10000
        Hospitality              0
        Equipment             5000
```

**Figure 9-16.** A printed report listing our "assumptions" on which the report is prepared.

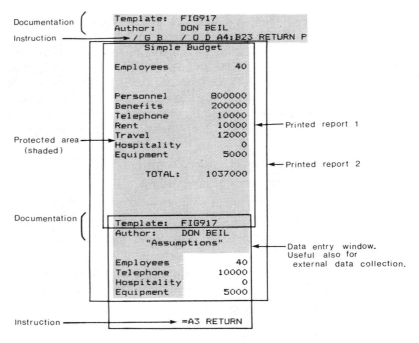

**Figure 9-17.** A summary of our template.

**Template Guideline 13:**   Provide documentation for the user other than that written onto the template.

Chapter 10, Documentation, discusses this topic and suggests methods appropriate for SuperCalc users.

## GUIDELINES FOR CREATING TEMPLATES: EXAMPLE 2

For the second example, assume that we need a template that will help us at our manufacturing plant to record our production activity on an hour-by-hour basis for one week and to establish hourly production goals for the coming week. Figure 9-18 shows the desired report that we want to produce.

The values for PRODUCTION THIS WEEK in Figure 9-18 are our actual production figures that we enter late Friday afternoon. Our FORECAST will use a simple goal mechanism. We want to increase production by a specific number of units per hour for every hour. The variables that we'll provide to the template include all the values enclosed in the two boxes of Figure 9-18. All other values will be computed by the template. Notice that we really have two reports on our template. Let's formalize this idea.

**Template Guideline 14:**   More than one report can be prepared on the same template.

If we wish, we can prepare several reports on the same sheet. We can add a simple graph of the same data if desired. On Figure 9-18, we can simply rearrange the axes of each of these reports and prepare both with the days of the week across the rows and the times down the columns.

Let's study the full template designed to prepare the two reports shown in Figure 9-18. The complete template is shown in Figure 9-19. The final report of the previous figure is marked. Also marked is the initial screen. Notice the location of the cursor as it appears when the template is loaded. It appears on the Monday 8:00 a.m. entry, ready for the first data to be entered. All shaded areas have been protected to limit access to the upper report area and to reduce the possibility of destroying formulas there.

Look at the screen in Figure 9-20. We have just moved down the column entering the values for production this week on Monday. As we finish the 4:00 p.m. time, we come to row 60, which shows:

TOTAL    0    !! CHECK MON. TOTAL

This line contains an instruction, the two exclamation points (!!) that ask for a recalculation. This sheet has been stored with a global recalculation

PRODUCTION THIS WEEK
(000)

|       | MON | TUES | WED | THUR | FRI | TOT |
|-------|-----|------|-----|------|-----|-----|
| 8:00  | 0   | 10   | 10  | 20   | 20  | 60  |
| 9:00  | 2   | 30   | 25  | 20   | 30  | 107 |
| 10:00 | 20  | 30   | 25  | 20   | 30  | 125 |
| 11:00 | 20  | 30   | 40  | 30   | 40  | 160 |
| 12:00 | 18  | 25   | 35  | 30   | 30  | 138 |
| 1:00  | 30  | 30   | 40  | 20   | 30  | 150 |
| 2:00  | 30  | 30   | 40  | 20   | 30  | 150 |
| 3:00  | 30  | 25   | 30  | 30   | 30  | 145 |
| 4:00  | 25  | 25   | 30  | 30   | 30  | 140 |
| TOTAL | 175 | 235  | 275 | 220  | 270 | 1175 |

FORECAST:
PRODUCTION NEXT WEEK
(000)

PLANNED INCREASE OF   10   UNITS/HR.

|       | MON | TUES | WED | THUR | FRI | TOT |
|-------|-----|------|-----|------|-----|-----|
| 8:00  | 10  | 20   | 20  | 30   | 30  | 110 |
| 9:00  | 12  | 40   | 35  | 30   | 40  | 157 |
| 10:00 | 30  | 40   | 35  | 30   | 40  | 175 |
| 11:00 | 30  | 40   | 50  | 40   | 50  | 210 |
| 12:00 | 28  | 35   | 45  | 40   | 40  | 188 |
| 1:00  | 40  | 40   | 50  | 30   | 40  | 200 |
| 2:00  | 40  | 40   | 50  | 30   | 40  | 200 |
| 3:00  | 40  | 35   | 40  | 40   | 40  | 195 |
| 4:00  | 35  | 35   | 40  | 40   | 40  | 190 |
| TOTAL | 265 | 325  | 365 | 310  | 360 | 1625 |

TEMPLATE: FIGURE 9-18
AUTHOR:   DON BEIL

**Figure 9-18.** The numbers enclosed in boxes are variables that we provide to this template to prepare our PRODUCTION THIS WEEK and our FORECAST for next week. All other values are calculated by the template.

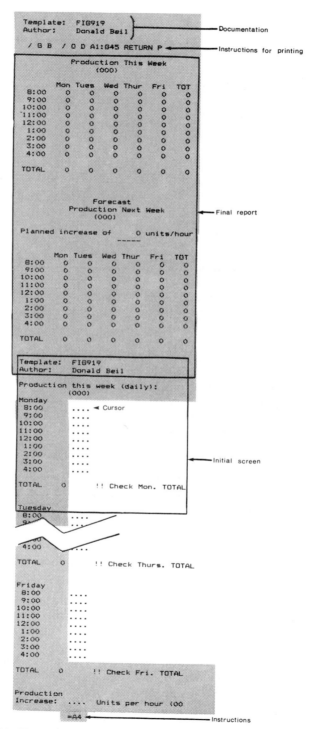

**Figure 9-19.** The full annotated template of our production example. The shaded area is protected.

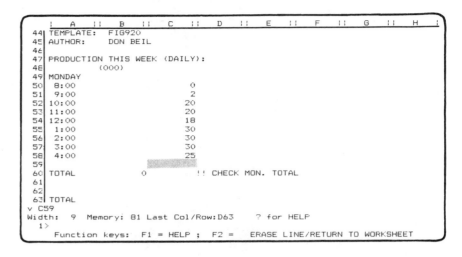

**Figure 9-20.** After moving down the column entering data, the user comes to an instruction to perform recalculations (!!).

mode of manual (M), so that data could be entered more quickly. Now the user is asked to recalculate twice. Doing so provides the screen shown in Figure 9-21.

Notice the entry at location B60, which now shows 175 instead of 0. The recalculations have provided a Monday TOTAL in the data entry area of the sheet, a "protected" entry. The user is also instructed to

CHECK MON TOTAL

meaning that a total has been provided for Monday and that the individual can use that as a method of verifying that the numbers for Monday have been entered accurately. We'll assume that the user has calculated this value as a control total used to check on the accuracy of the process. We can list this idea as a guideline.

**Template Guideline 15:** Provide the user with aids to verify that data are being entered properly.

This is important, especially since SuperCalc has only limited techniques to edit user input to ascertain validity. For example, we cannot easily check a value entered to see if it is a number, not a label. We are also very limited in communicating errors or potential errors to users since we can't print messages to users from the sheet (except for the words ERROR and NA). Therefore, it is important to include whatever capability we can to ensure that data are entered correctly. In this example, we are assuming that the user has previously totaled the

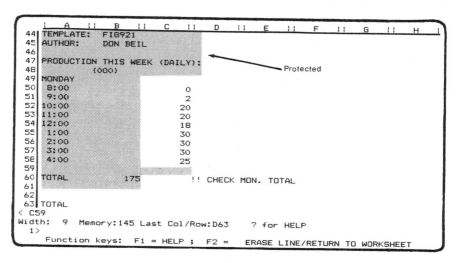

**Figure 9-21.** The recalculations provide a total for the day (here, 175) that gives the user a control total to be used to verify that accurate data have been entered.

production for each day and that this total is compared against our built-in sum as a way of controlling the accuracy of the data. We want the user to check the data entered so that accurate information is prepared.

Notice with this template, that the user is required to enter data vertically down the sheet. This was done with reason.

**Template Guideline 16:** When building the data entry area of a template, require the user to enter data while moving down the template in a single column.

There are several reasons for this. If we establish one direction (down) as the single movement required while entering data, we may reduce the possibility of error. If large amounts of data must be entered, we can still go down the sheet until the bottom is reached. At that point, the user can be directed (with a GO TO) to the top of another column at which additional data are entered down the sheet. Also, more rows than columns appear on the screen, making it easier to follow the action down the sheet, rather than across. Finally, the movement seems less abrupt when scrolling down the sheet instead of across it.

In our template, the user continues down the screen until the data for each day of the week have been entered; then the desired PRODUCTION INCREASE is entered as prompted.

Continuing down the sheet, the user finds an instruction,

=A4.

When issued, the user is sent to line 4 of our template. Here, the first instruction is to perform recalculations (!!) as shown in Figure 9-22. We'll review the reason next.

**Template Guideline 17:**    Recalculate before printing.

**Template Guideline 18:**    On spreadsheets requiring significant data entry, use the manual recalculation mode.

On this template, we placed the sheet into manual recalculation mode to speed the data entry process. Here, recalculations do occur after the data for each week are entered, but one is not included after the PRODUCTION INCREASE is entered at the bottom of the sheet. (We can, of course, include one if desired.) After the GO TO A4 is executed, our FORECAST table does not yet have the correct final values. The recalculation causes this. (Two exclamation points are not required, one is sufficient in this example.)

In Figure 9-22, the cursor is resting at position G19, where we have an incorrect entry. The formula at this entry, SUM(B19:F19), was generated when a Replicate command was used to copy the formula down the G column from entry G10. As discussed earlier, in the Replicate section of Chapter 4, Commands, this can happen often with spreadsheet creation. One method to avoid it follows.

```
|   A    ::   B   ::   C   ::   D   ::   E   ::   F   ::   G   ::   H   :
 1|TEMPLATE:   FIG922
 2|AUTHOR:     DON BEIL
 3|
 4| !! =A5 return   / O D A1:G45 return P
 5|
 6|                        PRODUCTION THIS WEEK
 7|                            (OOO)
 8|
 9|              MON      TUES     WED      THUR     FRI      TOT
10| 8:00          O        O        O        O        O        O
11| 9:00          O        O        O        O        O        O
12|10:00          O        O        O        O        O        O
13|11:00          O        O        O        O        O        O
14|12:00          O        O        O        O        O        O
15| 1:00          O        O        O        O        O        O
16| 2:00          O        O        O        O        O        O
17| 3:00          O        O        O        O        O        O
18| 4:00          O        O        O        O        O        O
19|                                                          ▓▓▓▓▓▓
20|3TOTAL         O        O        O        O        O        O
< G19          Form=SUM(B19:F19)
Width:   9  Memory: 79 Last Col/Row:G87    ? for HELP
   1>
     Function keys:  F1 = HELP ;   F2 =    ERASE LINE/RETURN TO WORKSHEET
```

**Figure 9-22.** The cursor highlights an error that could have been avoided if this blank row had been entered after all other work on the template was complete.

**Template Guideline 19:**   Insert blank rows and columns as the final step of creating the template.

Postponing this action can help avoid the work and potential problems associated with clearing individual entries that can occur when replicating as described.

## GUIDELINES FOR CREATING TEMPLATES: EXAMPLE 3

Our final example in the chapter will be a straightforward template used to estimate our electric utility bill per month for the year. We begin with records of the monthly usage last year which we enter as one column. Then we'll enter only two values:

- Percentage increase or decrease we anticipate in kilowatt usage for the year.
- Expected price.

We want to build an interactive template that allows us to change these two variables and observe the results of our actions. Figure 9-23 contains such a template. The opening screen contains two windows as shown. The two variables are entered in the lower window and the results are displayed in the upper window. As with other examples, protection is used, as indicated by the shading.

**Template Guideline 20:**   Split windows provide an important method of observing two areas of a template at once and extra protection in preserving sections of the sheet from accidental destruction.

This sheet also contains several other interesting sections. Notice in the illustration of the full sheet of Figure 9-23 that the last line contains instructions to begin printing if desired.  Then at location A4, we're told to

ENTER DATE AND TIME ON ROW 8.

Notice that row 8 contains

DATE: "MM/DD/YY  TIME: "00:00

If we tried to enter either without a double quote ("), we wouldn't be able to enter the slash (/) which would cause division since SuperCalc would assume that we are entering a value, or the colon (:) which would cause a FORMULA ERROR.  Thus, the instructions shown with the quote will, if followed, cause SuperCalc to accept the two items in the correct formats.

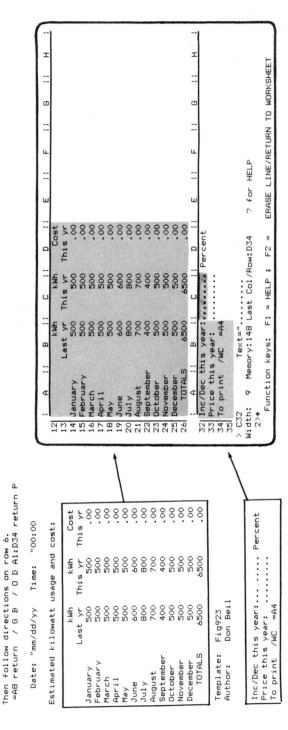

**Figure 9-23.** An interactive template that allows us to enter two variables and observe the impact on our electric consumption and cost.

**Template Guideline 21:** Format the data entry location so that it will be easy to enter the data correctly.

Here we've included explicit directions ("MM/DD/YY) for how the data are to be entered and thus helped the user. At other times, we can indicate that values are to be entered in ways other than using repeated periods; for example, we can use VVVVVV, VVVV.VV, or VALUE. Similarly, areas to receive a label could be marked TTTTTT, TEXT, etc.

How do we know if our templates work correctly? This is not a simple question to answer. Refer to Chapter 8, Recognizing, Preventing, and Correcting Errors, for a discussion of this topic and for a number of suggestions applicable to this discussion on creating templates. Here, let's briefly summarize our earlier advice of that chapter.

**Template Guideline 22:** Test templates before using them, check them while using them, and verify results after using them.

One of the major programming lessons of the last two decades has been to invest time and energy in designing a solution before beginning to code it. Coding is the process of actually writing and entering instructions. It should occur after we've mentally solved a problem and when we're ready to translate that solution to a format understandable to a computer system. This chapter began with an admonishment to understand the problem that we're solving. It ends with encouragement to understand the solution to be used before we begin to implement it.

# CHAPTER 10

# Documentation

## INTRODUCTION

Documentation provides a record of our activities that can be helpful when we want to reuse our work, or that can assist another person who uses spreadsheets that we prepare. Each of us must decide, using many factors, what is appropriate documentation for our efforts. Documentation of our work requires time and is often seen by those new to computers as unimportant; however, consider the importance of well-written manuals to guide in the use of computer hardware or accompanying software.

We hope the software that we use is well-documented both internally and externally. We'll explain both types in this chapter.

There are many examples of internal documentation. With SuperCalc this includes the information appearing on the prompt line to assist us in using SuperCalc correctly. As a specific example, when we enter the / (slash) to begin a command, letters appear on the prompt line. This documentation within the software makes it easier to use. SuperCalc contains a large number of these internal prompts.

As another example, the help screens that appear when we press the question mark (?) are very important internal documentation.

The manual accompanying SuperCalc is the external documentation provided for it. It is separate from the software but important to our understanding of how the software functions.

As we create software, in the form of SuperCalc spreadsheets, we'll want to prepare both internal and external documentation. Let's discuss both kinds of documentation for our SuperCalc activities and suggest methods of preparing both.

## PROVIDING INTERNAL DOCUMENTATION ON THE SPREADSHEET

When using SuperCalc, it is possible to include reference data, instructions, or other information within the sheet by entering this information as text on the spreadsheet. One example is a suggested standard documentation format that could appear within every one of our electronic sheets. Figure 10-1 provides a simple template layout for such internal documentation.

```
 !   A   !!    B    !!   C   !!   D   !!   E   !!   F   !!   G   !!   H   !
 1
 2  Template filename.
 3  Diskette Id-numb..
 4
 5  Description.......
 6
 7
 8
 9  Author...........
10  Date written......
11
12  Backup location:
13       Filename.....
14       Diskette id..
15
16  Contact person....
17         phone.....
18
19  To continue type..
20
 v  C2
Width:   9  Memory: 85 Last Col/Row:A19    ? for HELP
    1>
        Function keys:  F1 = HELP ;  F2 =    ERASE LINE/RETURN TO WORKSHEET
```

**Figure 10-1.** A template containing a format for internal documentation of a spreadsheet.

Figure 10-2 was built from Figure 10-1 to illustrate how we can complete the template for a specific spreadsheet.

Let's discuss the entries. On row 2 we've placed the file name of this spreadsheet (QTR4) and on row 3 the identification of the diskette (FORECAST-12). Rows 5 to 7 contain a brief description of the function of the electronic sheet. The next lines (rows 9 and 10) contain the name of the author of the sheet and the date written. These are followed by lines containing the location of the backup of this spreadsheet (the file and diskette names). As discussed earlier, the backup is a duplicate copy of this diskette (or one of several copies) retained in case this copy is inadvertently destroyed. The name and telephone number of the person to contact regarding the sheet follow.

```
   !  A  ¦¦  B  ¦¦  C  ¦¦  D  ¦¦  E  ¦¦  F  ¦¦  G  ¦¦  H  !
 1¦
 2¦ Template filename.QTR4
 3¦ Diskette Id-numb..FORECAST-12
 4¦
 5¦ Description.......PREPARES A FORECAST OF THE
 6¦                   FOURTH QUARTER BASED ON
 7¦                   THE 3rd QUARTER.
 8¦
 9¦ Author...........DONALD BEIL
1C¦ Date written......07/11/99
11¦
12¦ Backup location:
13¦      Filename.....BUQTR4
14¦      Diskette id..BU-FORECAST-12
15¦
16¦ Contact person....DONALD BEIL
17¦         phone.....716-475-6373
18¦
19¦ To continue type..=A40 RETURN
20¦
^ C19          Text="=A40 RETURN
Width:  9  Memory: 85 Last Col/Row:C19      ? for HELP
  1>
     Function keys:  F1 = HELP ;   F2 =    ERASE LINE/RETURN TO WORKSHEET
```

**Figure 10-2.** A specific example of our sheet with data for one of our budget spreadsheets.

Finally, there are directions to be followed to continue processing. In this example (Figure 10-2), the user is instructed to type

=A40 RETURN

When entered, this moves the cursor to position A40, where the user begins working with the sheet. Additional instructions then may be placed at that location. These commands have been written on the sheet by typing them as text, beginning each with the double quote (") character.

In another example, we'll have several commands embedded on the sheet as directions. Let's look at an example of this in Figure 10-3 and Figure 10-4. Notice that row 23 of Figure 10-3 contains a series of instructions to be followed when it's time to print a report from this spreadsheet. Assume that we were sent to location A23 by a GO TO instruction contained elsewhere on the sheet. Upon arriving at this location, we'll follow the instructions to print this report on the available printer. Here, following the directions on line 23, we move the cursor to location A26 and then by pressing

/GB

we remove the SuperCalc border.

Figure 10-4 shows a second line of instructions on row 24. If we follow these directions, we will print our report using the Output command. This line can be extremely useful since it can reduce the possibility for issuing an erroneous, and thus wasted, Output command.

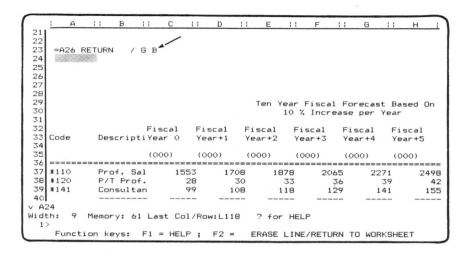

**Figure 10-3.** An example in which we've embedded instructions.

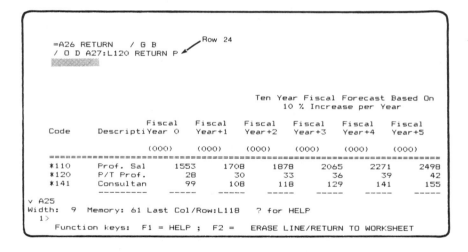

**Figure 10-4** We've added a second line of instructions to the sheet of Figure 10-3.

Figure 10-5 illustrates a more complicated example for the same report. Row 21 directs us to enter a date at location B28 by entering a double quotation mark and then the date in the format shown. This action will replace the guide

$$"MM/DD/YY$$

with the date that we enter.

Row 22 requests similar action for the time of day. Both the date and the time are commonly printed on computer reports and are important documentation elements. If many different reports are prepared, circulated, and filed from the same sheet, this action enables us to separate them based on date and time.

If we wish, we can insert instructions on the sheet directing the user to initiate a recalculation by entering an exclamation point, or we can include directions for how to save this sheet to a diskette. These instructions can be included on the sheet in the same way that rows 21, 22, 23, and 24 are included in the spreadsheet of Figure 10-5.

Finally, if we wish, we can include a full screen of documentation and directions on the spreadsheet or even have a full sheet consisting completely and only of documentation. To do so, we can establish the maximum column width available.

## PROVIDING EXTERNAL DOCUMENTATION FOR THE SPREADSHEET

In addition to the internal documentation that we develop, it's equally important to provide external documentation for the spreadsheet. In this section, we'll suggest information that could be provided to a user.

This additional documentation may consist of written pages including

- Sheet of directions and summary information.
- Sample copy of a report printed from the electronic sheet (if reports are printed).
- Sample copy of data collection forms on which the user writes data or assumptions that will be used with this sheet.
- Listing that includes usage of this spreadsheet (for example, the date used, the user name, files created, problems encountered).
- Other information needed, but not provided, on the spreadsheet, for example, a list of budget codes and their meanings as used on the template.
- Printed, annotated listing of the full template.

If documentation at this level is needed, then the use of simple plastic envelopes that can hold a diskette in one pocket, with accompanying do-

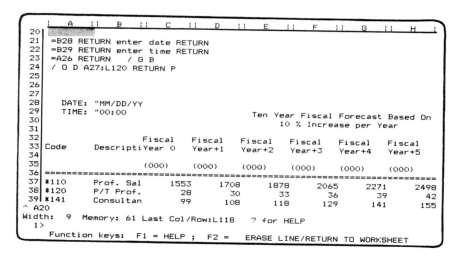

**Figure 10-5.** A window containing a series of embedded directions for the user of this spreadsheet.

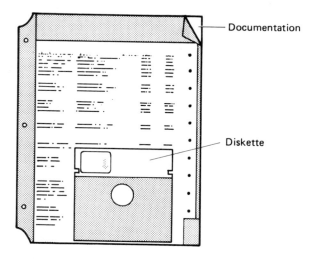

**Figure 10-6.** A convenient method of storing diskettes and documentation together.

cumentation in another, may be helpful. They are available with 3-hole punches, as shown in Figure 10-6, or designed to hang in a file cabinet.

Let's present a specific example of external documentation of a budget forecasting template. Page 1 of our documentation in Figure 10-7 contains

Worksheet
Documentation

Page _____ of _____

Template Filename: _____

Diskette Id-Number: _____

Description:        _____

                    _____

                    _____

Author:             _____

Date Written:       _____

Back-up Location

    Filename:       _____

    Diskette Id:    _____

Contact Person:     _____

      Phone:        _____

Note:   The information above should also appear on the first window
        shown when loading the spreadsheet. Be certain that the correct
        sheet is being used by comparing the top two lines here with those
        on the window.

Directions:

USAGE RECORD

| Date | User | New File Name | Notes, comments, problems |
|------|------|---------------|---------------------------|
|      |      |               |                           |
|      |      |               |                           |
|      |      |               |                           |
|      |      |               |                           |

**Figure 10-7.** A sample documentation sheet for our templates, page 1.

Worksheet
Documentation

Template Filename: __QTR4__
Diskette Id-Number: __FORECAST-11__

Description:     Prepares a report of projected vs. planned expenses.

Author:           Donald Beil
Date Written:     04/23/99

Back-up Location
     Filename:     BUQTR4
     Diskette Id:  BU-FORECAST-11

Contact Person:   Donald Beil
          Phone:  716-475-6373

Note:   The information above should also appear on the first window
        shown when loading the spreadsheet. Be certain that the correct
        sheet is being used by comparing the top two lines here with those
        on the window.

Directions:

1. Prepare input data on forms shown on page 3 of this documentation.
2. Boot SuperCalc.
3. Insert diskette "FORECAST-11."
4. Load file QTR4 (/LB:QTR4 RETURN A)
5. Verify that correct diskette and file have been loaded.
6. Follow "continue" instructions on bottom of the window.
7. Enter data collected in step 1 above.
8. Follow directions to move cursor and print.
9. Distribute copies of this report to Department 442, 481, and 530.

USAGE RECORD

| Date | User | New File Name | Notes, comments, problems |
|------|------|---------------|---------------------------|
|      |      |               |                           |
|      |      |               |                           |
|      |      |               |                           |

**Figure 10-7** continued.

a form on which we can record basic directions (as shown in Figure 10-7 Continued) as well as summary information for this particular spreadsheet.

Notice the directions included on this page. They explain steps required by an individual to use the template successfully. It also contains an area at the end of the page that can serve as an activity log of the use of the sheet. Problems encountered, if any, can be recorded here. The directions also indicate procedures, such as step 9, to be followed to distribute printed reports from the sheet.

Page 2 of our documentation, in Figure 10-8, shows a sample copy of the final report printed from this spreadsheet. This page is included as a reference for the user to illustrate the expected final report format.

The third page of our documentation, page 3 shown in Figure 10-9, contains the data collection layout form used with this sheet. On it the

|  | PROJECTED |
| CODE | EXPENSE |
| --- | --- |
| 120 | . . . . . . . . . . . . |
| 141 | . . . . . . . . . . . . |
| 145 | . . . . . . . . . . . |
| 150 | . . . . . . . . . . . . |
| 152 | . . . . . . . . . . . . |
| 155 | . . . . . . . . . . . . |
| 200 | . . . . . . . . . . . . |
| 210 | . . . . . . . . . . . . |
| 220 | . . . . . . . . . . . . |
| 232 | . . . . . . . . . . . . |
| 240 | . . . . . . . . . . . . |
| 260 | . . . . . . . . . . . . |
| 270 | . . . . . . . . . . . . |
| 310 | . . . . . . . . . . . . |
| 320 | . . . . . . . . . . . . |
| 408 | . . . . . . . . . . . |
| 430 | . . . . . . . . . . . |
| 470 | . . . . . . . . . . . |
| 515 | . . . . . . . . . . . |
| 520 | . . . . . . . . . . . |
| 620 | . . . . . . . . . . . |
| 630 | . . . . . . . . . . . |

**Figure 10-9.** A sheet that we can use to record the data to be used as input for this template, page 3 of our documentation.

| CODE | START-OF-YR BUDGET 442 | CURRENT BUDGET 442 | BUDGET-DIFFERENCE AMOUNT 442 | PERCENT 442 | YR-TO-DATE AMOUNT 442 | EXPENSES PERCENT 442 | PROJECTED EXPENSES 442 | TOTAL EXPENSES 442 | OVER/UNDER BUDGET 442 |
|---|---|---|---|---|---|---|---|---|---|
| #120 | 346700.00 | 341900.00 | -4800.00 | -1 | 164467.06 | 48 | 178002.00 | 342469.06 | 569.06 |
| #141 | 9800.00 | 9800.00 | 0.00 | 0 | 4800.00 | 49 | 5064.00 | 9864.00 | 64.00 |
| SUB. | 356500.00 | 351700.00 | -4800.00 | -1.38 | 169267.06 | 97.08 | 183066.00 | 352333.06 | 633.06 |
| 145 | 26600.00 | 26600.00 | 0.00 | 0 | 18232.11 | 69 | 15367.89 | 33600.00 | 7000.00 |
| SUB. | 26600.00 | 26600.00 | 0.00 | 0 | 18232.11 | 69 | 15367.89 | 33600.00 | 7000.00 |
| 150 | 2500.00 | 2300.00 | -200.00 | -8 | 4940.73 | 215 | 2559.27 | 7500.00 | 5200.00 |
| 152 | 2500.00 | 2500.00 | 0.00 | 0 | 889.97 | 36 | 410.03 | 1300.00 | -1200.00 |
| 155 | 7400.00 | 7400.00 | 0.00 | 0 | 2023.50 | 27 | 1976.50 | 4000.00 | -3400.00 |
| SUB. | 12400.00 | 12200.00 | -200.00 | -2 | 7854.20 | 64 | 4945.80 | 12800.00 | 600.00 |
| #200 | 63300.00 | 62600.00 | -700.00 | -1 | 0.00 | 0 | 0.00 | 0.00 | -62600.00 |
| 210 | 0.00 | 0.00 | 0.00 | 0 | 11909.32 | 0 | 9322.80 | 21232.12 | 21232.12 |
| 220 | 0.00 | 0.00 | 0.00 | 0 | 9725.60 | 0 | 7613.35 | 17338.95 | 17338.95 |
| 232 | 0.00 | 0.00 | 0.00 | 0 | 779.22 | 0 | 609.99 | 1389.21 | 1389.21 |
| 240 | 0.00 | 0.00 | 0.00 | 0 | 3505.21 | 0 | 2743.93 | 6249.14 | 6249.14 |
| 260 | 0.00 | 0.00 | 0.00 | 0 | 795.15 | 0 | 622.46 | 1417.61 | 1417.61 |
| 270 | 0.00 | 0.00 | 0.00 | 0 | 8398.50 | 0 | 6574.48 | 14972.98 | 14972.98 |
| SUB. | 63300.00 | 62600.00 | -700.00 | -1 | 35113.00 | 56 | 27487.00 | 62600.00 | 0.00 |
| 310 | 4000.00 | 4000.00 | 0.00 | 0 | 1818.05 | 45 | 2181.95 | 4000.00 | 0.00 |
| 320 | 6000.00 | 7000.00 | 1000.00 | 17 | 3363.15 | 48 | 4636.85 | 8000.00 | 1000.00 |
| SUB. | 10000.00 | 11000.00 | 1000.00 | 10 | 5181.20 | 47 | 6818.80 | 12000.00 | 1000.00 |
| 408 | 0.00 | 0.00 | 0.00 | 0 | 0.00 | 0 | 0.00 | 0.00 | 0.00 |
| SUB. | 0.00 | 0.00 | 0.00 | 0 | 0.00 | 0 | 0.00 | 0.00 | 0.00 |
| 430 | 300.00 | 400.00 | 100.00 | 33 | 321.94 | 80 | 178.06 | 500.00 | 100.00 |
| SUB. | 300.00 | 400.00 | 100.00 | 33 | 321.94 | 80 | 178.06 | 500.00 | 100.00 |
| 470 | 7800.00 | 0.00 | -7800.00 | -100 | 0.00 | 0 | 0.00 | 0.00 | 0.00 |
| SUB. | 7800.00 | 0.00 | -7800.00 | -100 | 0.00 | 0 | 0.00 | 0.00 | 0.00 |
| 515 | 0.00 | 0.00 | 0.00 | 0 | 0.00 | 0 | 0.00 | 0.00 | 0.00 |
| SUB. | 0.00 | 0.00 | 0.00 | 0 | 0.00 | 0 | 0.00 | 0.00 | 0.00 |
| 520 | 0.00 | 0.00 | 0.00 | 0 | 0.00 | 0 | 0.00 | 0.00 | 0.00 |
| SUB. | 0.00 | 0.00 | 0.00 | 0 | 0.00 | 0 | 0.00 | 0.00 | 0.00 |
| 620 | 13800.00 | 13800.00 | 0.00 | 0 | 10003.11 | 72 | 3796.89 | 13800.00 | 0.00 |
| SUB. | 13800.00 | 13800.00 | 0.00 | 0 | 10003.11 | 72 | 3796.89 | 13800.00 | 0.00 |
| 630 | 26000.00 | 23700.00 | -2300.00 | -9 | 12786.54 | 54 | 10913.46 | 23700.00 | 0.00 |
| SUB. | 26000.00 | 23700.00 | -2300.00 | -9 | 12786.54 | 54 | 10913.46 | 23700.00 | 0.00 |
| TOTALS | 526700.00 | 513000.00 | -13700.00 | -59.62 | 263940.36 | 51 | 259392.70 | 523333.06 | 10333.06 |

**Figure 10-8.** A sample report printed from our template. This report is page 2 of our documentation.

user can write the assumptions (data) to be used in preparing this sheet. This page has been printed directly from the template itself. It is the portion of the sheet on which the user will enter the data for the sheet. Using this exact layout as a data collection and layout form provides an important connection between the sheet and the data entry function.

Finally, Figure 10-10 contains an annotated listing of the full sheet we have prepared. Notes written on this page explain it to the user. This page can be important in our training session with the user to explain the sheet fully.

```
                    1  Template Filename..........QTRFOREC
                    2  Diskette Id-Number.........FORECAST-11
                    3
                    4  Description...............Prepares a report of projected vs
                    5                            planned expenses.
                    6
                    7  Author...................Donald Beil
                    8  Date Written..............04/23/99
                    9
                   10  Backup Location
                   11     Filename..........BUQTRFOR
                   12     Diskette..............BU-FORECAST-11
                   13
                   14  Contact Person............Donald Beil
                   15     Phone.............716-475-6373
                   16
                   17  To Continue Type..........=B107
                   18
                   19
                   20
                   21
                   22
                   23
                   24  =B28 RETURN (enter date) RETURN
                   25  =B29 RETURN (enter time) RETURN
                   26  / G B  / O D A27:J95 RETURN P
                   27
                   28  Date:  "MM/DD/YY
                   29  Time:  "00:00
                   30
```

First window { (lines 1–20)

Directions for printing { (lines 23–26)

| | START-OF-YR BUDGET | CURRENT BUDGET | BUDGET-DIFFERENCE AMOUNT | PERCENT | YR-TO-DATE AMOUNT | EXPENSES PERCENT | PROJECTED EXPENSES | TOTAL EXPENSES | OVER/UNDER BUDGET |
|---|---|---|---|---|---|---|---|---|---|
| 33 CODE | 442 | 442 | 442 | 442 | 442 | 442 | 442 | 442 | 442 |
| 36 #120 | 346700.00 | 341900.00 | -4800.00 | -1 | 164467.06 | 48 | 0.00 | 164467.06 | 569.06 |
| 37 #141 | 9800.00 | 9800.00 | 0.00 | 0 | 4800.00 | 49 | 0.00 | 4800.00 | 64.00 |
| 38 SUB. | 356500.00 | 351700.00 | -4800.00 | -1.38 | 169267.06 | 97.08 | 0.00 | 169267.06 | 633.06 |
| 40 145 | 26600.00 | 26600.00 | 0.00 | 0 | 18232.11 | 69 | 0.00 | 18232.11 | -8367.89 |
| 41 SUB. | 26600.00 | 26600.00 | 0.00 | 0 | 18232.11 | 69 | 0.00 | 18232.11 | -8367.89 |
| 43 150 | 2500.00 | 2300.00 | -200.00 | -8 | 4940.73 | 215 | 0.00 | 4940.73 | 2640.73 |
| 44 152 | 2500.00 | 2500.00 | 0.00 | 0 | 889.97 | 36 | 0.00 | 889.97 | -1610.03 |
| 45 155 | 7400.00 | 7400.00 | 0.00 | 0 | 2023.50 | 27 | 0.00 | 2023.50 | -5376.50 |
| 46 SUB. | 12400.00 | 12200.00 | -200.00 | -2 | 7854.20 | 64 | 0.00 | 7854.20 | -4345.80 |
| 48 #200 | 63300.00 | 62600.00 | -700.00 | -1 | 0.00 | 0 | 0.00 | 0.00 | -62600.00 |
| 49 210 | 0.00 | 0.00 | 0.00 | 0 | 11909.32 | 0 | 0.00 | 11909.32 | 11909.32 |
| 50 220 | 0.00 | 0.00 | 0.00 | 0 | 9725.60 | 0 | 0.00 | 9725.60 | 9725.60 |
| 51 232 | 0.00 | 0.00 | 0.00 | 0 | 779.22 | 0 | 0.00 | 779.22 | 779.22 |
| 52 240 | 0.00 | 0.00 | 0.00 | 0 | 3505.21 | 0 | 0.00 | 3505.21 | 3505.21 |
| 53 260 | 0.00 | 0.00 | 0.00 | 0 | 795.15 | 0 | 0.00 | 795.15 | 795.15 |
| 54 270 | 0.00 | 0.00 | 0.00 | 0 | 8398.50 | 0 | 0.00 | 8398.50 | 8398.50 |
| 55 SUB. | 63300.00 | 62600.00 | -700.00 | -1 | 35113.00 | 56 | 0.00 | 35113.00 | -27487.00 |
| 57 310 | 4000.00 | 4000.00 | 0.00 | 0 | 1818.05 | 45 | 0.00 | 1818.05 | -2181.95 |
| 58 320 | 6000.00 | 7000.00 | 1000.00 | 17 | 3363.15 | 48 | 0.00 | 3363.15 | -3636.85 |
| 59 SUB. | 10000.00 | 11000.00 | 1000.00 | 10 | 5181.20 | 47 | 0.00 | 5181.20 | -5818.80 |
| 61 408 | 0.00 | 0.00 | 0.00 | 0 | 0.00 | 0 | 0.00 | 0.00 | 0.00 |
| 62 SUB. | 0.00 | 0.00 | 0.00 | 0 | 0.00 | 0 | 0.00 | 0.00 | 0.00 |
| 64 430 | 300.00 | 400.00 | 100.00 | 33 | 321.94 | 80 | 0.00 | 321.94 | -78.06 |
| 65 SUB. | 300.00 | 400.00 | 100.00 | 33 | 321.94 | 80 | 0.00 | 321.94 | -78.06 |
| 67 470 | 7800.00 | 0.00 | -7800.00 | -100 | 0.00 | 0 | 0.00 | 0.00 | 0.00 |
| 68 SUB. | 7800.00 | 0.00 | -7800.00 | -100 | 0.00 | 0 | 0.00 | 0.00 | 0.00 |
| 70 515 | 0.00 | 0.00 | 0.00 | 0 | 0.00 | 0 | 0.00 | 0.00 | 0.00 |
| 71 SUB. | 0.00 | 0.00 | 0.00 | 0 | 0.00 | 0 | 0.00 | 0.00 | 0.00 |
| 73 520 | 0.00 | 0.00 | 0.00 | 0 | 0.00 | 0 | 0.00 | 0.00 | 0.00 |
| 74 SUB. | 0.00 | 0.00 | 0.00 | 0 | 0.00 | 0 | 0.00 | 0.00 | 0.00 |
| 76 620 | 13800.00 | 13800.00 | 0.00 | 0 | 10003.11 | 72 | 0.00 | 10003.11 | -3796.89 |
| 77 SUB. | 13800.00 | 13800.00 | 0.00 | 0 | 10003.11 | 72 | 0.00 | 10003.11 | -3796.89 |
| 79 630 | 26000.00 | 23700.00 | -2300.00 | -9 | 12786.54 | 54 | 0.00 | 12786.54 | -10913.46 |
| 80 SUB. | 26000.00 | 23700.00 | -2300.00 | -9 | 12786.54 | 54 | 0.00 | 12786.54 | -10913.46 |
| 85 TOTALS | 526700.00 | 513000.00 | -13700.00 | -59.62 | 263940.36 | 51 | 0.00 | 263940.36 | -65993.64 |

Final report { (lines 31–87)

| | CODE | PROJECTED EXPENSE |
|---|---|---|
| 107 | 120 | ............ |
| 108 | 141 | ............ |
| 110 | 145 | ............ |
| 112 | 150 | ............ |
| 113 | 152 | ............ |
| 114 | 155 | ............ |
| 116 | 200 | ............ |
| 117 | 210 | ............ |
| 118 | 220 | ............ |
| 119 | 232 | ............ |
| 120 | 240 | ............ |
| 121 | 260 | ............ |
| 122 | 270 | ............ |
| 124 | 310 | ............ |
| 125 | 320 | ............ |
| 127 | 408 | ............ |
| 129 | 430 | ............ |
| 131 | 470 | ............ |
| 133 | 515 | ............ |
| 135 | 520 | ............ |
| 137 | 620 | ............ |
| 139 | 630 | ............ |
| 140 | | >A24 |

Enter data here { (lines 104–140)

**Figure 10-10.** A printed list, page 4 of our documentation, of the full electronic sheet with written notes showing the relationships between sections of the sheet.

224

## SUMMARY

If a template will be used regularly, then attention to documentation when the sheet is created and first used will be of significant value later. As we'll see in Chapter 11, What Our Client, Secretary, or Supervisor Needs to Know, we must be prepared to train others who may use our sheets to understand and use our directions.

Let's emphasize that the length and format of the documentation may not be of importance; the quality and usefulness measure its value.

# What Our Client, Secretary, or Supervisor Needs To Know

## How Others Use Our Templates Successfully

---

## INTRODUCTION

This chapter is intended to be used by a knowledgeable SuperCalc user to train another person to use SuperCalc templates successfully. We'll assume that the trainee has no computer experience and that our training has a limited purpose: the trainee will learn how to use templates prepared by another person. It is not our intention here to teach an individual how to prepare templates, only how to use existing templates successfully.

However, this chapter could also be used as a starting point of more extensive training on the use of SuperCalc. An individual who's had the short training course of this chapter and who's gained experience from using our templates could be given this book for self-study on the full use of a SuperCalc System. In such an extended course, the Table of Contents of this book could serve as an outline, with this chapter used as a starting point.

This chapter is presented in outline form rather than narrative. As such, it provides a series of topics for a training session that we'll conduct. We'll elaborate on each item, or add items of our own, in meeting with trainees. The trainees can, of course, take notes on definitions, procedures, or other topics important to them.

A number of topics occur more than once on the outline since they are appropriate for discussion at several points, for general review, or for emphasis.

The training is intended to be performed at the computer with this outline in hand and with templates that the trainee will be expected to use. The trainee can be provided with the book for self study in getting started with our templates.

This training, and the communication established by it, is extremely important, for as we've recognized before, complete training of others who will use our templates is crucial to successful use of SuperCalc.

## TRAINING SESSION: OUTLINE

On Using Existing SuperCalc Templates
for Trainees Unfamiliar with Computers

### I. Training Goals

A. Develop knowledge to successfully use SuperCalc templates written by another person.

B. Develop an understanding that SuperCalc itself is a productive tool only as part of a system that involves the individual users, the computer hardware, the templates used, the accompanying documentation, the data used, and the way the data are entered.

C. Develop communication between the author of the template and the trainees regarding procedures of use, actions to take if problems occur, and methods for the trainees to communicate suggestions for revisions or improvement in the SuperCalc system.

### II. Hardware

(SuperCalc is used, or run, on a computer system; the components important for SuperCalc are discussed here.)

A. Communicating with the computer.
   1. Keyboard (input).
   2. Monitor or TV (output).
   3. Printer, if available (output).
   4. Other input or output devices.

B. Memory.

C. Disk drives and diskettes.

D. Turning the computer (and its components) on and off.

E.  Basic care required.
1. Respect for the hardware.
2. Simple cautions (don't open the hardware, no food or drink nearby, etc.).
3. Person to contact if trouble occurs.

## III.  SuperCalc

A.  SuperCalc is a software program with an accompanying manual enabling us to use the hardware for specific purposes.

B.  Loading SuperCalc.
1. Procedures for loading this program into memory from a diskette.
2. Cautions: Handle diskette carefully, avoid heat (do not place on top of equipment), avoid magnetic fields, do not bend, do not force into disk drive, load slowly and cautiously, handle the diskette only on the jacket, and do not touch the diskette surface.
3. Successful loading results in a screen like the top of Figure 11-1.

C.  The Worksheet (refer to a live screen or Figure 11-1, bottom).
1. Similarities to large accounting worksheets that can be moved ''under'' the screen like a sheet of microfiche or can be viewed through the screen like with a magnifying glass.
2. Columns, labeled A, B, C,...
3. Rows, labeled 1, 2, 3,...
4. Cells (intersection of columns and rows) are named A1, C30, G12, etc.
5. Cursor and Active Cell.
   a.  Defined.
   b.  Moving the cursor.
       Arrow keys.
       GO TO.

D.  Writing on the worksheet. This topic is presented under V. Entering Data.

## IV.  Templates

(The trainer may wish to discuss this section while referring to an actual template that the trainee will be using.)

A.  Templates—worksheets, like blank forms, on which text, some values, and relationships between entries (formulas) have been placed. An individual uses them by entering values (''fill in the blanks'') to obtain desired results.

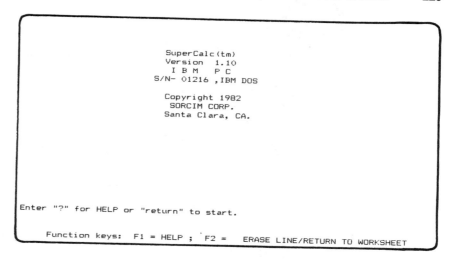

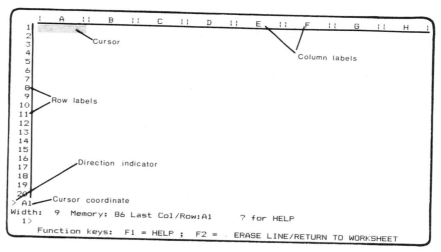

**Figure 11-1.** The screen, top, after SuperCalc has been successfully loaded into the memory of the computer (refer to Chapter 1, Introduction, for details of the specific hardware and SuperCalc versions used in this book).  The bottom screen shows the worksheet after pressing RETURN.

B.  Loading templates.
1.  First load SuperCalc (refer to III.B. of this outline).
2.  Procedures for loading a template from a diskette. (The documentation with the template may contain specific directions for this, as shown in steps 3, 4, and 5 of the directions portion of Figure 11-2.)
3.  Cautions with diskettes (refer to III.B.2. of this outline).

C.  Template documentation.
1.  Review documentation format of existing templates.
    a.  Documentation on the sheet itself (for example, refer to V.H.3. of this outline).
    b.  Written documentation accompanying the template.
2.  Procedures when problems occur. Record problems on usage section of the documentation.

## V.  Entering Data

(The trainer may wish to discuss this section while referring to an actual template the trainee will be using.)

A.  This is the process of communicating with the template and writing data onto the electronic sheet from a paper sheet or other source.

B.  Keyboard.
1.  Letters. Availability of upper and lower case.
2.  Numbers.
3.  Special characters (. ! " * + -, etc.).
4.  Control keys (as available):
    Arrow keys
    Return
    Repeat capability
    Shift
    Escape
    Control
    Reset
    = (GO TO)
    ;
    /
    ? (help)
    Function keys (if available)
    "
    Space bar

C.  Protected/unprotected cells.

D.  Entering numbers.
1.  Commas and dollar signs are not acceptable. Therefore,

$112.16 or 1,000 or $12,617.28 all are incorrect. Enter
112.16 or 1000 or 12617.28 instead.

2. Leading or trailing zeros are acceptable but are unnecessary. Thus, 12.6 and 0012.6 and 12.60, etc., all are
evaluated identically.

3. A decimal point, positive or negative sign, and scientific
notation (42E-10) are acceptable.

E.  Entering text.

1. Availability of upper and lower case letters.

2. Use of the double quote (") for entering text items as
prompted by the template, for example, "MM/DD/YY.

F.  Correcting typing errors.

1. The arrow keys.

2. The insert and delete keys (if available).

3. If the return key has been entered, correct the error by simply reentering.

4. Use of control-Z or function (if available) to erase the line.

G.  Cautions.

1. Reset key.

2. Keys that are often confused:

   1 (number) and I (letter).

   0 (number) and O (letter).

3. SuperCalc Error Messages (refer to VI.A. of this outline).

4. When interrupted (telephone, coffee break, lunch), do not
turn off or unplug the computer unless all work is completed (files saved or printed as required), because this will
destroy all data in memory.

H.  Printing (if appropriate).

1. Perform a recalculation (!) as needed.

2. Preparing the printer.

   a.  Power on (if necessary).

   b.  Load and align paper.

   c.  Set controls (if necessary).

3. Follow directions for the template as appropriate.

4. Verify output as appropriate: was a full report (from top to
bottom, left to right) printed? Do numbers, totals, etc., appear reasonable?

5. Distribute copies of the report if necessary.

I.  Storage and backup of files.

1. Store templates with data entered on diskettes as directed.
Changing the templates in memory does not alter the stored
file; we must do that deliberately if required.

2. Handle diskettes with care (see III.B.2.).

Worksheet
Documentation

Page _____ of _____

Template Filename_____

Diskette Id-Number:_____

Description:     _____

                _____

                _____

Author:         _____

Date Written:   _____

Back-up Location

    Filename:   _____

    Diskette Id: _____

Contact Person: _____

       Phone:   _____

Note:   The information above should also appear on the first window
        shown when loading the spreadsheet. Be certain that the correct
        sheet is being used by comparing the top two lines here with those
        on the window.

Directions:

USAGE RECORD

| Date | User | New File Name | Notes, comments, problems |
|------|------|---------------|---------------------------|
|      |      |               |                           |
|      |      |               |                           |
|      |      |               |                           |

**Figure 11-2.** Part of the documentation prepared for a SuperCalc template.

Template Filename: __QTR4__
Diskette Id-Number:__FORECAST-11__

Description:    Prepares a report of projected vs. planned expenses.

Author:    Donald Beil
Date Written:    04/23/99

Back-up Location
    Filename:    BUQTR4
    Diskette Id:    BU-FORECAST-11

Contact Person:    Donald Beil
    Phone:    716-475-6373

Note:    The information above should also appear on the first window shown when loading the spreadsheet. Be certain that the correct sheet is being used by comparing the top two lines here with those on the window.

Directions:

1. Prepare input data on forms shown on page 3 of this documentation.
2. Boot SuperCalc.
3. Insert diskette "FORECAST-11."
4. Load file QTR4 (/LB:QTR4 RETURN A)
5. Verify that correct diskette and file have been loaded.
6. Follow "continue" instructions on bottom of the window.
7. Enter data collected in step 1 above.
8. Follow directions to move cursor and print.
9. Distribute copies of this report to Department 442, 481, and 530.

## USAGE RECORD

| Date | User | New File Name | Notes, comments, problems |
|------|------|---------------|---------------------------|
|      |      |               |                           |
|      |      |               |                           |
|      |      |               |                           |
|      |      |               |                           |

**Figure 11-2** continued.

          3. Prepare backup copies of the files as directed.

J.    Other procedures.

       1. Perform recalculations (!) as directed.

       2. If the same template is to be used with multiple sets of data, consider clearing memory and reloading the template for each to prevent the possibility that a relationship (formula) or text inadvertently destroyed in one step of data entry will create errors in subsequent uses.

       3. Steps to complete the use of a template.

          a. Power off.

          b. Record activity in usage record (log) of documentation.

          c. Store diskettes.

## VI. Handling Problems

A.    Cells show ERROR unexpectedly or other problems.

       1. Recalculate (!).

       2. Verify that all required values have been entered.

       3. Reload the sheet and enter all data again.

B.    Screen shows FORMULA ERROR or other message.

       1. Verify that first character of text is a double quote (").

       2. Verify that numbers entered do not contain dollar signs ($) or commas (,).

       3. Use the help capability (press the ? key).

C.    Machine inadvertently powered off.

D.    Record problems in the usage record (log) of the documentation as required.

E.    Name and telephone number of person to contact with questions or problems.

## VII. Other Topics

A.    Suggestions for improvement or revisions in the template, documentation, or procedures should be made to: person, phone number.

# CHAPTER 12

# The Limitations
# of a SuperCalc System

## INTRODUCTION

Each of us might want to be aware of SuperCalc's limitations so that we'll know if SuperCalc can be used to solve the problems facing us. We'll find, however, that we'll need to consider more than simply this software. We'll need to think in terms of a computer system composed of

- SuperCalc and the worksheets we create.
- The hardware we use.
- The data we prepare.
- The users (ourselves or others).

Within this general framework let's develop limitations for such a system. They are interrelated; the discussion will not neatly divide into the following headings. In each case, we'll try to concentrate on the limitations from a perspective of a user of a SuperCalc System, which means the SuperCalc program plus the other components already listed.

In addition to the limitations below, the other chapters of this book also discuss limitations of these systems.

In examining these limitations, it should be clear that the success of this product result from its *capabilities*. A reader evaluating this product needs to balance the contents of this chapter against the capabilities described throughout the remainder of this book.

Some of the SuperCalc system limitations are listed next. For each of us, they are limitations only if they interfere with our ability to solve the individual problems facing us. Some of the items listed could be described as desired enhancements.

## SUPERCALC AND OUR WORKSHEETS

Within this framework, let's examine some limitations of the SuperCalc software.

In some instances, the system of nested capabilities within commands means that we need to know where to start to accomplish some lower level operations. SuperCalc is well designed in this area, but each of us may have trouble remembering where particular operations are to be found.

There is only limited capability provided to manipulate character data (as opposed to the powerful capabilities with numeric data). For example, we can enter characters as text but cannot process them. We cannot communicate well from our sheets to the person using them, except in awkward ways. We cannot print English messages when certain events occur.

A label cannot be automatically copied from one location to another, although a value can be. For example, if we want to copy the numeric value from D30 to location F14, we can place D30 at F14 and thus copy its value. But a label cannot be copied in this way. This can be a limitation during the data entry process with templates.

Although some versions do contain an "execute" capability (see the Execute command section in Chapter 4, Commands), all versions do not.

SuperCalc does not have sorting capabilities or sophisticated selection capabilities. We cannot get a list of the top salespeople from each department in descending order by their sales.

The limitation on significant digits that can be stored can cause a problem in some applications. There is only limited control on the number of decimal places displayed (two with /F...$ or none with /F...I). Dollar and cents formatting does not include capability for commas, for display of dollar signs, for an accounting-like display of negative numbers within parentheses, etc. There is only very limited graphing capability.

SuperCalc does contain software problems, though they seem to be extremely few in number.

## HARDWARE

The limitations of a SuperCalc system, when considered from a hardware perspective, are included in this section.

Computers have limited memory. We'll need to know if problems that we typically encounter will "fit" within the memory of our hardware system. This is a limitation for any computer system, for the problem that we want to solve may simply be too large for it. This is a limitation on both the individual problem that can be solved and on the role that SuperCalc can play in part of a larger system.

Some computers only have directional arrows for left and right, or have no directional arrows. To move the cursor we must use combinations of the CONTROL and other keys, which can be awkward.

Only a limited number of characters from the sheet may be displayed horizontally, and only a limited number of rows may be displayed vertically. With all systems only a small part of the largest potential sheet can be displayed. However, SuperCalc overcomes this well with the Window and Title Lock commands.

Because of the limited number of characters on most keyboards many keys must perform different functions depending on when they are entered. As an extreme example, the character R is used

- To initiate the Replicate command.
- As an indicator of a row in several commands.
- To indicate right justification (twice) in the Format command.
- Within the Global command to change the recalculation mode.

The Output command can be awkward to use for some printers. We are not asked what printer we are using and we are not then prompted regarding carriage control, etc. Instead, we must learn and use what may be a strange string of characters that must be repeated each time we want to print. However, for a user with a single printer, the required operation may quickly become a habit. The wide variety of printers available and their separate methods of operation are in part responsible for this.

## DATA WE PREPARE

The checking capabilities necessary to verify that accurate data have been provided are not fully present. For example, if a formula requires the entry of a numeric value and text is inadvertently entered, the label will be evaluated as a number (zero) and results will be obtained although they will not be flagged as incorrect. The process of verifying data in many computer systems often occupies a major portion of user prepared software. This capability is only provided in very limited ways with SuperCalc.

The SuperCalc system may be difficult to use with data over time. Year-to-date totals, in week-after-week processing, can be awkward to accumulate. This is also true for many file processing systems where this is a complicated problem.

The data entry process is not distinct from other aspects of using SuperCalc (however, see the suggestions in Chapter 9, Creating Templates). This means that preparing trails of activity is difficult and also implies that more reliance is placed on the person doing data entry than on the prepared sheet since it's awkward to verify data entry activity as in other computer systems.

## USERS (OURSELVES OR OTHERS)

As with other computer systems the users are the crucial element. We must fully understand what we have established, must be aware of all of the limitations, and must regularly verify that results upon which we act and make decisions which are indeed accurate. Regular vigilance is necessary with SuperCalc.

We must focus full attention on our task, especially data entry.

If others use our electronic sheets, they must be trained and their training must be more than cursory. They must understand the full system and their part within it. They must know how to handle problem situations. SuperCalc systems place heavy responsibilities on the users and these must be understood.

# CHAPTER 13

# Practice Problems

## INTRODUCTION

This chapter presents a wide variety of problems that can be used for practice in developing skill with SuperCalc. Work with these problems may suggest new ways in which this software tool can help us solve problems that we encounter.

This chapter can also be used for an educational training activity in a company, a school, or a university or for a seminar or workshop on SuperCalc for which this book is used.

Finally, this chapter can serve as a source of pleasure for those who simply enjoy solving problems with SuperCalc.

The sheets that we prepare may be of use later and therefore may be of value to save.

## PROBLEMS

**1.** Prepare a worksheet to be used to determine the total price of a microcomputer system. In one column list the name of each item of hardware and software to be purchased. In the next column list the price of each. Subtotal and total the sheet as shown in Figure 13-1.

**2.** Produce a template containing a documentation format that will serve as the standard beginning for all your template preparation. Such a template might look like the one in Figure 13-2 and should be composed of data important for your environment.

**3.** Prepare a spreadsheet with the days of the week (Figure 13-3),

```
              Microcomputer Costs

Hardware                          COSTS
        Microcomputer
        Disk Drives
        TV or Monitor
        Printer
                                 _____

        Subtotal


Software
        SuperCalc
        Word Processor
        Data Base
                                 _____
        Subtotal

        TOTAL
```

**Figure 13-1.** An electronic sheet that helps calculate the cost of a microcomputer system.

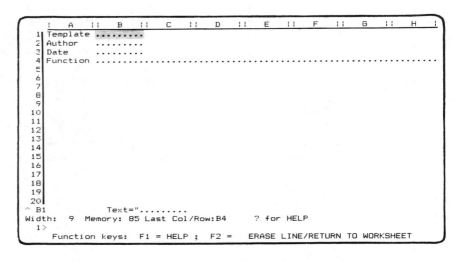

**Figure 13-2.** A suggested model template that can serve to start all our SuperCalc applications.

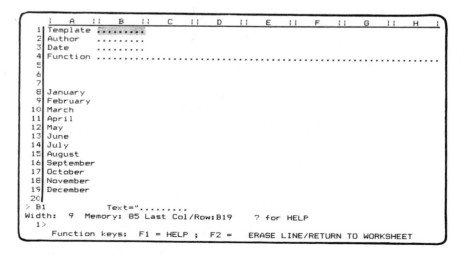

```
   |   A   !!   B   !!   C   !!   D   !!   E   !!   F   !!   G   !!   H   !
 1| Template ........
 2| Author   ........
 3| Date     ........
 4| Function ...............................................................
 5|
 6|
 7|
 8| Monday
 9| Tuesday
10| Wednesday
11| Thursday
12| Friday
13| Saturday
14| Sunday
15|
16|
17|
18|
19|
20|
>  B1            Text="........
Width:   9   Memory: 85 Last Col/Row:B14      ? for  HELP
    1>
      Function keys:  F1 = HELP ;   F2 =    ERASE LINE/RETURN TO WORKSHEET
```

**Figure 13-3.** A starter template containing days of the week.

another with the months of the year (Figure 13-4), and two others with weeks labeled from Week 1 across to Week 52 as shown in Figure 13-5 and Figure 13-6. For Figure 13-6 use the Replicate command for both rows. If you wish, prepare the 52-week template with the labels down the rows instead of across the columns as shown in Figure 13-7 and Figure

```
   |   A   !!   B   !!   C   !!   D   !!   E   !!   F   !!   G   !!   H   !
 1| Template ........
 2| Author   ........
 3| Date     ........
 4| Function ...............................................................
 5|
 6|
 7|
 8| January
 9| February
10| March
11| April
12| May
13| June
14| July
15| August
16| September
17| October
18| November
19| December
20|
>  B1            Text="........
Width:   9   Memory: 85 Last Col/Row:B19      ? for  HELP
    1>
      Function keys:  F1 = HELP ;   F2 =    ERASE LINE/RETURN TO WORKSHEET
```

**Figure 13-4.** A template containing months of the year.

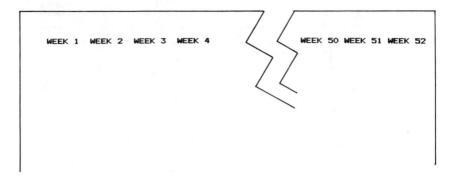

**Figure 13-5.** A template containing weeks of the year numbered horizontally across the sheet.

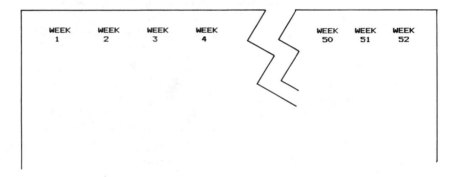

**Figure 13-6.** This template, containing weeks of the year numbered horizontally, can be prepared with the the Replicate command.

```
WEEK  1
WEEK  2
WEEK  3
WEEK  4
WEEK  5
WEEK  6
WEEK  7
WEEK  8
       .
       .
       .
WEEK  48
WEEK  49
WEEK  50
WEEK  51
WEEK  52
```

**Figure 13-7.** One version of a vertical presentation of the weeks of the year.

```
WEEK    1
WEEK    2
WEEK    3
WEEK    4
WEEK    5
WEEK    6
WEEK    7
WEEK    8

        .
        .
        .

WEEK    48
WEEK    49
WEEK    50
WEEK    51
WEEK    52
```

**Figure 13-8.** A second version of a vertical presentation of the weeks of the year.

13-8. In Figure 13-8, right justify the word WEEK and left justify the number.

**4.** Prepare a spreadsheet, such as Figure 13-9, listing names of individuals. For your sheet, use the names shown, or use a set of names important to you, for example, employees, customers, students, members of your family, etc. Store this sheet for possible later use in reports that you may need to prepare. If you report on activities by organizational unit, then establish a worksheet by unit such as shown in Figure 13-10.

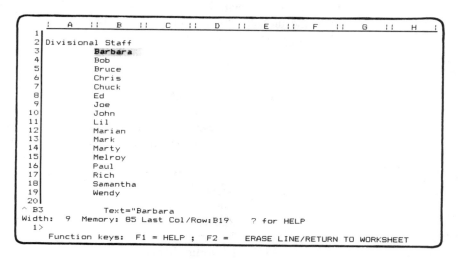

**Figure 13-9.** A prewritten template containing the names of divisional employees.

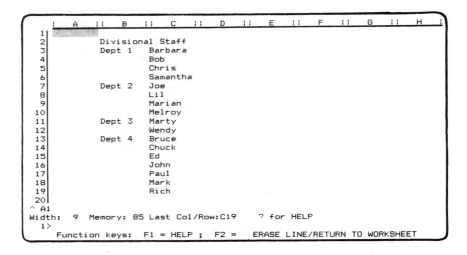

**Figure 13-10.** A file containing the names of divisional employees by department.

SuperCalc does not have sorting capability; however, by inserting rows it is possible to prepare the report of Figure 13-9, beginning with an external unsorted list and sorting as the names are entered.

Prepare Figure 13-10 from Figure 13-9, using the Move command.

**5.** The salary and benefits expense codes, and their titles, for one organization are shown. Build a template which has this information. If you're the budget authority at your company or organization, build this table from your codes and definitions.

| Code | Title |
|------|-------|
| 110 | Salaries, administrative and professional |
| 120 | Salaries, other full-time |
| 130 | Salaries, technical, clerical and secretarial |
| 141 | Salaries, part-time, permanent admin/prof |
| 142 | Salaries, part-time, permanent genr'l/hourly |
| 170 | Salaries, other part-time, temporary |
| 210 | Social security expense |
| 215 | Unemployment insurance |
| 220 | Retirement contributions |
| 230 | Workmen's compensation |
| 235 | Disability benefits |
| 240 | Group health insurance |
| 250 | Group major medical |

260    Group life insurance
270    Tuition

**6.** Prepare a spreadsheet with times of the day shown in intervals appropriate to a scheduling activity on which you prepare reports, for example, as in Figure 13-11.

```
TIME

 8:00
 8:30
 9:00
 9:30
10:00
10:30
11:00
11:30
 NOON
12:30
 1:00
 1:30
 2:00
 2:30
 3:00
 3:30
 4:00
 4:30
 5:00
 5:30
 6:00
 6:30
 7:00
 7:30
 8:00
 8:30
 9:00
 9:30
10:00
10:30
```

**Figure 13-11.** This sheet shows scheduled times of the day from which a report can be prepared.

7. On occasion it is desirable to be able to count columns on the worksheet, for example, to know how many columns there are from column M to column AR. Prepare a reference report like the one of Figure 13-12, which numbers each column identifier as shown. Right and left justify the data as shown in the columns. Change the column widths until you have a report that you feel is easy to read. This table can be used to compute "distances" between columns.

| A | 1 | AA | 27 | BA | 53 |
|---|----|----|----|----|----|
| B | 2 | AB | 28 | BB | 54 |
| C | 3 | AC | 29 | BC | 55 |
| D | 4 | AD | 30 | BD | 56 |
| E | 5 | AE | 31 | BE | 57 |
| F | 6 | AF | 32 | BF | 58 |
| G | 7 | AG | 33 | BG | 59 |
| H | 8 | AH | 34 | BH | 60 |
| I | 9 | AI | 35 | BI | 61 |
| J | 10 | AJ | 36 | BJ | 62 |
| K | 11 | AK | 37 | BK | 63 |
| L | 12 | AL | 38 | | |
| M | 13 | AM | 39 | | |
| N | 14 | AN | 40 | | |
| O | 15 | AO | 41 | | |
| P | 16 | AP | 42 | | |
| Q | 17 | AQ | 43 | | |
| R | 18 | AR | 44 | | |
| S | 19 | AS | 45 | | |
| T | 20 | AT | 46 | | |
| U | 21 | AU | 47 | | |
| V | 22 | AV | 48 | | |
| W | 23 | AW | 49 | | |
| X | 24 | AX | 50 | | |
| Y | 25 | AY | 51 | | |
| Z | 26 | AZ | 52 | | |

**Figure 13-12.** A reference table that can be used to "measure" the distance from one column to another.

8. Prepare a spreadsheet that will provide you with a record of your home or business consumption of electricity for a one-year period on a month-by-month basis. List the months down a column and then in another column record the consumption for each month in kilowatt-hours (kWh). Finally, add a third column that shows the year-to-date consumption. Include a total value for the second and third columns.

9. Develop a template on which you could record your consumption of natural gas for your business or home. Include report headings and then columns containing

- Month.
- Gas usage in hundreds of cubic feet (Ccf) used.
- Conversion to therms of the gas used, obtaining this value by multiplying Ccf by a 1.026 conversion factor.

Total the second and third columns.

**10.** Revise the last problem to include the three columns for last year, and then add two new columns for this year. These new columns should contain Ccf used and the conversion to therms. Finally add a column that calculates the difference between Ccf last year and this year.

**11.** Prepare a spreadsheet like the one in Figure 13-13, which contains a monthly record of your last year kilowatt (KWH) consumption, your forecast for this year, your actual consumption this year, and the difference to date between your forecast and actual usage. Your forecast for this year should be a variable that can be revised as shown by entering different values on the last line. Use the NA value for coming months.

|       | KWH LAST YEAR | FORE-CAST KWH THIS YEAR | ACTUAL TO DATE | DIFF |
|-------|------|------|------|------|
| JAN   | 800  | 720  | 700  | 20   |
| FEB   | 850  | 765  | 650  | 115  |
| MAR   | 920  | 828  | 700  | 128  |
| APR   | 750  | 675...... |  | 675  |
| MAY   | 600  | 540...... |  | 540  |
| JUN   | 300  | 270...... |  | 270  |
| JUL   | 300  | 270...... |  | 270  |
| AUG   | 400  | 360...... |  | 360  |
| SEP   | 500  | 450...... |  | 450  |
| OCT   | 550  | 495...... |  | 495  |
| NOV   | 750  | 675...... |  | 675  |
| DEC   | 750  | 675...... |  | 675  |
|       | 7470 | 6723 | 2050 | 4673 |

FORECAST FOR THIS YR AT:    −10 %

**Figure 13-13.** A record of actual and projected kilowatt usage.

**12.** A utility company allows customers to divide an estimated annual bill into equal amounts to be paid monthly. Prepare a spreadsheet, like the one in Figure 13-14, that can be used to compare actual against planned billing.

**13.** A large retail store maintains close records on weekly sales by department, such as the partial report shown in Figure 13-15. Complete the report for department A, B, C, D, and E for 52 weeks.

```
                                            DIFF.
                                           (EQUAL
                      EQUAL     ACTUAL      MINUS
                    PAYMENT       BILL    ACTUAL)

          JAN       100.00      80.00      20.00
          FEB       100.00     140.00     -40.00
          MAR       100.00      95.00       5.00
          APR       100.00     .......    100.00
          MAY       100.00     .......    100.00
          JUN       100.00     .......    100.00
          JUL       100.00     .......    100.00
          AUG       100.00     .......    100.00
          SEP       100.00     .......    100.00
          OCT       100.00     .......    100.00
          NOV       100.00     .......    100.00
          DEC       100.00     .......    100.00
        TOTAL      1200.00     315.00     885.00
```

**Figure 13-14.** This spreadsheet compares actual billing against a planned equal payment billing.

```
                    RETAIL SALES BY DEPARTMENT
                    LAST YEAR VS. THIS YEAR

        WEEK                   DEPT A  DEPT B  DEPT C
                               ------  ------  ------
          1        LAST YR     14000
                   THIS YR     15100
                     DIFF:      1100

          2        LAST YR       850
                   THIS YR       400
                     DIFF:      -450

          3        LAST YR
                   THIS YR
                     DIFF:
```

**Figure 13-15.** The beginning of a departmental comparison of retail sales this year against last year.

**14.** Figure 13-16 shows six weeks of a weekly sales report for one department of a retail store. Implement this report for 52 weeks.

**15.** A retail music store will be placing on sale all records whose original selling price was from $5 to $10. The store is planning a sale at 80% of the original price. Prepare a table like that in Figure 13-17, which can be posted and placed by the cash register to display the sale price. Print the dollar sign ($) as shown.

```
             GROSS RETAIL SALES FOR:
                DEPARTMENT: ** A **
                     BY WEEK
                              YEARLY            TO DATE
                       DIFF. SALES TO DATE    DIFFERENCE
      WEEK    LAST   THIS  THIS  --- YEAR ----  ------------
              YR     YR    WEEK    LAST   THIS    $      %
              -----  ----- -----  -----  -----  -----  -----
       1      14000  15100  1100  14000  15100   1100    8
       2       1000    800  -200  15000  15900    900    6
       3       2000   2000  1000  17000  17900    900    5
       4          0   1000  1000  17000  18900   1900   11
       5        500    100  -400  17500  19000   1500    9
       6      20300  21400  1100  37800  40400   2600    7
```

**Figure 13-16.** Weekly departmental sales report.

```
       ORIGINAL           80 %
       SELLING          "SALE"
        PRICE            PRICE

      $   5.00        $   4.00
      $   5.05        $   4.04
      $   5.10        $   4.08
      $   5.15        $   4.12
      $   5.20        $   4.16
      $   5.25        $   4.20
      $   5.30        $   4.24
      $   5.35        $   4.28
      $   5.40        $   4.32
      $   5.45        $   4.36
      $   5.50        $   4.40
            .                .
            .                .
            .                .
      $   9.75        $   7.80
      $   9.80        $   7.84
      $   9.85        $   7.88
      $   9.90        $   7.92
      $   9.95        $   7.96
      $  10.00        $   8.00
```

**Figure 13-17.** Part of a chart of original and sale prices.

**16.** Expand the spreadsheet of the last problem so that it calculates tax at 7% and then the total price, all prepared as in Figure 13-18.

| ORIGINAL SELLING PRICE | 80 % "SALE" PRICE | TAX 7% | TOTAL PRICE |
|---|---|---|---|
| $  5.00 | 4.00 | 0.28 | $  4.28 |
| $  5.05 | 4.04 | 0.28 | $  4.32 |
| $  5.10 | 4.08 | 0.29 | $  4.37 |
| $  5.15 | 4.12 | 0.29 | $  4.41 |
| $  5.20 | 4.16 | 0.29 | $  4.45 |
| $  5.25 | 4.20 | 0.29 | $  4.49 |
| $  5.30 | 4.24 | 0.30 | $  4.54 |
| $  5.35 | 4.28 | 0.30 | $  4.58 |
| $  5.40 | 4.32 | 0.30 | $  4.62 |
| $  5.45 | 4.36 | 0.31 | $  4.67 |
| . | . | . | . |
| . | . | . | . |
| . | . | . | . |
| $  9.75 | 7.80 | 0.55 | $  8.35 |
| $  9.80 | 7.84 | 0.55 | $  8.39 |
| $  9.85 | 7.88 | 0.55 | $  8.43 |
| $  9.90 | 7.92 | 0.55 | $  8.47 |
| $  9.95 | 7.96 | 0.56 | $  8.52 |
| $ 10.00 | 8.00 | 0.56 | $  8.56 |

**Figure 13-18.** An expanded sales price table that includes tax and total price.

**17.** Revise problem 15 so that the information is presented in four columns, not two.

**18.** Prepare an energy audit report template that can be used by a utility company to prepare a summary of savings and payback from various insulating activities. Use Figure 13-19 as your guide.

**19.** Prepare a template, such as the one in Figure 13-20, that can be used by a homeowner to estimate the average monthly consumption and cost of an electrical appliance. In the third column place a 1 (one) or a 0 (zero), with

| value | meaning |
|---|---|
| 1 | in the home |
| 0 | not in the home |

Then in the fourth column multiply column 2 by the cost per kWh (entered at the top of the report) and by the number in column 3 (either a zero or a one). This will place the approximate cost per month in the fourth column if the appliance is in the home and will place zero in the

ENERGY AUDIT

Name      _____
Address   _____
Town/City _____
Date      _____

| Summary of Savings and payback period | Est. Cost | Yearly Savings | Payback* Years |
|---|---|---|---|
| A.  Ceiling or Attic Insulation...... | _____ | _____ | _____ |
| B.  Wall Insulation.................. | _____ | _____ | _____ |
| C.  Storm Windows.................... | _____ | _____ | _____ |
| D.  Storm Doors...................... | _____ | _____ | _____ |
| E.  Weather Stripping................ | _____ | _____ | _____ |
| F.  Caulking......................... | _____ | _____ | _____ |
| G.  Basement Wall Insulation......... | _____ | _____ | _____ |
| H.  Floor Insulation................. | _____ | _____ | _____ |
| | | | |
| I.  SUBTOTAL......................... | _____ | _____ | _____ |
| | | | |
| J.  Automatic Thermostat............. | _____ | _____ | _____ |
| K.  Water Heater Insulation.......... | _____ | _____ | _____ |
| | | | |
| TOTAL......................... | _____ | _____ | _____ |

*Estimated Cost divided by Yearly Savings equals Payback Years.

**Figure 13-19.** A form from which an energy audit template can be prepared.

fourth column if it is not in the home. Compute yearly costs for each item, and total the monthly and yearly costs.

**20.** Develop a template that you can use to record individual medical expenses for family members. For every expense include the date, a description, the total cost, insurance payment if any, and net amount (total cost minus insurance payment). Subtotal for each family member and prepare a grand total. Establish subtotals so that new expenditures can be added without completely revising the formulas.

**21.** An employer prepares an annual summary of benefits for each employee. Prepare a single template to be used repeatedly for each individual with areas on which to enter a dollar value for each benefit. The benefits are group life insurance, long-term disability insurance, Social

Electrical Consumption and Cost
(Excluding Heat and Lighting)

Enter cost per KWH:

| Appliance | Approx. kWh/mo. | Used? Yes = 1 No = 0 | Approx. Cost/ Mo. | Approx. Cost/ Yr. |
|---|---|---|---|---|
| FOOD PREPARATION: | | | | |
| Microwave Oven | 16 | | | |
| Electric Range/oven | 58 | | | |
| Dishwasher | 30 | | | |
| Roaster | 5 | | | |
| Slow Cooker | 11 | | | |
| Toaster Oven | 7 | | | |
| Toaster | 3 | | | |
| Baby Food Warmer | 2 | | | |
| Electric Fry Pan | 8 | | | |
| SUB:  Food Preparation: | | | | |
| | | | | |
| FOOD PRESERVATION: | | | | |
| Freezer (manual defrost) | 100 | | | |
| 100 Freezer (auto. defrost) | 115 | | | |
| Refrig-Freezer (manual defrost) | 125 | | | |
| Refrig-Freezer (auto defrost) | 188 | | | |
| SUB:  Food Preservation | | | | |
| | | | | |
| LAUNDRY: | | | | |
| Clothes Dryer (electric) | 82 | | | |
| Washer (automatic) | 9 | | | |
| Iron (hand) | 5 | | | |
| SUB:  Laundry | | | | |
| | | | | |
| HEALTH AND COMFORT: | | | | |
| Air cleaner (electronic) | 43 | | | |
| Air Conditioner (room) | 71 | | | |
| Dehumidifier (300 watts) | 150 | | | |
| Fan, Furnace | 125 | | | |
| Water Bed (heater) | 150 | | | |
| Water Heater (80 gal.) | 600 | | | |
| SUB:  Health & Comfort | | | | |
| | | | | |
| HOME ENTERTAINMENT: | | | | |
| Radio | 7 | | | |
| Radio/Record Player | 9 | | | |
| Television | | | | |
| (b&w tube) | 18 | | | |
| (b&w solid state) | 8 | | | |
| (color, tube) | 44 | | | |
| (color, solid state) | 26 | | | |
| Pool filter | 360 | | | |
| SUB:  Home Entertainment | | | | |
| | | | | |
| TOTALS | | | | |

**Figure 13-20.** A template design that can be used to estimate electrical consumption from home appliances.

Security (FICA), retirement and annuity plan, health care, other benefits, and gross salary. Include a grand total.

**22.** A basic record keeping system for shares of stock owned includes stock name, date purchased, number of shares, certificate number, price per share, stock cost, purchase fees, total cost, date sold, number of shares sold, selling price per share, total selling price, sales fees, net received, and profit/loss. Create a template with columns for each of these, with totals in appropriate columns.

**23.** A teacher must record grades for each student in a class on four examinations. Prepare a template with columns for student name, for the scores on each test, for the total, and for the percentage.

**24.** Revise the spreadsheet from the previous problem to display the high and low score (use MAX and MIN) and the average (use AVERAGE) for each test.

**25.** Use the LOOKUP function to build a table of months of the year (1, 2, ... 12) and which can be used to look up the number of days in each month.

**26.** The market value of a treasury bill is computed by subtracting the discount from the face value. The discount is the face value times the number of days to maturity times the rate (which is the amount bid expressed as a decimal) divided by 360. Prepare an electronic sheet that accepts the variables in this formula and produces the discount and market value.

**27.** Some people say that a rough rule of thumb in computing life insurance and other death benefits is that they should total at least six times annual salary. Create the template shown in Figure 13-21 to assist in computing these values for a husband and wife.

```
                      Life Insurance
                "Six-times-Salary" Formula.


                                    HUSBAND              WIFE

1.  Enter present annual salary      $____               $____
2.  Multiply by six                       x6                  x6
3.  Minimum protection goal          $____               $____
4.  Enter coverage now held:
    (a) Personal policies         $____               $____
    (b) Group insurance
    (c) Pension plan death benefits
5.  Subtract total of (a) (b) (c)   -$____              -$____
6.  Additional insurance needed (if any)
```

**Figure 13-21.** Assumptions for estimating adequacy of life insurance holdings.

**28.** Equity holdings are often shown in reports clustered by industry group. Figure 13-22 contains the beginnings of such a report. Using a similar report from a fund or other institution prepare a spreadsheet to track the holdings. The sheet should include a separate sum for each industry group and should show a group subtotal and the percentage (to two decimal places) that this group represents of the total holdings. The sheet should compute market value as the product of the number of shares and the price per share. The price per share should be on the sheet but should not be printed.

```
                Holdings By Industry Group

                                  Market
                        Shares     Value      Percent
        Aerospace:
            Stock 1      2040      125756
            Stock 2      8685      223641
            Stock 3      3667      403430
                                   752827      4.88%

        Aluminum (and non-ferrous metals)
            Stock 1        .          .          .
                           .          .     .     .
                           .          .     .     .
```

**Figure 13-22.** The beginning of an equity holding report that shows diversification among industry groups.

**29.** A realtor maintains records of the homes sold by the company in the city. For comparison purposes, data are maintained for the current year and last year on a weekly basis. Prepare a spreadsheet with columns for the two years and one row for each of the 52 weeks of the year. For each week list the number of homes sold, their total price (enter this as an expression, for example, 70000+112000+29000), the average price, and the year-to-date sales. Include these columns for this year and last year.

Develop an end-of-year procedure to "roll" the report from one year to the next. Basically all of the columns from this year should become comparison data, that is, data for last year.

**30.** Individuals with sole proprietorships use tax Schedule C of Form 1040, shown in Figure 13-23, to report business profit or loss. Set up a template in a format equivalent to the deductions portion of that form. If SuperCalc is used for tax preparation, be certain to use a form for the current year.

**SCHEDULE C**
(Form 1040)
Department of the Treasury
Internal Revenue Service

# Profit or (Loss) From Business or Profession
(Sole Proprietorship)
Partnerships, Joint Ventures, etc., Must File Form 1065.
▶ Attach to Form 1040 or Form 1041.   ▶ See Instructions for Schedule C (Form 1040).

Name of proprietor

Social security number of proprietor

**A** Main business activity (see Instructions) ▶ _____ ; product ▶ _____

**B** Business name ▶

**C** Employer identification number

**D** Business address (number and street) ▶ _____
City, State and ZIP Code ▶

**E** Accounting method: **(1)** ☐ Cash   **(2)** ☐ Accrual   **(3)** ☐ Other (specify) ▶ _____

**F** Method(s) used to value closing inventory:
**(1)** ☐ Cost   **(2)** ☐ Lower of cost or market   **(3)** ☐ Other (if other, attach explanation)

|  | Yes | No |
|---|---|---|
| **G** Was there any major change in determining quantities, costs, or valuations between opening and closing inventory? . . If "Yes," attach explanation. | | |
| **H** Did you deduct expenses for an office in your home? . . . . . . . . . . . . . . . | | |
| **I** Did you elect to claim amortization (under section 191) or depreciation (under section 167(o)) for a rehabilitated certified historic structure (see Instructions)? . . . . . . . . . . . . . . . . (Amortizable basis (see Instructions) ▶ _____ ) | | |

## Part I  Income

| | | | |
|---|---|---:|---|
| **1 a** Gross receipts or sales . . . . . . . . . . | **1a** | | |
| **b** Returns and allowances . . . . . . . . . . | **1b** | | |
| **c** Balance (subtract line 1b from line 1a) . . . . . . . . . | | **1c** | |
| **2** Cost of goods sold and/or operations (Schedule C–1, line 8) . . . . . . . . | | **2** | |
| **3** Gross profit (subtract line 2 from line 1c) . . . . . . . . . . . | | **3** | |
| **4** Other income (attach schedule) . . . . . . . . . . . . . | | **4** | |
| **5** Total income (add lines 3 and 4) . . . . . . . . . . . . . . ▶ | | **5** | |

## Part II  Deductions

| | | 31 | |
|---|---|---|---|
| **6** Advertising . . . . . . . . | | **a** Wages . . | |
| **7** Amortization . . . . . . . | | **b** Jobs credit | |
| **8** Bad debts from sales or services . | | **c** WIN credit | |
| **9** Bank charges . . . . . . . | | **d** Total credits | |
| **10** Car and truck expenses . . . . | | **e** Subtract line 31d from 31a . | |
| **11** Commissions . . . . . . . | | **32** Other expenses (specify): | |
| **12** Depletion . . . . . . . . | | **a** _____ | |
| **13** Depreciation (explain in Schedule C–2) . | | **b** _____ | |
| **14** Dues and publications . . . . | | **c** _____ | |
| **15** Employee benefit programs . . | | **d** _____ | |
| **16** Freight (not included on Schedule C–1) . | | **e** _____ | |
| **17** Insurance . . . . . . . . | | **f** _____ | |
| **18** Interest on business indebtedness . | | **g** _____ | |
| **19** Laundry and cleaning . . . . | | **h** _____ | |
| **20** Legal and professional services . | | **i** _____ | |
| **21** Office supplies . . . . . . | | **j** _____ | |
| **22** Pension and profit-sharing plans . | | **k** _____ | |
| **23** Postage . . . . . . . . | | **l** _____ | |
| **24** Rent on business property . . . | | **m** _____ | |
| **25** Repairs . . . . . . . . . | | **n** _____ | |
| **26** Supplies (not included on Schedule C–1) . | | **o** _____ | |
| **27** Taxes . . . . . . . . . | | **p** _____ | |
| **28** Telephone . . . . . . . . | | **q** _____ | |
| **29** Travel and entertainment . . . | | **r** _____ | |
| **30** Utilities . . . . . . . . . | | **s** _____ | |

| | |
|---|---|
| **33** **Total deductions** (add amounts in columns for lines 6 through 32s) . . . . . . . . . ▶ | **33** |
| **34** Net profit or (loss) (subtract line 33 from line 5). If a profit, enter on Form 1040, line 13, and on Schedule SE, Part II, line 5a (or Form 1041, line 6). If a loss, go on to line 35 . . . . . | **34** |

**35** If you have a loss, do you have amounts for which you are **not** "at risk" in this business (see Instructions)? . . ☐ Yes ☐ No

**Figure 13-23.** IRS Form 1040, Schedule C.

**31.** Revise the previous problem so that the template is enlarged to have a separate area in which monthly expenses are recorded during the year in a column for each of the items listed. The yearly totals from each column total should then be automatically moved into the deductions format of the template. If SuperCalc is used for tax preparation, be certain to use a form for the current year.

**32.** Prepare a template that will complete Form 1040A of the U.S. Individual Income Tax Return shown in Figure 13-24. Assume that numeric values from other forms or from a table are entered here by hand. Include line number, brief description, and then columns as needed for the form. If SuperCalc is used for tax preparation, be certain to use a form for the current year.

**33.** Prepare a template as in the previous problem; however, prepare it for the Form 1040 shown in Figure 13-25. If SuperCalc is used for tax preparation, be certain to use a form for the current year.

**34.** Prepare a spreadsheet to help decide on a source from which to purchase a microcomputer. Prepare a row for each item to be purchased, for example, microcomputer, disk drives, monitor, software, etc. Then prepare a column with the manufacturer's suggested retail price. For each source prepare three columns: the quoted price, the dollar discount from the suggested retail price (if any), and the percentage discount. Total columns as appropriate.

**35.** To gain practice in entering labels, prepare a template that you can use as the format of a weekly calendar. In one column include the times of day broken into convenient units (for example 8:00, 8:15, 8:30, etc.). Then include columns titled Monday, Tuesday,...Sunday. Include an area to enter the dates for the week.

**36.** Prepare a template which can be used to determine salary increases for department members. It should have columns like those in Figure 13-26. The ''Proposed Percentage Increase'' column should be used in ''what if...'' fashion, meaning that when we change these values we'll get new values in the last two columns. Include column totals where appropriate.

**37.** As a student, suppose that you want to record a running average of your grade for the course. Prepare a template with columns for the assignment or test number (for example, assignment 1, test 4, etc.), your score, the possible score, your total to date, the total possible to date, and your average. An example is shown in Figure 13-27.

**38.** An animal hospital provides boarding services for cats ($4 per day), small dogs ($5 per day) and large dogs ($6 per day). Prepare a table with four columns, one column for the length of the stay in days, and then one column for each type of animal that lists the total cost of a stay at the hospital. Print the table for lengths of stay from 1 to 60 days.

Form **1040A**  Department of the Treasury—Internal Revenue Service
**U.S. Individual Income Tax Return**

| Use IRS label. Otherwise, please print or type. | Your first name and initial (if joint return, also give spouse's name and initial) | Last name | Your social security number |
|---|---|---|---|
| | Present home address (Number and street, including apartment number, or rural route) | | Spouse's social security no. |
| | City, town or post office, State and ZIP code | Your occupation ▶ | |
| | | Spouse's occupation ▶ | |

**Presidential Election Campaign Fund** ▶

Do you want $1 to go to this fund? . . . . . . . . . . . . . . .   Yes ☐  No ☐

If joint return, does your spouse want $1 to go to this fund? . . .   Yes ☐  No ☐

**Note:** Checking "Yes" will not increase your tax or reduce your refund.

**Requested by Census Bureau for Revenue Sharing** ▶

**A** Where do you live (actual location of residence)? (See page 6 of Instructions.) State _____ City, village, borough, etc. _____

**B** Do you live within the legal limits of a city, village, etc.? ☐ Yes ☐ No

**C** In what county do you live?

**D** In what township do you live?

For Privacy Act Notice, see page 27 of Instructions

For IRS use only

**Filing Status**
Check Only One Box.

1 ☐ Single
2 ☐ Married filing joint return (even if only one had income)
3 ☐ Married filing separate return. Enter spouse's social security no. above and full name here ▶ ........
4 ☐ Head of household. (See pages 7 and 8 of Instructions.) If qualifying person is your unmarried child, enter child's name ▶ ........

**Exemptions**
Always check the box labeled Yourself. Check other boxes if they apply.

5a ☐ Yourself   ☐ 65 or over   ☐ Blind
b ☐ Spouse   ☐ 65 or over   ☐ Blind

Enter number of boxes checked on 5a and b ▶

c First names of your dependent children who lived with you ▶ ........

Enter number of children listed on 5c ▶

| d Other dependents: (1) Name | (2) Relationship | (3) Number of months lived in your home. | (4) Did dependent have income of $1,000 or more? | (5) Did you provide more than one-half of dependent's support? | |
|---|---|---|---|---|---|
| | | | | | Enter number of other dependents ▶ |

Add numbers entered in boxes above ▶

6 Total number of exemptions claimed . . . . . . . . . . . . . . . .

7 Wages, salaries, tips, etc. (Attach Forms W–2. See page 10 of Instructions) . . . . . . .   **7**

8 Interest income (See pages 3 and 10 of Instructions) . . . . . . . . . . . . . . . .   **8**

9a Dividends _____ (See pages 3 and 10 of Instructions) 9b Exclusion _____ Subtract line 9b from 9a   **9c**

10a Unemployment compensation (insurance). Total received from Form(s) 1099–UC _____

b Taxable amount, if any, from worksheet on page 10 of Instructions . . . . . . . . .   **10b**

11 Adjusted gross income (add lines 7, 8, 9c, and 10b). If under $10,000, see page 12 of Instructions on "Earned Income Credit" . . . . . . . . . . . . . . . . . . . .   **11**

12a Credit for contributions to candidates for public office.
(See page 11 of Instructions) . . . . . . . . . . . .   **12a**

IF YOU WANT IRS TO FIGURE YOUR TAX, PLEASE STOP HERE AND SIGN BELOW.

b Total Federal income tax withheld (If line 7 is more than $25,900, see page 11 of Instructions) . . . . . . . . . . .   **12b**

c Earned income credit (from page 12 of Instructions) . . .   **12c**

13 Total (add lines 12a, b, and c) . . . . . . . . . . . . . . . . . . . . . .   **13**

14a Tax on the amount on line 11. (See page 13 of Instructions; then find your tax in the Tax Tables on pages 15–26) . . . .   **14a**

b Advance earned income credit (EIC) (from Form W–2) . . .   **14b**

15 Total (add lines 14a and 14b) . . . . . . . . . . . . . . . . .   **15**

16 If line 13 is larger than line 15, enter amount to be **REFUNDED TO YOU** . . . . . . . ▶   **16**

17 If line 15 is larger than line 13, enter **BALANCE DUE.** Attach check or money order for full amount payable to "Internal Revenue Service." Write your social security number on check or money order . ▶   **17**

**Please Sign Here**

Under penalties of perjury, I declare that I have examined this return, including accompanying schedules and statements, and to the best of my knowledge and belief, it is true, correct, and complete. Declaration of preparer (other than taxpayer) is based on all information of which preparer has any knowledge.

▶ Your signature        Date   ▶ Spouse's signature (if filing jointly, BOTH must sign even if only one had income)

**Paid Preparer's Use Only**

| Preparer's signature and date ▶ | Check if self-employed ▶ ☐ | Preparer's social security no. |
|---|---|---|
| Firm's name (or yours, if self-employed) and address ▶ | E.I. No. ▶ | |
| | ZIP code ▶ | |

☆ U.S. GOVERNMENT PRINTING OFFICE: 1980—O-313-267 13-2687299

Form **1040A** (1980)

**Figure 13-24.** IRS Form 1040A.

Form **1040** Department of the Treasury—Internal Revenue Service
**U.S. Individual Income Tax Return**

| For Privacy Act Notice, see Instructions | For the year January 1–December 31, 1980, or other tax year beginning | , 1980, ending | , 19 |
|---|---|---|---|

| Use IRS label. Otherwise, please print or type. | Your first name and initial (if joint return, also give spouse's name and initial) | Last name | Your social security number |
| | Present home address (Number and street, including apartment number, or rural route) | | Spouse's social security no. |
| | City, town or post office, State and ZIP code | Your occupation ▶ | |
| | | Spouse's occupation ▶ | |

**Presidential Election Campaign Fund**

Do you want $1 to go to this fund? . . . . . . . . . . . . . . . .  Yes ☐ No ☐

If joint return, does your spouse want $1 to go to this fund? . . .  Yes ☐ No ☐

**Note:** Checking "Yes" will not increase your tax or reduce your refund.

**Requested by Census Bureau for Revenue Sharing**

**A** Where do you live (actual location of residence)? (See page 2 of Instructions.) State : City, village, borough, etc.

**B** Do you live within the legal limits of a city, village, etc.? ☐ Yes ☐ No

**C** In what county do you live?

**D** In what township do you live?

**Filing Status**

Check only one box.

1 ☐ Single
2 ☐ Married filing joint return (even if only one had income)
3 ☐ Married filing separate return. Enter spouse's social security no. above and full name here ▶ ------
4 ☐ Head of household. (See page 6 of Instructions.) If qualifying person is your unmarried child, enter child's name ▶ ------
5 ☐ Qualifying widow(er) with dependent child (Year spouse died ▶ 19     ). (See page 6 of Instructions.)

For IRS use only

**Exemptions**

Always check the box labeled Yourself.
Check other boxes if they apply.

6a ☐ Yourself     ☐ 65 or over     ☐ Blind
 b ☐ Spouse       ☐ 65 or over     ☐ Blind

} Enter number of boxes checked on 6a and b ▶

c First names of your dependent children who lived with you ▶ ------

Enter number of children listed on 6c ▶

| d Other dependents: (1) Name | (2) Relationship | (3) Number of months lived in your home | (4) Did dependent have income of $1,000 or more? | (5) Did you provide more than one-half of dependent's support? |
|---|---|---|---|---|
| | | | | |
| | | | | |

Enter number of other dependents ▶

7 Total number of exemptions claimed . . . . . . . . . . . . . . . . .

Add numbers entered in boxes above ▶

**Income**

Please attach Copy B of your Forms W–2 here.

If you do not have a W–2, see page 5 of Instructions.

Please attach check or money order here.

| | | |
|---|---|---|
| 8 | Wages, salaries, tips, etc. . . . . . . . . . . . . . . . . | 8 |
| 9 | Interest income (attach Schedule B if over $400) . . . . . . . . . . . | 9 |
| 10a | Dividends (attach Schedule B if over $400)_____ , 10b Exclusion_____ | |
| c | Subtract line 10b from line 10a . . . . . . . . . . . . . . | 10c |
| 11 | Refunds of State and local income taxes (do not enter an amount unless you deducted those taxes in an earlier year—see page 9 of Instructions) . . . . . . . | 11 |
| 12 | Alimony received . . . . . . . . . . . . . . . . . . . . | 12 |
| 13 | Business income or (loss) (attach Schedule C) . . . . . . . . . . . . | 13 |
| 14 | Capital gain or (loss) (attach Schedule D) . . . . . . . . . . . . . | 14 |
| 15 | 40% of capital gain distributions not reported on line 14 (See page 9 of Instructions) . | 15 |
| 16 | Supplemental gains or (losses) (attach Form 4797) . . . . . . . . . . | 16 |
| 17 | Fully taxable pensions and annuities not reported on line 18 . . . . . . . | 17 |
| 18 | Pensions, annuities, rents, royalties, partnerships, etc. (attach Schedule E) . . . . | 18 |
| 19 | Farm income or (loss) (attach Schedule F) . . . . . . . . . . . . . | 19 |
| 20a | Unemployment compensation (insurance). Total received_____ | |
| b | Taxable amount, if any, from worksheet on page 10 of Instructions . . . . . . | 20b |
| 21 | Other income (state nature and source—see page 10 of Instructions) ▶_____ | 21 |
| 22 | Total income. Add amounts in column for lines 8 through 21 . . . . . . . . ▶ | 22 |

**Adjustments to Income**

(See Instructions on page 10)

| 23 | Moving expense (attach Form 3903 or 3903F) . . . . | 23 | |
| 24 | Employee business expenses (attach Form 2106) . . | 24 | |
| 25 | Payments to an IRA (enter code from page 10 ........) . | 25 | |
| 26 | Payments to a Keogh (H.R. 10) retirement plan . . . | 26 | |
| 27 | Interest penalty on early withdrawal of savings . . . | 27 | |
| 28 | Alimony paid . . . . . . . . . . . . . . . . | 28 | |
| 29 | Disability income exclusion (attach Form 2440) . . . | 29 | |
| 30 | Total adjustments. Add lines 23 through 29 . . . . . . . . . . . ▶ | | 30 |

**Adjusted Gross Income**

31 Adjusted gross income. Subtract line 30 from line 22. If this line is less than $10,000, see "Earned Income Credit" (line 57) on pages 13 and 14 of Instructions. If you want IRS to figure your tax, see page 3 of Instructions . . . . . . ▶   31

☆ U.S. GOVERNMENT PRINTING OFFICE: 1980—O-313-250 13-2687299

Form **1040** (1980)

**Figure 13-25.** IRS Form 1040.

Form 1040 (1980)

Page **2**

| | | | |
|---|---|---|---|
| **Tax Computation** (See Instructions on page 11) | 32 Amount from line 31 *(adjusted gross income)* . . . . . . . . . . . . . . . . . . . . . . | **32** | |
| | 33 If you do not itemize deductions, enter zero . . . . . . . . . . . . . . . . . . . . . . } | **33** | |
| | If you itemize, complete Schedule A (Form 1040) and enter the amount from Schedule A, line 41 . . . . } | | |
| | **Caution:** If you have unearned income and can be claimed as a dependent on your parent's return, check here ▶ ☐ and see page 11 of the Instructions. Also see page 11 of the Instructions if: <br> • You are married filing a separate return and your spouse itemizes deductions, OR <br> • You file Form 4563, OR <br> • You are a dual-status alien. | | |
| | 34 Subtract line 33 from line 32. Use the amount on line 34 to find your tax from the Tax Tables, or to figure your tax on Schedule TC, Part I . . . . . . . . . . . . . . . . . . . <br> Use Schedule TC, Part I, and the Tax Rate Schedules ONLY if: <br> • Line 34 is more than $20,000 ($40,000 if you checked Filing Status Box 2 or 5), OR <br> • You have more exemptions than are shown in the Tax Table for your filing status, OR <br> • You use Schedule G or Form 4726 to figure your tax. <br> Otherwise, you MUST use the Tax Tables to find your tax. | **34** | |
| | 35 Tax. Enter tax here and check if from ☐ Tax Tables or ☐ Schedule TC . . . . . . . . | **35** | |
| | 36 Additional taxes. (See page 12 of Instructions.) Enter here and check if from ☐ Form 4970, } <br> ☐ Form 4972, ☐ Form 5544, ☐ Form 5405, or ☐ Section 72(m)(5) penalty tax . . . } | **36** | |
| | 37 **Total.** Add lines 35 and 36 . . . . . . . . . . . . . . . . . . . . . . . . . . . . . ▶ | **37** | |

| | | | | |
|---|---|---|---|---|
| **Credits** (See Instructions on page 12) | 38 Credit for contributions to candidates for public office . . . | **38** | | |
| | 39 Credit for the elderly *(attach Schedules R&RP)* . . . . . | **39** | | |
| | 40 Credit for child and dependent care expenses *(attach Form 2441)* . | **40** | | |
| | 41 Investment credit *(attach Form 3468)* . . . . . . . . . . | **41** | | |
| | 42 Foreign tax credit *(attach Form 1116)* . . . . . . . . . . | **42** | | |
| | 43 Work incentive (WIN) credit *(attach Form 4874)* . . . . . . | **43** | | |
| | 44 Jobs credit *(attach Form 5884)* . . . . . . . . . . . . | **44** | | |
| | 45 Residential energy credits *(attach Form 5695)* . . . . . . | **45** | | |
| | 46 **Total credits.** Add lines 38 through 45 . . . . . . . . . . . . . . . . . . . . . | | **46** | |
| | 47 **Balance.** Subtract line 46 from line 37 and enter difference (but not less than zero) . ▶ | | **47** | |

| | | | |
|---|---|---|---|
| **Other Taxes** (Including Advance EIC Payments) | 48 Self-employment tax *(attach Schedule SE)* . . . . . . . . . . . . . . . . . . . . | **48** | |
| | 49a Minimum tax. Attach Form 4625 and check here ▶ ☐ . . . . . . . . . . . . . . . | **49a** | |
| | 49b Alternative minimum tax. Attach Form 6251 and check here ▶ ☐ . . . . . . . . . . | **49b** | |
| | 50 Tax from recomputing prior-year investment credit *(attach Form 4255)* . . . . . . . . | **50** | |
| | 51a Social security (FICA) tax on tip income not reported to employer *(attach Form 4137)* . . | **51a** | |
| | 51b Uncollected employee FICA and RRTA tax on tips *(from Form W–2)* . . . . . . . . . . | **51b** | |
| | 52 Tax on an IRA *(attach Form 5329)* . . . . . . . . . . . . . . . . . . . . . . | **52** | |
| | 53 Advance earned income credit (EIC) payments received *(from Form W–2)* . . . . . . . | **53** | |
| | 54 **Balance.** Add lines 47 through 53 . . . . . . . . . . . . . . . . . . . . . . . ▶ | **54** | |

| | | | |
|---|---|---|---|
| **Payments** Attach Forms W–2, W–2G, and W–2P to front. | 55 Total Federal income tax withheld . . . . . . . . . . . | **55** | |
| | 56 1980 estimated tax payments and amount applied from 1979 return . . | **56** | |
| | 57 Earned income credit. If line 32 is under $10,000, see pages 13 and 14 of Instructions . . . . . . . . . . . . . | **57** | |
| | 58 Amount paid with Form 4868 . . . . . . . . . . . . . | **58** | |
| | 59 Excess FICA and RRTA tax withheld (two or more employers) | **59** | |
| | 60 Credit for Federal tax on special fuels and oils *(attach Form 4136 or 4136–T)* . . . . . . . . . . . . . . | **60** | |
| | 61 Regulated Investment Company credit *(attach Form 2439)* | **61** | |
| | 62 **Total.** Add lines 55 through 61 . . . . . . . . . . . . . . . . . . . . . . . ▶ | **62** | |

| | | | |
|---|---|---|---|
| **Refund or Balance Due** | 63 If line 62 is larger than line 54, enter amount **OVERPAID** . . . . . . . . . . . . . ▶ | **63** | |
| | 64 Amount of line 63 to be **REFUNDED TO YOU** . . . . . . . . . . . . . . . . . . ▶ | **64** | |
| | 65 Amount of line 63 to be applied to your 1981 estimated tax . . . ▶ | **65** | |
| | 66 If line 54 is larger than line 62, enter **BALANCE DUE.** Attach check or money order for full amount payable to "Internal Revenue Service." Write your social security number on check or money order . . ▶ <br> (Check ▶ ☐ if Form 2210 (2210F) is attached. See page 15 of Instructions.) ▶ $ | **66** | |

| | |
|---|---|
| **Please Sign Here** | Under penalties of perjury, I declare that I have examined this return, including accompanying schedules and statements, and to the best of my knowledge and belief, it is true, correct, and complete. Declaration of preparer (other than taxpayer) is based on all information of which preparer has any knowledge. <br><br> ▶ Your signature _____ Date ____ ▶ Spouse's signature (if filing jointly, BOTH must sign even if only one had income) |

| | | | |
|---|---|---|---|
| **Paid Preparer's Use Only** | Preparer's signature and date ▶ | Check if self-employed ▶ ☐ | Preparer's social security no. |
| | Firm's name (or yours, if self-employed) and address ▶ | E.I. No. ▶ | |
| | | ZIP code ▶ | |

**Figure 13-25** continued.

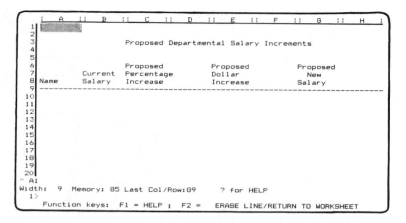

**Figure 13-26.** A template that can be used to determine salary increments for department members.

```
                          CLASSROOM
      NAME _____ GRADING SHEET

                                   TOTAL    TOTAL
      DESCRIPTION  MY SCORE  POSSIBLE TO DATE POSSIBLE  %

      ASSIGN. 1-1  _____    20    _____    20   ____
      ASSIGN. 1-2  _____    20    _____    40   ____
      ASSIGN. 1-3  _____    25    _____    65   ____
      ASSIGN. 1-4  _____    25    _____    90   ____
      ASSIGN. 1-5  _____    60    _____   150   ____
      TEST 1       _____   100    _____   250   ____
      ASSIGN. 1-6  _____    25    _____   275   ____
      ASSIGN. 1-7  _____    70    _____   345   ____
      ASSIGN. 1-8  _____    40    _____   385   ____
      TEST 2       _____   100    _____   485   ____
      ASSIGN. 1-9  _____    50    _____   535   ____
      ASSIGN. 1-10 _____    25    _____   560   ____
      TEST 3       _____   100    _____   660   ____
      ASSIGN. 1-11 _____    90    _____   750   ____
      ASSIGN. 1-12 _____    50    _____   800   ____
      FINAL EXAM   _____   200    _____  1000   ____
```

**Figure 13-27.** A sample recordkeeping sheet for individual grades.

**39.** A gas and electric company charges rates as below:

|  |  | Rate |
|---|---|---|
| First | 3 therms, or less | $2.90000 |
| Next | 997 therms, per therm | .43709 |
| Next | 99,000 therms, per therm | .37672 |
| Over | 100,000 therms, per therm | .34191 |

The minimum monthly charge is $2.90.

Prepare a template on which the number of therms consumed is entered and that computes the total charge. (A review of the MAX and MIN functions may be helpful.)

**40.** Prepare a report like the one in Figure 13-28 which shows projected space requirements for several departments of a data processing division. The column, Staff Total, is entered by the user. The Type-of-Office column is a code which is used to look up an office size in square feet (SF) which is then placed in the Unit-SF column. The codes and their associated areas are

| Type of Office | Unit SF |
|:---:|:---:|
| 1 | 160 |
| 2 | 140 |
| 3 | 120 |
| 4 | 100 |
| 5 | 80 |

Using a table allows us to vary office size by changing these values in the table and then immediately determining the impact on the total space requirements.

DATA PROCESSING DIVISION       SPACE REQUIREMENTS

| Code No. | Space Title | Staff Total | Type of Office | Unit SF | Total Square Feet |
|---|---|---|---|---|---|
| 448 | ADMIN. | | | | |
| | - Division Director | 1 | 1 | 160 | 160 |
| | - Secretary | 5 | 5 | 80 | 400 |
| | | 6 | | Subtotal | 560 |
| 442 | SYSTEMS | | | | |
| | - Manager | 1 | 3 | 120 | 120 |
| | - Offices | 10 | 5 | 80 | 800 |
| | - Users' Area | | | 1,300 | 1,300 |
| | - Gen'l Area | | | 2,500 | 2,500 |
| | - Storage | | | 160 | 160 |
| | | 11 | | Subtotal | 4,880 |
| 442 | PROGRAMMING | | | | |
| | - Manager | 1 | 3 | 120 | 120 |
| | - Offices | 21 | 5 | 80 | 1,680 |
| | - Terminal Area | | | 1,000 | 1,000 |
| | - Gen'l Area | | | 3,000 | 3,000 |
| | | 22 | | Subtotal | 5,800 |
| 448 | OPERATIONS | | | | |
| | - Manager | 1 | 3 | 120 | 120 |
| | - Offices | 7 | 5 | 80 | 560 |
| | | 8 | | Subtotal | 680 |
| 450 | OTHER | | | | |
| | - Reception Area | | | 260 | 260 |
| | - Resource Area/Supply Area | | | 80 | 80 |
| | - Terminal Room | | | 80 | 80 |
| | - Storage | | | 160 | 160 |
| | - Mail Box Area | | | 80 | 80 |
| | - Coffee/Break Area | | | 80 | 80 |
| | | | | Subtotal | 740 |
| | | | | NET TOTAL | 12,660 |

**Figure 13-28.** A space requirements planning sheet.

# CHAPTER 14

# Products Related To SuperCalc

## INTRODUCTION

A number of commercial products are marketed for SuperCalc users or marketed for multiple purposes but of value to users. Since products are regularly introduced, modified, and sometimes removed from the market, none is identified by name. Instead, items below are identified by capability and grouped by classification: software, hardware, and written aids and users' groups.

## SOFTWARE

**Worksheets:** Several vendors are offering prepared templates that can be used with SuperCalc for purposes like individual and business tax preparation, business forecasting and financial planning, cash flow projections, etc. Several users' groups also offer or plan to market templates with a variety of capabilities.

**Data-handling programs:** There are programs capable of using data generated by SuperCalc to produce graphics and plots, perform statistical analysis, prepare output in formats not available with SuperCalc, sort data in a variety of ways, send sheets over phone lines, and provide for regular updating of files in batch-processing modes.

Some word processing programs, data base programs, etc. can accept SuperCalc files directly for further manipulation.

**Competing programs:** A number of software products with capabilities similar to SuperCalc are available.

## HARDWARE

**Memory:** Additional memory, if available in some form for our computer, can substantially increase the potential size of our spreadsheets.

**Keypads:** Keypads provide for data entry with one hand with a key configuration that usually matches that of a numeric calculator. They offer speed for a trained operator. Some computers are marketed with a built-in keypad in the keyboard. When not available in this format, manufacturers are producing them as hardware accessories for some systems. Since they are connected by a cable, and are usually hand size, they also offer limited portability.

**Printers:** Some printers can print several hundred characters per row, a capability that can provide a significant advantage for many SuperCalc sheets.

## WRITTEN AIDS AND USERS' GROUPS

**Articles and other written material:** The Bibliography contains references to articles and books published on SuperCalc.

**Users' groups:** Users' groups have formed and published newsletters for spreadsheet users. These contain articles on these products and reviews of related products. They are also a forum for users to share ideas and concerns. Several are listed in the Bibliography.

# SuperCalc Summary Reference

## COMMANDS

(For SuperCalc version 1.10 on the IBM Personal Computer)

| Symbol | Name | Purpose |
|--------|------|---------|
| /B | the Blank command | Blank a cell or group of cells. |
| /C | the Copy command | Copy one area of the sheet to another of equal size. |
| | RETURN | Copy entered range with automatic adjustment. |
| | , (comma) | Request "Options." |
| | N | No adjustment of coordinates. |
| | A | Ask for adjustment on a coordinate by coordinate basis. |
| | Y | Yes, adjust this coordinate. |
| | N | No, do not adjust this coordinate. |
| | V | Values only should be copied, not formulas. |
| /D | the Delete command | Delete a row, column, or file. |
| | R | Row. |
| | C | Column. |
| | F | File. |
| | filename | Delete this file. |
| | RETURN | Display the disk directory. |
| | C | Choose another drive. |
| | x | Enter desired drive prefix. |
| | D | All files should be listed. |
| | S | SuperCalc files only should be listed. |

| | | |
|---|---|---|
| /E | the Edit command | Edit an entry without completely retyping. Copy from one cell to the current cell with editing. |
| /F | the Format command | Format the appearance of a range of cells on the screen. |
| | G | Global. |
| | C | Column |
| | R | Row. |
| | E | Entry (range). |

For each option above the following format selections are available.

| | | |
|---|---|---|
| | I | Integer. |
| | G | General. |
| | E | Scientific notation. |
| | $ | Dollars and cents. |
| | R | Right justify, numeric. |
| | L | Left justify, numeric. |
| | TR | Right justify, text. |
| | TL | Left justify, text. |
| | * | Graph |
| | D | Default. |
| | column width | Enter desired column width. (Available only for a previous choice of Global or Column.) |
| /G | the Global command | Globally affect the sheet. |
| | F | Formula and text contents displayed (not current values). Toggles on/off. |
| | N | Next cell on RETURN (auto-advance). Toggles on/off. |
| | B | Borders displayed. Toggles on/off. |
| | T | Tab on RETURN (skip blank and protected entries). Toggles on/off. |
| | R | Rowwise order of recalculation. |
| | C | Columnwise order of recalculation. |
| | M | Manual recalculation on ''!''. |
| | A | Automatic recalculation. |
| /I | the Insert command | Insert a row or column. |
| | R | Row |
| | C | Column |

| /L | the Load command | Load a file. |
| | filename | Load this file. |
| | RETURN | Display the disk directory. |
| | C | Choose another drive. |
| | x | Enter desired drive prefix. |
| | D | All files should be listed. |
| | S | SuperCalc files only should be listed. |

For each option above (filename or RETURN), the following choices apply.

| | A | All. |
| | P | Part, followed by range and TO location. |

| /M | the Move command | Move a row or column. |
| | R | Row move. Followed by FROM and TO rows. |
| | C | Column move. Followed by FROM and TO columns. |

| /O | the Output command | Output all or part of a worksheet to a device. |
| | D | Display. Output items as displayed on the screen. |
| | C | Contents. Output text and formulas as entered on the worksheet. |

For each option above, enter the range, or ALL and then choose from the options below.

| | P | Printer. |
| | S | Setup. |
| | L | Length. Change page length. |
| | W | Width. Change page width. |
| | S | Setup. Enter setup strings. |
| | P | Print. |
| | filename | Output to a disk with this name. |
| | RETURN | Display the disk directory. |
| | C | Choose another drive. |
| | x | Enter desired drive prefix. |
| | D | Directory. All files should be listed. |
| | S | SuperCalc files only should be listed. |
| | C | Console |
| | D | Disk. |

| /P | the Protect command | Protect a range of cells. |
|---|---|---|
| /Q | the Quit command | Quit SuperCalc. |
| /R | the Replicate command | Replicate a range onto another area of the worksheet. Then enter the FROM and TO ranges. |
| | RETURN | Replicate entered range with automatic adjustment. |
| | , (comma) | Request "Options." |
| | N | No adjustment of coordinates. |
| | A | Ask for adjustment on a coordinate by coordinate basis. |
| | Y | Yes, adjust this coordinate. |
| | N | No, do not adjust this coordinate. |
| | V | Values only should be copied, not formulas. |
| /S | the Save command | Save all or part of the worksheet. |
| | filename | Save the file, giving it this name. |
| | RETURN | Display the disk directory. |
| | C | Choose another drive. |
| | x | Enter desired drive prefix. |
| | D | All files should be listed. |
| | S | SuperCalc files only should be listed. |

For each choice above (filename or RETURN), the following options appear if the file already exists on this diskette.

| | C | Change name, by editing entry line. |
|---|---|---|
| | B | Backup. Save this as another copy with a suffix indicating backup. |
| | O | Overwrite. Write this file over the existing file, replacing the original file with the current worksheet. |

For each option above (filename or RETURN), the following choices apply.

| | A | All. |
|---|---|---|
| | V | Values only should be saved. |
| | P | Part, followed by range and TO location. |

| | | |
|---|---|---|
| /T | the Titles Lock | Lock titles in place. |
| | H | Horizontally. |
| | V | Vertically. |
| | B | Both. |
| | C | Clear. |
| /U | the Unprotect command | Unprotect a range of cells. |
| /W | the Window command | Affect the window display. |
| | H | Horizontal split. |
| | V | Vertical split. |
| | C | Clear the split. |
| | S | Synchronized scrolling. |
| | U | Unsynchronized scrolling. |
| /X | the eXecute command | Execute a file of commands and data. |
| /Z | the Zap command | Zap (clear) the entire worksheet. |
| | Y | Yes. |
| | N | No. |

## BUILT-IN FUNCTIONS

| | |
|---|---|
| ABS(argument) | the absolute value |
| ACOS(argument) | the arccosine |
| AND(argument1,argument2) | logical AND |
| ASIN(argument) | the arcsine |
| ATAN(argument) | the arctangent |
| AVERAGE(argument1,argument2,...) | the average |
| COS(argument) | the cosine |
| COUNT(argument1,argument2...) | count how many |
| ERROR | the error function and error value |
| EXP(argument) | $e$ to a power |
| IF(argument1,argument2,argument3) | logical IF |
| INT(argument) | integer |
| LN(argument) | natural logarithm |
| LOG10(argument) | logarithm, base 10 |
| LOOKUP(argument1,argument2) | look up a value in a table |
| MAX(argument1,argument2,...) | the maximum value |
| MIN(argument1,argument2,...) | the minimum value |
| NA | not available |
| NOT(argument) | the logical NOT |
| NPV(argument1,argument2) | the net present value |
| OR(argument1,argument2) | the logical OR |
| PI | value of $\pi$ |
| SIN(argument) | the sine |
| SQRT(argument) | the square root |
| SUM(argument1,argument2,...) | sum the values |
| TAN(argument) | the tangent |

# SuperCalc Bibliography

Ahl, David H. "Digital Equipment Corporation Rainbow 100 Personal Computer." *Creative Computing* 8, no. 11 (November 1982): 10-12, 14, 18, 20, 24, 26, 30-31. An equipment evaluation of the DEC Rainbow 100, including a discussion of Multiplan with brief mention of SuperCalc.

Alsop II, Stewart. "Software Arts Wrote the First Best-Seller." *INC*. 4, no. 1 (January 1982): 71, 73, 75. Article on the development of VisiCalc by Dan Bricklin and Bob Frankston and its marketing by Dan Fylstra, which includes mention of SuperCalc and other competing products.

Barry, Tim. "SuperCalc Spread-Sheet Simulator from Sorcim Corp." *InfoWorld* 3, no. 20 (October 5, 1981): 30-32. Describes SuperCalc and gives it a 'software report card' of excellent.

Bayer, Barry D. "Visulating." *Desktop Computing* (November 1981): 84-88. Includes brief mention of SuperCalc.

Bayer, Barry. "Visulating." *Desktop Computing* 2, no. 6 (June 1982): 74-49. Includes brief mention of SuperCalc use for accounting applications on a Zenith system.

Berger, Myron. "Scenarios For Success: The Vision of Spreadsheeting." *Personal Computing* 6, no. 4 (April 1982): 58-59, 61-63. General discussion of spreadsheet programs (with listings of 22 programs including SuperCalc), and several specific business applications.

"Between the Lines." *Computer Retail News* 005 (September 27, 1982): 4. Discussion of the price of PlannerCalc from Comshare Target Software with brief price comparison to SuperCalc.

270

Brunt, Deryk Van and Julian Henkin. "The Bridge." *DEC Professional* 1, no. 1 (July 1982): 30, 32-33. A description of the Bridge which allows CP/M software to run on mainframes. The article refers to the large pool of inexpensive creative software available for the CP/M environment and mentions the high quality of SuperCalc documentation. A letter to the editor from Arnold Cohen, 1, no. 2 (September 1982): 6, 70, including a comparison of DIGICALC and SuperCalc when run with the Bridge.

Bunnell, David and Lawrence J. Magid. "An Interview With VisiCalc Entrepreneur Daniel Fylstra." *PC* 1, no. 4 (August 1982): 28-33, 35-37. Includes Fylstra's response to the absence of copy protection on SuperCalc and the ability to copy it to a hard disk, and the lack of these capabilities with VisiCalc.

"CDC Set to Roll Out Software." *Datamation* 28, no. 1 (January 1982): 13. Announces SuperCalc for the CDC 110 business system.

Chin, Kathy. "Firms Approach the Business of Employee Computer Training." *InfoWorld* 4, no. 48 (December 6, 1982): 51, 53. Discusses training by several firms, including Software Training Company, with reference to their SuperCalc training package.

"Choosing Micro Software." *Computerworld Extra: The Changing Software Environment* 16, no. 35A (September 1, 1982): 47. Reports that Standard Software Co. lists SuperCalc as number 2 (after Wordstar) on the CP/M top 10 best-sellers list.

Cohen, Arnold. (*See* Brunt *entry above*.)

"Computer-Based Business Planning." *Small Business Computers* 6, no. 3 (May/June 1982): 38-47. Presents the capabilities of spreadsheets, and includes SuperCalc among over thirty planning programs.

"CP/M-Compatible Electronic Worksheet Accommodates Any Terminal." *EDN* June 10, 1981: . Describes general capabilities of Super-Calc.

Dahmke, Mark. "The Osborne 1." *Byte* 7, no. 6 (June 1982): 348, 350, 352, 354, 356, 358, 360, 362. Includes discussion of SuperCalc with the comment 'SuperCalc may be the best buy on the system'.

"Dedicated to Modeling." *Which Computer?* October 1982: 85-86. Describes the Prophet 2 microcomputer from Busicomputers that contains a worksheet product in ROM. The product is compared to Super-Calc.

Ditlea, Steve. "Getting More Out of VisiCalc." *INC* 4, no. 10 (October 1982): 154, 156. Includes references to SuperCalc and to templates available for it.

Ditlea, Steve. "The New Software: A Powerful Ally." *INC* 3, no. 11 (November 1981): 103-105, 108. Discusses a variety of business software, including brief mention of SuperCalc.

Ditlea, Steve, ''VisiCalc and 'Visiclones.''' *Popular Computing*. Part 1, 1, no. 11 (September 1982): 48, 50-52, 54. Includes a discussion of SuperCalc, and other spreadsheet programs, including a strong endorsement from a user who converted to it from VisiCalc.

Dvorak, John C. ''The Dimwit-Delay Phenomenon.'' *InfoWorld* 4, no. 49 (December 13, 1982): 26. Discusses ''copycat programs,'' including SuperCalc following VisiCalc.

Dvorak, John C. ''Inside Track.'' *InfoWorld* 4, no. 15. (April 19, 1982): 34. Mentions SuperWriter, its interface with SuperCalc, and the availability of a color version of SuperCalc for the IBM Personal Computer.

''Episode Computer Work Station.'' *Popular Computing* 1, no. 5 (March 1982): 22. Announces SuperCalc for the Eric Computer Corporation's Episode.

Ferris, Michael. ''Detective Story: A PC Confidential.'' *Softalk for the IBM Personal Computer* 1, no. 6 (November 1982): 38-42, 44. Describes the use of a computer by a private investigation firm, including SuperCalc use for invoicing and record keeping.

Fisher, Shirley. ''The Profit Plot.'' *SOFTALK for the IBM Personal Computer* 1, no. 5 (October 1982): 18-19. Describes the bar chart capabilities of SuperCalc and VisiCalc and compares other features of the two products.

Fisher, Shirley. ''The Profit Plot.'' *Softalk for the IBM Personal Computer*, all issues. Regular column on spreadsheets.

Fluegelman, Andrew. ''Calc Wars.'' *PC* 1, no. 4 (August 1982): 71-78, 80. Lengthy and thorough comparison of VisiCalc and SuperCalc for the IBM Personal Computer, resulting in ''a split decision-two winners'' from the author.

Fluegelman, Andrew. ''The Challenger: Multiplan.'' *PC* 1, no. 4 (August 1982): 85-86. Includes the comment that SuperCalc was studied in developing Multiplan.

Freiberger, Paul. ''Sorcim's SuperWriter Makes a Three-Point Landing.'' *InfoWord* 4, no. 48 (December 6, 1982): 3. Announces SuperWriter and an enhanced version of SuperCalc.

Freiberger, Paul. ''A Spreadsheet Program for $50.'' *InfoWorld* 4, no. 25 (June 28, 1982): 1, 5. Discussion of the marketing of PlannerCalc by Comshare, with comparison to SuperCalc.

Good, Phillip. ''VisiCalc, An Electronic Worksheet.'' *Popular Computing* 1, no. 2 (December 1981): 34, 36, 38. General product description with references to several specific uses and comparisons to SuperCalc.

Hart, Glenn A. "The Little Computer That Could." *Creative Computing* 8, no. 6 (June 1982): 11-12, 14. Includes brief discussion of SuperCalc for the Osborne 1 microcomputer.

Heintz, Carl. "Evaluation of Financial Planning Packages." *Interface Age* 7, no. 7 (July 1982): 78-79, 81-82, 84, 86, 91-93. Compares features of over thirty products.

*INTERCALC* (see *S P R E A D S H E E T* below).

Latamore, Bert. "Monroe Sells Solutions." *Desktop Computing* 2, no. 6 (June 1982): 12-17. Describes the Monroe 8820 microcomputer and its use of SuperCalc.

Mace, Scott and John Markoff. "Comparing the Portables and Looking for Trends." *InfoWorld* 4, no. 3 (August 2, 1982): 22-25. Includes reference to the availability of SuperCalc on the Courier.

Magid, Lawrence J. "MBA: Putting It All Together." *PC* 1, no. 4 (August 1982): 74-75. Description of the MBA product with the comment that it's slower than SuperCalc.

Magid, Larry. "Surrender at the Faire." *PC* 1, no. 3 (June/July 1982): 59-60. Discussion of the 7th West Coast Computer Faire including availability of spreadsheets like SuperCalc.

Magid, Lawrence J. and David Bunnell. "VisiCalc Creators Look Forward to Future Glory." *PC* 1, no. 4 (August 1982): 30-31. Includes Dan Bricklin's comments on comparisons of SuperCalc and VisiCalc.

*Micro-Calc Business Users' Group Newsletter.* 1, no. 1 (May 1981). (P.O. Box 12039, Salem, Oregon 97309).

Morgan, Chris. "The 'Visiclones' Are Coming." *BYTE* 7, no. 2 (February 1982): 6, 8. Brief mention of several spreadsheets that compete with VisiCalc.

Needle, David. "VisiCalc Creators Unveil 'No-Program' Problem Solver." *InfoWorld* 4, no. 23 (June 14, 1982): 6, 9. Description of TK!Solver, from Software Arts, with comments from Richard Frank of Sorcim.

Needle, David. "'What is this CP/M?' Seminar Introduces Micros to the Public." *InfoWorld* 4, no. 15 (April 19, 1982): 27. Describes courses offered about microcomputers, including a course on SuperCalc.

Neuringer, Jules K. "Praise and Advice (letter to the editor)." *BYTE* 7, no. 11 (November 1982): 20, 22. Describes users' satisfaction with SuperCalc and with the customer support at Sorcim.

"A New Alternative to Buying on Faith." *INC.* 4, no. 7 (July 1982): 20, 23. Describes SuperCalc as offered through Soft-Link, which allows users to use software on a demonstration basis, and then if purchase is desired, obtain a code to unlock the full software package.

Norton, Robert E. "Microcomputer Exhibit Draws SRO Crowds." *American Banker* October 20, 1982: 3, 38. Describes the strong interest in microcomputers at the ABA convention, including mention of SuperCalc.

O'Connor, Rory J. "PC Applications, OSs, Languages." *Computer Business News* 5, no. 16 (April 19, 1982): 6. Includes discussion of SuperCalc for the IBM Personal Computer.

Pournelle, Jerry. "ADA, MINCE, CP/M Utilities, Overpriced documentation, and Analiza II." *BYTE* 7, no. 7 (July 1982): 290, 292, 294, 298, 300, 302, 304, 306, 308, 310. Contains brief comments on the documentation of SuperCalc ("...good examples and tutorial...but include a demonstration financial analysis and two or three other such programs.").

Pournelle, Jerry. "The Osborne 1, Zeke's New Friends, and Spelling Revisited." *Byte* 7, no. 4 (April 1982): 212-214, 216, 218, 220, 222, 224, 226, 228, 230, 234, 236, 238. Includes brief mention of SuperCalc.

Pournelle, Jerry. "SuperCalc, Spelling Programs, BASIC Compilers, and Home-Grown Accounting." BYTE 7, no. 5 (May 1982): 226, 228-230, 232, 234, 236, 238, 240, 242-243. Description of SuperCalc and a tale of installing it on a Godbout 8085/88 with a Zenith Z-19 terminal.

"R2E Offers 8-, 16-Bit Micros." *MIS Week* 3, no. 46 (Wednesday, November 17, 1982): F. Announces the R2E microcomputer and the availability of SuperCalc for it.

Rust, W. J. "p-Soup and Baloney Sandwich? (letter to the editor)." *Softalk for the IBM Personal Computer* 1, no. 6 (November 1982): 4. Discusses the p-System, and mentions SuperCalc reading PC-DOS files.

SATN (Software Arts Technical Notes). *The Journal for VisiCalc Users*, Software Arts, Inc., P.O. Box 815, Quincy, MA 02169. Bimonthly journal for VisiCalc users which may be of value for SuperCalc users.

Seiver, Ben. "Guessing Game (Letter to the Editor)." *InfoWorld* 4, no. 5 (February 8, 1982): 21. Describes, without naming, a microcomputer including SuperCalc available for $2995.

"*SOFTALK* Presents the Bestsellers." *SOFTALK for the IBM Personal Computer* 1, no. 4 (September 1982): 51-52. Lists SuperCalc as number 3 in "the top thirty" after VisiCalc and WordStar.

Spohr, Mark. "A Comparison of SuperCalc and VisiCalc." *S P R E A D S H E E T* 10 (May-June 1982): 10. Describes features of SuperCalc not available in VisiCalc. *Also* issue 11 (July-August 1982):11, correctly stating that SuperCalc does allow "pointing the cursor" with the ESC key.

*S P R E A D S H E E T .* VisiGroup 1, no. 1 (November 1980 and sub-sequent issues). Newsletter from VisiGroup, National VisiCalc Users' Group (P.O. Box 1010, Scarsdale, NY 10583). Published through March-April 1982, Issue 9, after which the group name was changed to InterCalc, the International Electronic Spreadsheet Users' Group, to re-flect a membership "over several different computers and several dif-ferent spreadsheet programs."

Steffin, Sherwin. "New Technology, New Thinking." *Softline* 1, no. 6 (July 1982): 31. Brief mention of SuperCalc as a simulation tool.

Stein, Donna. "The Calc Wars." *Business Computer Systems* September 1982: 68-70, 72-76. Describes the growth of VisiCalc and mentions capabilities of its competitors including SuperCalc.

"SuperCalc for CP/M." *Byte* 7, no. 1 (January 1982): 442. Announces SuperCalc for the Apple CP/M, Xerox 820, North Star, Superbrain, Micropolis, Zenith, Osborne, and Vector Graphic microcomputers.

"SuperCalc to the Rescue." *Popular Computing* 1, no. 2 (December 1981): 36. Describes features of SuperCalc not available in VisiCalc.

*SuperCalc User's Guide & Reference Manual.* San Jose, CA; Sorcim, 1981. The product manual by Bryant Associates.

*SuperNews.* Sorcim newsletter which began with issue number 1, Second Quarter, 1982. (Sorcim, 405 Aldo Avenue, Santa Clara, CA 95050).

Tannenbaum, Michael. "Tax-Preparation Software for Professionals." *Popular Computing* 2, no. 1 (November 1982): 38, 42, 44, 46. Brief mention of SuperCalc use to generate tax returns.

Taylor, Robert H. and Bruce D. Juhlin. "Versatile Electronic Spreadsheet Program." *Small Business Computers* 6, no. 4 (July/August 1982): 18-20. A review of SuperCalc—"with a little study and imagination it can become an indispensable management tool."

Thé, Lee. "More Computer Muscle to Power the Machine." *Personal Computing* 6, no. 10 (October 1982) 88-89, 93, 96, 98, 101, 102, 104, 109. Describes microcomputer memory products and worksheet guidelines with them for SuperCalc.

Thé, Lee. "Self Improvement Beyond Productivity." *Personal Comput-ing* 6, no. 7 (July 1982): 89-90, 93-94, 134-135, 137-139. Includes reference to several spreadsheet programs, including SuperCalc, and their use to improve productivity.

Tommervik, Allan. "Exec Lotus, A New Caper for Mitch Kapor." *Sof-talk* 2, no. 5 (January 1982): 46-48, 50. Includes mention of SuperCalc application models from Pansophics.

"What is this VisiCalc, Anyway?"" *Personal Computing* 6, no. 2 (February 1982): 154. Brief description of VisiCalc capabilities with mention of SuperCalc.

''Which Financial Planning Package?'' *Which Computer?* August 1982: 23, 25, 29-30, 33. Contains a table of approximately 75 financial planning products, including SuperCalc.

Williams, Robert E. and Bruce J. Taylor. *The Power of SuperCalc.* Portland, OR: Management Information Source, 1982.

Wrege, Rachael. ''Software Trends.'' *Popular Computing* 2, no. 1 (November, 1982): 82-86. Includes mention of SuperCalc among the ''fastest selling programs...in the financial genre'' and mentions its availability with Softlok.

Zussman, John Unger. ''Battle of the Spreadsheets.'' *InfoWorld* 4, no. 10 (March 15, 1982): 20-21. Discussion of several spreadsheet programs.

# Index